Relevance of Self in THE BHAGAVAD GĪTĀ to the Modern World

Relevance of Self in THE BHAGAVAD GĪTĀ to the Modern World

J. Rangaswami

SHARADA

Sharada Publishing House
Delhi-110085
2008

First Published 2008

ISBN : 978-81-88934-46-1

Published by
B.L. Bansal
Sharada Publishing House
111, Vidya Vihar Apartment
Sector-9, Rohini
Delhi-110085
Phones: +91-11-3292 1560, 2755 2102
E-mail: bansal_sph@rediffmail.com

Printed at
Salasar Imaging Systems
Delhi

Dr. C. Subramaniam
Vice Chancellor
Tamil University

FOREWORD

It is a world known fact that the greatness of *Bhagavad Gītā* is beyond the words of appreciation. It crosses the national boundaries and guides humanity for its moral and spiritual upheaval. From it, the plausible answers for metaphysical along with the multifarious socio-political and economical, including the scientific problems, could be deduced for the *summum bonum* of the life *per se*. Minding this cosmopolitan perspectives of religious and philosophical outlook, Aldous Huxley commends, "The *Gītā* is one of the clearest and most comprehensive summaries of the Perennial Philosophy ever to have been made" (Mukerjee1999:xxi). Apart from them, it maintains the secularist trends and provides available means for societal welfare. Dr. S. Radhakrishnan affirms this: "The chief problem facing us today is the reconciliation of mankind. The *Gītā* is specially suited and purpose, as it attempts to reconcile varied and apparently antithetical forms of the religious consciousness and emphasises the root conceptions of religion which are neither ancient nor modern but eternal and belong to the very flesh of humanity, past, present, and future" (Radhakrishnan 1977:6-7).

Though the esoteric text is analysed through multifarious dimensions by the international scholars, the approach of the present publication is specific; in which, the author focuses upon the nature of self within the worldly flux and conveys its contemporary relevance. The Celestial Song states, "Let a man lift himself by himself; let him not degrade himself; for the self alone is the friend of self and self alone is the enemy of the self" (7:5). He excavates the uniqueness of the text within the background of the Indian Philosophical systems and exhaustively elucidates the thematic conceptions of the self and clarifies the practical means to overcome the hurdles to realize its divinity.

Dr. Surendranath Dasgupta, while explaining the originality of the text, firmly remarks, "a large number of commentaries have been written on it by the adherents of different schools of thought, each of which explained the *Gītā* in its own favour" (Dasgupta 1988:ii.347). The author approaches the work through the commentaries of Śrī Śaṅkara and Śrī Rāmānuja, where he compares them with his own reasoning and supports the latter's view in concern with its modernity. He authoritatively examines the drastic conditions of the world community caused by its material attachments; by scientifically invented sophisticated equipments for comfortable life; and by wrong identification of name and fame in the tune of hypocrisy. Since the scientific tempo upheavals the non-materialistic aspect of the life force as the spiritual and necessity of metaphysical prospect through the physical theories, the author points out of the proper investigation of the true self and its relevance are dare in need of at present rather than before. The author recommends the practise of *niṣkāmyakarma yoga* and right attitude of the law of *karma*, the individual could exercise the apt means towards the higher spiritual order. Also, he reasonably focuses his vision, i.e., detachment towards materialism; awareness of the Universal Self through love; harmonious tendency against different *yogas;* steadfast in self-determinism; and the apprehension of Universal Brotherhood with *sāttvika jñāna,* the society could become a heaven on earth. Hence, through this work, the writer unveils the secret, that, the Supreme Force is always directing the mankind towards its spiritual perfection, within which all the humanly manifested differences are nullified. It is relevant to remember Mahatma Gandhi's words, "while trying to act up to *Gītā* we find that the effort fails. In this way failure we see the rays of the success which is coming like the rising sun" (Satwalikar 1977:3). Yes!, let us walk with hope to the success.

May my wishes shower upon Dr. J. Rangaswami to come up with more works. I whole heartedly commend this intellectual task.

C. SUBRAMANIAM

ACKNOWLEDGEMENTS

I experienced, that, the success is not certain for an individual's effort, but with the help extended by the experts who surround him; in it, if he fails, it would be because of his sheer inefficiency. I have completed this task not all of a sudden, but as my hobby along with the stipulated academic endeavors. Whenever I found time, I used to discuss the central theme of the text with Dr. S. Kodantaraman, Professor of Sanskrit, Raja's College, Thiruvaiyaru. He without minding my unbearable academic itches, always interacted and shared his thinking; and helped me to derive some constructive conclusions. I ought to owe much, because without his intellectual help; specifically related with the field of Sanskrit, it would not be possible to complete this volume. As such to Dr. A. Veeraraghavan, Sanskrit Pandit, Sarasvathi Mahal Library, Thanjavur, who checked the portions of the transliteration.

I am always indebted to Dr. Raju Kalidos, Retired Professor, Department of Sculpture, Tamil University, who recommended this manuscript to Mr. B.L. Bansal, the Publisher. If not, it would not be a successful endeavor as the second publication in the name of Sharada Publishing House. Equal credit goes to Mr. Bansal, who as my brother affectionately encouraged and trained me as an eminent writer cum efficient editor. Ms. Shikha Bansal, daughter of him finalized the output to neatly publish this volume.

I wholeheartedly express my sincere reverence and gratitude with bowing head to Dr. C. Subramaniam, Vice Chancellor, Tamil University, who is very kind enough to write a foreword; in it, he excellently explicated the nutshell of this record. It honestly adds a feather to my cap. Dr. G. Bhaskaran, Director, School of Philosophy; and Registrar-in-charge, Tamil University also personally and officially helped to achieve this goal. Much regards to him.

I am with appreciation remembering Dr. B. Sundaresan and Dr. K. Thirumaran, the Librarians of Tamil University Library and School of Philosophy. They kindly helped me to get the necessary collections on the *Bhagavad Gītā* to complete this work; particularly in the last phase, they provided the back volumes and journals from the old collections.

If this book possesses minimum flaws and faults, the credit goes to Dr. B. Jambulingam, Tamil University, who looked after the proof correction and proper presentation. Though he is a Superintendent in the administrative side, I respect his academic interest.

Yes, I thank Mr. B. Ravi, Thiruvalluvar Offset Printers, Thanjavur who accurately perceived my imagination and expressed it through the images of the wrapper and inner pages, which positively expose the theme grand galore.

Last, but not the least, Mrs. R. Parimala, my wife; R. Muraleedharan and R. Giridharan, my sons are the source of my inspiration, who by all means help me to achieve the academic ventures. I solicitly thank my kiths.

By mentioning the couplet of *Thirukkuṟaḷ*, 'World Ethical Code' (110), "*ennaṉṟi koṉṟārkkum uyvuṇṭu uyviḷḷai; ceynaṉṟi koṉṟa maharkku*" — 'He who has killed every virtue may yet escape; there is no escape for him who killed a benefit', I am sincerely expressing my veneration to all who helped for this publication.

J. RANGASWAMI

CONTENTS

NOTE REGARDING TRANSLITERATION

Roman	*Devanagri*
a	अ
ā	आ
i	इ
ī	ई
u	उ
ū	ऊ
e	ए
ē	
ai	ऐ
o	
ō	ओ
au	औ
ḥ	अः
k	क्
kh	ख्
g	ग्
gh	घ्
ṅ	ङ्
c	च्
ch	छ्
j	ज्
jh	झ्
ñ	ञ्
ṭ	ट्
ṭh	ठ्

ḍ	ड्
ḍh	ढ्
ṇ	ण्
t	त्
th	थ्
d	द्
dh	ध्
n	न्
p	प्
ph	फ्
b	ब्
bh	भ्
m	म्
y	य्
r	र्
l	ल्
v	व्
ḻ	ल
ḷ	ळ
ṟ	
ṉ	
ś	श्
ṣ	ष्
s	स्
h	ह्
kṣ	क्ष्
tr	त्र
Jñ	ज्ञ्

ABBREVIATIONS

A	-	*Aitareya Upaniṣad*
An.ni.	-	*Aṅguttara-nikāya*
BG	-	*Bhagavad Gītā*
BU	-	*Bṛhadāraṇyaka Upaniṣad*
Ca.saṁ	-	*Caraka-saṁhitā*
ChU	-	*Chāndogya Upaniṣad*
Di.ni.	-	*Digha-nikāya*
IU	-	*Īśā Upaniṣad*
KU	-	*Kaṭha Upaniṣad*
MaiU	-	*Maitreyī Upaniṣad*
Maj.ni.	-	*Majjhima-nikāya*
MU	-	*Muṇḍaka Upaniṣad*
Ṛg	-	*Ṛg-Veda*
Sāṃ.kā	-	*Sāṃkhya-Kārikā*
Sāṃ. ni.	-	*Sāṃkhya-nikāya*
SU	-	*Śvetāśvatara Upaniṣad*
Su	-	*Suttanipāta*
TU	-	*Taittirīya Upaniṣad*
VP	-	*Viṣṇu Purāṇa*

CHAPTER-1

INTRODUCTION

The truth is unanimously accepted, that, all the religions depend upon their scriptural support to anchor their faith for ever. As it is understood, Christianity, Islam and Hinduism are supported by Bible, Quran and *Prasthānatrayam* respectively.[1] Among the *Prasthānatrayam, Upaniṣads* are considered to be the essence of the *Vedas*. They are all in toughest and archaic language and enriched with the diversified, enigmatic and paradoxical truths. Since they demand for an extraordinary intellectual caliber and comprehensive understanding, indeed the ordinary intellectuals may not have the chance to realize their truths. Though *Brahma Sūtras* also absorbs the salient features from the *Upaniṣads* and forms a general dialectical and substantial basement, they hold the different doctrines by interconnecting the numerous theological as well as the philosophical views. But one cannot understand the *sūtras* and *Upaniṣads* directly except with the help of the textual commentaries. Even though *Upaniṣads* and *Brahma Sūtras* are considered to be the wonderful treasure troves of philosophical doctrines, they are not so popular as expected among the intellectual masses because a very few only take pains to grasp the truths. Comparatively since the *Bhagavad Gītā* condenses all the rationalistic essence of *Vedānta* and covers the philosophical wisdom of the *Brahma Sūtras*[2], and expresses the truths directly with reference to the societal needs and current socio-economical and religious problem of the individual as well as it always stands as the beacon light to the ships of the sea.

S. Radhakrishnan holds the view, that, the *Bhagavad Gītā* penetrates and forms a harmonious reconciliation within the diversified truths proclaimed by *Vedas* and the *Upaniṣads*.[3] So, even though the philosophical truths of *Vedic* religion disintegrate from the intellectual as well as the ordinary masses, the science of the *Bhagavad Gītā* certainly could maintain the principles and place them before the society[4] for its onward march towards the humanistic order. The *Gītā-dhyānam* expresses this fact, 'All the *Upaniṣads* are the cows, the milker is Kṛṣṇa, the cowherd boy, Pārtha is the calf, men of purified intellect are the drinkers, the milk is the supreme nectar of the *Gītā*.[5]

The *Bhagavad Gītā* contains seven hundred verses. They have been divided into eighteen chapters, which are included between the twenty-fifth and forty-second chapters of the *Mahābhārata*. The treatment of the text may be brought under three major divisions: (i) The first six chapters are *karma khaṇḍa* which deals with the rituals. (ii) The second six chapters are *bhakti khaṇḍa* which explains the meaning about the devotion. (iii) The last six chapters are *jñāna khaṇḍa* which describes the meaning and the way to acquire the full fledged wisdom and the values and the necessity of self-surrender.[6]

A multifarious discussion upon the Kurukṣetra war-field prove, that, the eternal, infinite, moral and universal spiritual law which is invariably pervading within the empirical activities; within which, the individual struggles to follow the eternal principle throughout his span of life. After realizing his inner nature of the self within the worldly flux, he understands the transcendental essence of God who is permeating within this empirical reality. So, the war-field is nothing but the symbolic representation of the human body where the cousins, the Pāṇḍavas and the Kauravas are nothing but the good and bad inclinations, which coexist in human life. Evil forces emerge out of blind ignorance and the good tendencies emerge from the pure heart; and they try to dominate one over the other; eventually the goodness alone triumphs the kingdom of victory, i.e., the attainment of the Supreme God.

The *Bhagavad Gītā* is not a weapon for the dialectical warfare of human life. Instead, the esoteric text opens the gate to the spiritual truth and even to experience the same. It advocates a supreme divine plane, through which, one could be realized the taste of the Supreme spiritual ecstasy in one's life time itself. A synthetic conception of Kurukṣetra war-field explains the phenomenal fact, that, everybody should fight in his life battle within the two extremes of good and bad. If it is so, the divinity within him guides the individual to get self discipline which paves the way for total emancipation through his perfect sense of duty for duty-sake, rather the duty for deity-sake. If so, he could certainly be reached over the spiritual reach of the Kṛṣṇa-hood[6] and attained the sense of completeness in his life.[7]

With an incredible confidence, one could confess, that, even person with delusion and confusion can get proper guidance to lead a spiritually advanced life. For this, *Gītā* lifts animistic attitudes of the aspirant from the lower level to a humanistic extreme, within which, he renounces all the desires and experiences calm in ceaseless contemplation. The text multifariously investigates the Ultimate Reality through the eternal spiritual values and the steadied wisdom with reason and moral intuition. Franklin Edgerton reasonably advocates that, the *Gītā* is the world scripture and proclaims it as the India's favourite Bible. He conveys the fact, 'It has permeated the collective religious consciousness of the people, from one end of India to the other . . . . not to know it means among them, almost what it would mean for an English speaking person not to know the Bible'[8]. His statement is correct and explicates the truth *per se.*

The spiritual treatments in concern with the social order, the *Gītā* is considered to be the divine, synthetic and universal. The divinity regards God as the supreme and perfect person, 'Puruṣottama'. The synthetic and universal refer to the reconciled approach upon the contradictory views with respect to different religious sects and practices of the modes of life pattern of the world.[9] It is also compared to a diamond among the scriptures because it approaches the all kinds of crisis of human beings. The individual's mind and its struggle within the society to acquire self fulfillment within the multifaceted problems of the humanity.[10] The universal message of the *Gītā* advises the human beings to face the odd situations as there are and shows the ways of action to get success in all walks of life. In this aspect, this work helps even to the ordinary persons to realize the nature of the world as well as themselves within the context of the divinity, which guides the humanity towards the spiritual order.[11] By understanding this, Svāmi Vivekānanda commends upon the scripture, 'the end of all religions is the realizing of God in soul. That is the universal religion'.[12]

The supreme belief in the entire religious attitude invariably refers to the importance of realization of the self from the valuable statement, 'Self-reverence, self-knowledge, self-control. These three lead life to sovereign power'.[13] It is understood about the value of one's own self-realization. Also, a deep analysis of the nature of self would be helpful to get proper perspective, i.e., the subjective realization of the self within the materialistic entanglement of the worldly attachment. Moreover, 'know thyself' is a famous dictum contributed to the world by the Greek Philosopher Socrates. He argues, that, everybody should know himself, because through the knowledge of self alone a person can know his nature, potentialities, propensities, needs, aims; and out of them, he could acquire a reasoning power to get the self-confidence and self-reliance with divine blessings.[14]

Systematized perceptions upon the Western philosophical systems reveal the unavoidable inclinations and human warrant to understand the study of the self. Ionic School of thought assumes, that, the material elements are the basic ones for our life. For example, Thales represents the water, Anaxe-menes refers to the air and Heraclitus believes in fire. The atomists-Leucippus, Democritus and Permenides argue the finer atoms as self. Anaxagoras, the first dualist distinguishes the self as a moving force apart from the material substance.[15] Phthagorian considers the self as a totality and harmony of the body which is movable from one body to another.[16] In the Greek period, Homer argues, that, the self is identical with the breath and it is separable at the time of death. Socrates considers it as consciousness which is the seat of character, knowledge and ignorance.[17] Plato regards it as a self moving force evolving from God which is indestructible and the efficient cause of good and bad.[18] Aristotle explains the self as a related term to the body, where the latter exists for the realization of the self.[19] In the Stoic system, Zeno treats the self as matter.[20] The scholastic system considers the self as an undivided spiritual substance, which is associated with the body.[21] The rationalists Descartes, Spinoza and Leibnitz approach the nature of self in their own way. Among them, Descartes describes the existence of the self through his famous dictum, '*cogito ergo sum*'-'I think therefore I exist';[22] and Spinoza considers the self as an individual modal fraction of either the divine or the natural force.[23] Through the allied mode of thinking, Descartes assumes the mind and matter as substances; and Spinoza treats both as divine attributes. But Leibnitz explains, that, the mind and matter are ultimately constituted by monads.

Each monad represents a minute cosmos which is different from one another.[24] Here the monad may be considered as in some sense of the self.

The British Empiricists Locke, Berkeley and Hume analyse the self in a different manner. Along with the history of analysis, though Descartes asserts, that, the self is a thinking substance with consciousness, Locke empirically verifies, that, the knowledge of the self is not persisting in conception but in apprehension because the self is *'tabula rasa'* a white paper.[25] Berkeley rejects both Descartes and Lockian conception of substance through the epistemological ground. Epistemologically, he rejects the material objects by stating, that, the idea of the material objects may not arise by itself to constitute our knowledge but the Infinite Spirit, which is the background, would be the main cause for the emergence of the ideas.[26] Here the 'idea' would have some reference with the self.

In the core of the thinking, Hume in his own methodologically explains the self as a collective bundle of different perceptions which rapidly moving here and there with perpetual flux and movement.[27] Though his understanding possess his genuine reasoning, they have to be valued along with the opinion of the other scholars. Immanuel Kant, the German Philosopher putforths his view of the self by analyzing the process of knowledge. He considers, that, the self and mind are combined with different sensations and confirm the total object.[28] His epistemological approach towards the self bears two ways. In one way, he states, that, the data of our knowledge which arise from the stimulation of the unknown and unknowable thing-in-itself. With the background, he further proceeds, that, the unknown and the unknowable self is the synthesizing unity of our experiences through the rationalistic faculty and the various activities of our mind.[29] In the history, slowly the thinking towards the idea of God expressively emerged out. In its intellectual way of rationalistic perspective, Fitch, Schopenhauer, St. Augustine, Dun Scouts, William of Occam and Wundt are genuinely considering the 'Free Will' as the constituents of the self; and the Absolute Will is considered to be the God.[30] Herbert confirms the self as a basic entity of simple and absolute concept, which transcends the space and time.[31] Hermaun Lotze defines the self or mind as a higher part of nature, which develops from the grossest matter.[32] Mc Taggart assumes, that, the self by itself is revealing its refined and adequate truths of the Ultimate Reality. F.H. Bradley treats the self as a combination of feelings and thoughts. In the history, he reasonably professes, that, there is absence of the possibility of conceiving the actual nature of self because it may not be located properly.[33] Fechner, a panpsychist confirms the hierarchical order of many selves towards the World Self, 'God'; and within it, God's body is considered to be the material world.[34]

Henry Bergson considers the natural force 'elan vital' is running within the individual and the universe. The actual self can be realized by transcending the ego through intuition but not through the intellect. He also professes, that, the damming up of the stream of life force upon the concomitant matter results in the individual self.[35] William James and Holts are considering the self under neutral monism. They explain the self as an entity which is neither physical nor psychical.[36] Bertrand Russell also supports the explanation of the neutral monism.[37]

So, if we pursue the western history, the reputed thinkers spent much of their time to analyse the nature of self. Moreover, if we perceive them properly, it is unanimously resolved, that, they focused their other venue of thinking only by considering the study of self as the basic factor upon which all other existences depend.

The speciality of the *Gītā* lies in its versatile knowledge in every field, particularly the pivotal problems of human beings. Scholars and intellectuals have observed the limitations of the scientific development and the mystery of the infinitude in the nature. In this respect, the ancient sages have expounded the knowledge of the *Brahma Vidyā*. So, the teachings of the *Bhagavad Gītā* help to acquire the *Brahma Vidyā* to realize the constant state of the self within the continuous flux of the nature.[38] Our day-to-day life consists of two spiritually motivated aspects, that, there is an undoubted eternal and changeless noumenal truth which reveals through *śruti*, where all phenomenal truths have merged and is explained by *smṛti*; and the timeless and eternal truth expresses itself through the time and mind of the human beings. The *Bhagavad Gītā* is considered to be superb because it consists of the above mentioned aspects of temporary and transient ideas which are relevant to current existing problem; and the eternal truth would applicable to all countries beyond the spacio-temporal factors.[39]

The *Gītā* preaches a message for the human beings to have a self-purified life through the means of *bhakti, jñāna, karma* and other *yogas*. Generally if a scripture propounds spiritual knowledge for self-perfection, it ignores our earthly life and differentiates the transcendental life from that of the mundane. But it treats both in a balanced approach. It makes the best use of our mundane existence and draws the inspirations from the transcendental existence.[40] Habitually all our human activities are divided into two types as the spiritual and temporal or the sacred and secular. But the *Gītā* is away from these artificial distinctions because it treats the life as the spiritual force, which experiences the moral world. As such, through the spiritual and moral fulfillment, automatically the force transcends the material world and leads towards the centre of the divinity. Normally, change in a body does not add anything to the total personality of a human being, but change of an attitude towards the action decides the person. Here, an action in the hands of spiritual person becomes sacred but the same one with the material attitude sinks down to the secular and vulgar plane. Being an universal scripture, the *Gītā* elevates all our activities into the spiritual plane through the modification of one's materialistic attitude from lower to higher spiritual plane. At the same time, it gives much importance to will, emotion and cognition for the constitution of a perfect mind. If the mind performs its function, then automatically spirituality will be hailed down from the divinity. So, one can say, that, the *Gītā* covers the human endeavors in all walks of life and leads him towards perfection.

The *Gītā* guides a man to build up a perfect personality with harmonious development in a three dimensional way: (i) *Acquiring Strong Physique*: helping the aspirant to acquire a strong body with stable mind and to develop an efficient character. (ii) *Developing Compassion*: preaching the supreme and intensified love and emanate sweetness to the entire living beings. (iii) *Meaningful Life*: Helping to acquire the highest knowledge, they enable one to lead a right and perfect life. So, this universal measure provides the opportunity to evolve a complete personality which merges with the Divinity.[41] The theme of the *Gītā* is beyond the time series; and from it, it could be inferred that, it for ever will direct the humanity towards the right direction. To illustrate this, Lord Kṛṣṇa says to Arjuna, 'That same ancient *Yoga* has been to-day taught to thee by Me, seeing that thou art My devotee and friend; for, this is the Supreme Secret'.[42] Following this, He continues, 'For this protection of the good, for the destruction of the evil-doers, for the firm establishment of religion, I am born in every age'.[43] So, from this discussion, it is verified, that, an in-depth research upon the self as expounded in the *Gītā* would be a necessary one and the result may guide the society as well as the individual for the total emancipation of the worldly order to the spiritual order with the moral and spiritual perfection.

The above perspectives necessarily may initiate over-flowing interest to acquire a deep and wide knowledge of the self in the *Gītā*. For this, the following objectives would be outlined; so that, the entire theme upon the treatment of the *Gītā* would be understood. So, this research would be conducted with following methodology.

To understand the nature of self in Indian Philosophy, a bird's eye-view is systematized. Out of it *Gītā's* treatment of the self and its specific place in Indian Philosophy and the way of approach by the text towards self would be understood.

The relation of the *Gītā* with *Sāṅkhya*, *Yoga*, Jainism and *Buddhism* is argued; so that, one could easily understand how the text talks its basic themes from the tradition and how it justifies the treatment with the necessary theistic as well as philosophical background. Through the study, by knowing the explanation of the self in relation with the body, the means could be understood, so that, the maturity of the self could be reasonably elucidated. Along with the study, the value of God's grace and the destiny of the self; and the identity between the higher self and God could be treated well. Out of them, the greatness of the divinity could be realized.

Herewith, an important point should be added. It is the opinion, that, though we with much care and intellectual background which included with modern technique of methodology, to understand the central core of the traditional text is very tough, perhaps, the *modus operandi* of the text may not be accurately perceived. Instead the indication of the central core of the text may be missed; otherwise, quite even misunderstood. But the traditional scholars who wrote commentaries upon it perceives the central theme without fail; and even that could be appreciated. Along with the perception, they also add many more authentic views with reference to the self. Apart from this, if one go along with the notion of the traditional commentator of the text, it is easily possible to understand the themes as they are; and could easily enjoy the in-depth meanings of the text with its current references. If it is to be convened, that, to ensure this research more successful and original to the text; and to make it useful to the society as well to the individual; an intellectual exercise is executed to review the important traditional commentaries of the *Bhagavad Gītā* by Śrī Śaṅkara and Śrī Rāmānuja within the comprehensive preview of the metaphysical treatment of the self. In it, the analysis is intrinsically valued with respect to their viability, easiness and pertinent to the current relevance towards the modernity.

Moreover, for any research, the discussions would be relevant to the individual as well as to society; if not, it could be considered as the mere intellectual exercise and utmost useless to the common people. So, the study could be referred to the reference to the upliftment of the individual and the improvement of the society as well.

With this background, by following this discussion, the second chapter touches upon the concept of self as expounded in heterodox and orthodox systems of Indian Philosophy. In the heterodox systems, *Cārvāka's* treatment of matter as self, *Buddhistic* concept of *anātmavāda* and *Jaina's* self as growing entity are sharply analysed. In the orthodox systems, the self in *Vedas, Upaniṣads* and in Śrī Śaṅkara's *Advaita* are analysed under 'Absolutism'; the self by Śrī Rāmānuja, Śrī Madhva, Śrī Nimbārka and Śrī Vallabha are examined under 'Theistic Absolutism'; and the self in *Nyāya Vaiśeṣika, Mīmāṁsā* and *Sāṅkhya* are explained under 'Realism'. In the end, metaphysics of self in the *Bhagavad Gītā* and its place in Indian Philosophy is academically codified.

The third chapter is a comparative study of the self in the *Bhagavad Gītā* and Indian Philosophical systems of *Sāṅkhya, Yoga, Jainism* and *Buddhism* where a special attempt is made to elucidate their philosophical and terminological affinities among the said systems.

In the fourth chapter, a comprehensive attempt is being made to thoroughly study the metaphysics of the self with respect to the text, the *Gītā*. The discussion is started with the analysis of manifestated, *vyakta* and the unmanifested, *avyakta* state of the self; and in what way they are controlled under the wishful command of the Ultimate Reality. For that, the *Vedic, Upaniṣadic,* Biblical and Islamic views are discussed, where the drawbacks are also appropriately discussed. Along with these views, the *Gītā's* opinion is elucidated through its perception of the manifested and the unmanifested states. Then, the study stresses the self as 'agent' in the empirical order and as 'non-agent' in the transcendental sphere. To unveil the unique features of the self from all the psychophysical complex as *buddhi, manas, indriyas* and the individual's worldly activities, a proper study is included. Out of the study, the fact, that, the self as a transmigrating entity which is undergoing metempsychosis from one generation to another is properly elucidated. To catch the actual gist, the spiritual nature of the self is necessarily debated. While studying the spiritual maturity of the self towards perfection, the nature of lower grade of the self as carnal self and its maturation of higher position as spiritual are genuinely examined. To raise the lower self to higher spiritual self, the means as *karma yoga, jñāna yoga* and *bhakti yoga* are discussed. Along with the study, the self in moral order and its nature of obedience to the grace of God are accurately discussed with the relevant verses of the *Bhagavad Gītā*. Lastly, an investigation is being undertaken to examine the destiny of the self and the way of its activities within the materialistic order of the universe.

In the fifth chapter, a comparative account has been drawn between Śrī Śaṅkara's conceptions of the self and that of Śrī

Rāmānuja. A careful analysis of rigidity of Śrī Śaṅkara's *Advaitic* approach and the flexibility of Śrī Rāmānuja's *Viśiṣṭādvaitic* approach are verified. Here the latter view is justified with reference to the needs of the society and the easiest way to regulate them towards the divinity.

In the sixth chapter, the cardinal points are dealt with regarding the dissatisfaction and misunderstanding of the humanity in the field of metaphysics, philosophy and science. In it, the inequality of religious, social, political and economical ground in which the necessity of the metaphysics of the self for renovation of the society towards the spiritual order are analysed. Through the *Gītā's* teachings, a study is attempted for a life of *summum bonum* to the individual in particular and the society in general. For the individuals, the value of *niṣkāmyakarma yoga*, the ways of raising the lower carnal self to the higher spiritual self, versatile views of *svadharma* and the right perspectives of the law of *karma* and *paradharma* are discussed. For the society, the message of the value of non-attachment towards the material side, evolution of the universal self through love, value of the middle path, harmonization of the different *yogas*, the necessity of *sātvika jñāna* and the needs of the world religion are discussed. Also, the drawbacks of the scientific invention which indirectly directs the humanity towards the wrong side of destruction are practically analysed. Out of them, the necessity of the understanding of the inner spiritual nature of the self with reference to the Supreme command of the God for the fulfillment of the goodness within the world is critically discussed.

The conclusion gives a gist of the findings that have been elaborately dealt within the five chapters with a special emphasis on the importance and relevance of this study for the modern world, along with its scientifically tempered and guide it towards the spiritual order.

REFERENCES

1. Chidbhavananda Swami, *The Bhagavad Gītā*, pp. 1-2.
2. Ragavachar, S.S., *Sri Ramanuja on the Gītā*, pp. vi-ix.
3. Radhakrishnan, S., *Bhagavad Gītā*, p. 14.
4. Satwalekar Shripad Damodar, *Shrimad Bhagavad Gītā*, Vol. I, p. 4.
5. *sarvoupaniṣado gāvo dogdhā gopālanandanaḥ/*
pārtho vatsaḥ sudhīr bhoktā dugdhaṁ gītāmṛtaṁ mahat//
-Gītādhyānam.
6. Chidbhavananda, Swami, *op.cit.*, p. 9.
7. *Ibid.*, p. 17.
8. Edgerton, Franklin, *The Bhagavad Gītā*, p. vii.
9. Adhedananda, Swami, *op.cit.*, pp. 4-5.
10. Vadekar, D.D., *Bhagavad Gītā*, p. 4.
11. Wood, Ernest, *The Bhagavad Gītā*, pp. 3-4.
12. Vivekananda, Swami, *The Complete Works of Swami Vivekananda*, p. 324.
13. *The Oxford Dictionary of Quotations* (Second Edition), p. 537.
14. Phillipson, Coleman, *The Trail of Socrates*, pp. 107-109.
15. *The Encyclopedia Americana* — The International Reference Works, Vol. 25, p. 259.
16. Hastings, James, (Ed.), *Encyclopedia of Religion and Ethics*, Vol. 10, p. 523.
17. Hastings, James. (Ed.), Vol. II, *op. cit.*, p. 741.
18. *Ibid.*
19. *Ibid.*
20. Hastings, James. (Ed.), *op.cit.*, Vol. 5, p. 327.
21. *The Encyclopaedia Americana*, *op. cit.*, Vol. 25, p. 269.
22. Edwards, Paul (Editor in chief), *The Encyclopaedia of Philosophy*, Vol. 2, p. 347.
23. *Ibid.*, pp. 535-536.
24. *Ibid.*, pp. 429-430.
25. *Ibid.*, pp. 490-491.
26. *Ibid.*, Vol. 1, pp. 300-301.

27. *Ibid.*, Vol. 4, pp. 88-89.
28. Banerjee, V.V., *History of Western Philosophy*, p. 261.
29. Edwards, Paul (Ed.in chief), *op.cit.*, Vol. 4, pp. 314-317.
30. *The Encyclopaedia Americana*, Vol. 25, pp. 270-271 and Hastings James, Vol. 5, *op.cit.*, p. 907.
31. Edwards, Paul, (Ed. in chief), *The Encyclopedia of Philosophy*, Vol. 3, pp. 481-482.
32. Hastings, James (Ed.), *op.cit.*, Vol. 3, pp. 148-150.
33. Laird, John, *The Idea of the Soul*, p. 42.
34. Edwards, Paul (Ed. in chief), *op.cit.*, Vol. 3, p. 185 and *The Encyclopaedia Americana*, *op. cit.*, Vol. 25, p. 270.
35. Edwards, Paul (Ed. in chief), *op.cit.*, Vol. 1, pp. 293-294.
36. Runes, Dogbert, D. (Ed.), *The Dictionary of Philosophy*, p. 209.
37. *The Encyclopaedia Americana*, Vol. 25, *op.cit.*, p. 271 and Edwards Paul (Ed.-in-Chief), *op.cit.*, Vol. 7, pp. 255-256.
38. Chidbhavananda, Swami, *op. cit.*, pp. 30-31.
39. Roy, Anilbaran (Ed.), *The Message of the Gita —As Interpreted by Sri Aurobindo*, p. xv.
40. Chidbhavananda, Swami *op.cit.*, p. 63.
41. *Ibid.*, p. 65.
42. *sa evāyaṁ mayā te adya yogaḥ proktaḥ purātanaḥ/*
    bhakto asi me sakhā ceti, rahasyaṁ hyetad uttamam//—BG, 4. 3.
43. *paritrāṇāya sādhūnāṁ vināśāya ca duṣkṛtām/*
    dharma-saṁsthāpanārthāya saṁbhavāmi yuge yuge// —Ibid., 4. 8.

CHAPTER-2

METAPHYSICS OF SELF IN INDIAN PHILOSOPHY

Generally, Indian Philosophy defines the self as spiritual entity and it is described as *avināśi*, 'indestructible', *nitya*, 'eternal', *sarvagata*, 'all pervasive' and *vikārya*, 'immutable'. The self is considered to be *jñātā*, 'knower', *bhoktā*, 'enjoyer', *karttā*, 'doer' and it is associated with one's *buddhi, manas* and *jñāna-karma-indriyas*. The self acts as the basis for our experiences, sensuous desires, instincts, emotions, sentiments and the motives of likes and dislikes. Transcendentally, the self is a counterpart of the ultimate reality and immanently it varies with respect to its connection with worldly activities. The essence of the self in transcendental sphere is the same as the universal spirit. But its differences in the worldly level are one temporary because its nature depends upon its empirical activities. The essence of the self as Reality in the transcendental realm has been derived from the deviation of the immanent study of the self in its practical experiences and the external condition of the world. Various studies of the self represent the different approaches and apprehensions made by the particular system, with respect to the infinite conditions of the phenomenal order.[1] These divergent characters of Indian Philosophy reject the negative and pessimistic description but explain the self through several stages of development with optimistic attitude.[2]

Indian Philosophy includes two division namely *Āstika* and *Nāstika* systems; the former develops from *Vedas* and the latter being independent of it. The *Āstika* systems are the offshoot of the belief in the highest power which in turn is revealed through our spiritualistic intellect.[3] The *Nāstika* systems reject the orthodox beliefs because they embrace only feelings, thoughts and the right conduct.[4] The *Nāstika* systems help self-realisation through worldly activities. The *Āstika* systems advise the human beings to know the divinity in self-realisation through *brahmacarya, gṛahastha, vānaprastha* and *saṁnyāsa*.[5]

Generally the *Nāstika* systems reject the authority of the *Vedas* and neither deny nor accept the existence of God by professing the absence of anything apart from the self; rather, no need of the discussion about Him. These systems except *Cārvāka* accept the law of *karma* which is working without any external guidance and command. *Cārvāka* considers the entire body itself as self, where the consciousness is the by-product of the body and liberation means the mere extinction of the body. This system totally rejects the law of *karma*, heaven and hell and gives way for total enjoyment in the phenomenal order for every possible ways. Jaina system accepts the realities of the external world with many selves where even the dust particles, plants and animals are also having the selves with consciousness but varied in qualities. The system refers to the self as a growing entity i.e., condensation and expansion as in the size of the bodies. In Buddhism, the self is represented as a stream of consciousness; which is always changing from one state to another; *nirvāṇa* means the positive bliss and the law of *karma* works by itself without any permanent self. Among the four schools of Buddhism, the first two schools of the *Theravāda Buddhism* describe the self as a changing series but their explanations are not fulfilled and answerable for all the doubts. Those doubts are rectified in the next two schools of *Mahāyāna Buddhism*. Though the *Nāstika* systems explain the nature of self as such; they in themselves fulfilled the requirement of the arguments.

In the *Āstika* systems, the explanations of the spiritual self pave the way to realize the nature of ultimate reality. These systems assume *atmānaṁ viddhi*, 'by knowing the spiritual self everything can be known'[6] as the dictum, which is relevant to the religious needs of society. Every *Āstika* system analyses the nature of self in its own distinct way with logic reason. The treatment transcends our self consciousness through intuition, revelation, cosmic consciousness and divine vision.[7] They are approaching the stable and permanent Reality as selves, atoms, *puruṣa* and *prakṛti* and Brahman. All the systems independently aim at the practical end of salvation through natural integration with fulfilled mental poise and freedom from the sufferings and sorrows of the worldly flux. So, this system gives importance to worldly activities, rebirth, pre-existence and the progressive development of the self which merges into the God. Ordinarily, human beings pass through *saṁsāra* with clinging hopes. They are expecting the divinity to dominate over the passions and the unreal world. For this, the *Āstika* systems provide the facilities to realize the actual self through selfless love, disinterested activities and *cittaśuddhi*, 'cleaning of heart'; which clean the self, where at the final the divinity with its Grace hails down to fulfill the spiritual needs of it.

In order to analyse and understand the metaphysics of self the orthodox systems is classified into three types. They are: (i) Spiritualistic Absolutism treats the self as an ultimate entity and which is identical with God. This system includes *Upaniṣads* and *Advaita Vedānta*. (ii) Theistic Absolutism considers the innumerable finite selves which are independently existing as the bodies of the ultimate reality but not identical with Him. This school includes *Viśiṣṭādvaita, Dvaita, Dvaitādvaita* and *Śhuddhādvaita*. (iii) Realism regards the self infinite and real entities. This system includes *Nyāya Vaiśeṣika* and *Mīmāṁsā's* pluralistic realism and the *Sāṅkhya's* dualistic realism. So, with this above classification, the research upon the metaphysic of self will be preceded.

Āstika systems of Indian Philosophy beyond doubt reject the resemblance of self with *indriyas, manas, buddhi* and *anubhūti*. It accepts the resemblance between the divinity and the self but only in gradations. According to the absolutist Śrī Śaṅkara, the self mingles within the sphere of non-self through the process of understanding, knowing, thinking and it is acting as a basic model entity. Transcendentally, it is identifying with the ultimate reality rather it is in all respects. Śrī Rāmānuja, Śrī Madhva, Śrī Vallabha and Śrī Nimbārka, the theistic absolutists differ from Śrī Śaṅkara. They state that at any situation the self does not leave its selfhood. But they accept the dualistic notion of self and non-self where the self resembles the divinity in certain respects only. So, *mukti* means the annihilation of non-self and realization of actual self through elimination of *avidya* with the help of God's grace. But Śrī Śaṅkara differs where *mukti* means the realization of the *vyāvahārika* nature of God through proper *jñāna*. So, through the *jñāna* the illusory appearance of individual self disappears and the God is completely absorbed in the self.[8]

As for the *Nyāya Vaiśeṣika* and *Mīmāṁsā* systems *mukti* means the realization of the selfhood. But *Sāṅkhya* system deviates from the above two systems and treats *mukti* as the conceiving the self as essentially consciousness.[9] Absolutism regards the self as ultimate reality and so God is only an efficient cause of the world. The theistic absolutism treats God as efficient as well as material cause because the self is only a part of the ultimate reality. Within this, Śrī Rāmānuja's view differs from other's view. He argues that God is superior to world which is the material cause and the self as the efficient cause. Absolutists are considering the ultimate reality as beyond the subjective and the objective elements. Non-absolutists consider the reality as a spiritual entity pervading within the being and the non-being, i.e. the subjective as well as objective sides. In *Sāṅkhya* system, the self acts as a spectator only and not as an agent or an enjoyer but in *Nyāya* and *Vaiśeṣika* the self wills, feels and acts.

2.1. *NĀSTIKA* SYSTEMS

2.1.1. *Cārvāka*

Cārvāka accept that the *lokāyata* is their scripture; perception is authority; four *bhūtas* of earth, water, fire and air are the only elements; human existence is intended for enjoyment; mind is nothing but the combination of the four elements; there is no heaven or hell; and death alone liberates the self. The self means nothing but the *caitanya*, 'conscious body' which is an epi-phenomenon, a by-product of matter. It arises from the emergent and dialectical evolution. The nature of self is like the formation of the intoxicative wine from fermented yeast which associates with the body and disappears at the time of its disintegration[10]. *Cārvākas* are categorized into three kinds of materialists. They are *dekhātmavādin,* who identifies the self with the *sthūla śarīra; indriyātmavādin,* who regards the self as the senses; and *prāṇātmavādin,* who realizes no difference between *manas* and *ātma*. There is also another kind of division, the *dhūrta,* 'cunning' and the *suśikṣita,* 'educated'; where the former considers the conscious body itself as self and the latter visualizes the self as external knowledge and enjoys the different experiences. The self perishes with body and it does not migrate from one body to another or from one birth to the next birth.

Cārvāka rejects the immortality of the self, the doctrine of *karma,* the transmigration of self, the results of good and bad actions; and the belief in the *adṛṣṭa.*[11] According to them, the virtuous activities are only delusions and the enjoyment alone is real. This system totally rejects the immortality because there is no self apart from body. Morality in materialism is nothing but seeking pleasure to the maximum and the moral values are only phantoms because they are unreal arising out of the diseased mind and virtues are mere false belief. This system teaches the doctrine of *svabhāva* as self-existence which is neither the cause nor the effect leading to total rejection of the causality and the good and bad effects of our activities.[12]

Indian Philosophy criticizes the materialism especially on the concept of the consciousness as expounded in the *Cārvāka*. Human beings are having the rational consciousness but animals are having only ordinary consciousness. For this, *Cārvāka* asserts that the reason is a particular combination of the elements. If one accepts this view, then, the body and consciousness should have inseparable connection. But actually it is not so because in certain time like swoons, fits, epilepsy and dreamless sleep, consciousness is absent from the body. Moreover, consciousness may not be the effect of the particular combination of the elements because within the walking, dreaming and dreamless state the consciousness controls the material body. The enjoyer and the subjective knower will never persist as the enjoying object because the objects are existing before the particular object. So, consciousness alone helps to realize the body and which may not be identical with body. Moreover, consciousness and body should have some differences within it like sight and light. Without light sight is impossible, for that the light and sight are not synonymous like consciousness and body. A careful study reveals, that, this system does not deny the spiritual principle but it does not hold it as ultimate. But this system regards it as a by-product of physical aggregative and it disappears when the body disintegrates.[13]

If one accepts the *Cārvāka's* view of consciousness as body, he should perceive the consciousness itself as our body. But actually it is not so. Practically, in consciousness, there is some individual variation but *Cārvāka* system does not accept it. So materialistic philosophy of self is unacceptable because it denies the human values such as *dharma* and *mokṣa*. But, without the belief upon the values our life may be comparable with animal life. Even though, man is a biological animal and he is rational with moral values.

2.1.2. Jainism

According to *Jaina*, there are nine kinds of *padārthas;* within these, the *jīva* and the *ajīva* are two major *padārthas*. Jainism advocates dualism of mind and body. Within the individual, the external *indriyas* are distinguished as *dravya-indriyas* 'physical sense organs' and the *bhāva-indriyas*, 'psychical counterparts that which constitute the *jīva*'.[14]

Jaina considers the self as spiritual substance which is immaterial, incorporeal and distinct from the body and the sense-organs. At the same time, the self is *svataḥpramāṇya*, 'self co-exists with the material body'. The self phenomenally unites with *karmic* forces which undergo many births and deaths but ontologically the self is existing as eternal without any beginning and end. Like *Sāṅkhya* system, *Jaina* holds the many selves divided into two types namely *saṁsāra*, 'bounded' and *mukta*, 'liberated self'. The *saṁsāra* selves are limited by *upādhi*, 'adjuncts' bearing gross or subtle bodies and they are having impure and finite knowledge because of its *karmic* forces. The *mukta* selves are free from material bodies and the limitations of the *karmic* forces because they possess pure and infinites knowledge.[15]

The Jaina system accepts the self as substance and the qualities as its attributes. The qualities are something different from the other systems of Indian Philosophy. In *Advaita Vedānta* the substance is real and the qualities are its false appearance. The Buddhistic view regards the substance as unreal but the aggregate of the five *skandhas* is real. The *Nyāya Vaiśeṣika* admits that there is no identity between the substance and attribute. Unlike *Sāṅkhya's puruṣa, Jaina's jīva* is not only a knower takes responsibility for its acts to the worldly activities. This system proclaims that the *jīva* as an agent or active being possesses the freedom of will. If the freedom of will is tide up with the *karmic* force, the self is in bondage. But at the same time if the self separates itself from the *karmic* forces the self will be in the state of liberation.

In the *Nāstika* systems, *Cārvāka* rejects God as well as the authority of the *Vedas*. But Jainism is not so because it accepts the theistic element, i.e., the system emphasizes the intensive spiritual quality of *jīva* and treats the liberated self as God. If the word, *nāstika* refers to the rejection of God, then one should also consider *Sāṅkhya* and *Mīmāṁsā* as *Nāstika* because they also reject God. So, *Jainism* and *Buddhism* are termed as *Nāstika* because they deny only the authoritativeness of the *Vedas*.

Jaina system regards the consciousness as the main spiritual essence of the *jīva*, which pervades throughout the body. They are qualitatively same but quantitatively differed. The former refers to the spiritual nature of the self and the latter shows the dimension of the *jīva* with respect to the body.[16] *Jaina's jīva* is invariably mingling as intermediate dimension of finite and infinite or eternality and non-eternality- *'madhyama-parimāṇa'*. The eternality of the *jīva* refers to the consciousness which is the result of the union of the different parts of the body. When the union is destroyed, the nature of consciousness becomes non-eternal but this *madhyamaparimāṇa* is untenable because this system denies the destruction of the *jīva*.[17] The Jaina system accepts dualism as spiritual and non-spiritual within the *jīva* and *ajīva*. But they are related with each other in the specific realm of *'madhyamaparimāṇa'*. The *Jaina* system describes the universe as ranging from the material elements of earth, water, fire and air to the human beings which are spiritual in nature. But they differ in their degrees of perfection.[18]

The very important characteristic feature of the self in Jaina philosophy is the pervading feature of consciousness throughout the body of living beings. The self is having the capacity of expansion and contraction with respect to the dimension of the physical body within the time series.[19] In this respect, the self is pervading as light rays illuminating within the space of closed room whether small or big. Like this, many selves are occurring within the space without any collapse or contraction. Eventhough there is the absence of form, it has acquired the form as the form of the body. Moreover, the *jīva* is having the feature of expansion and condensation, i.e., the *jīva* of an elephant having a larger form with expansion and during its next birth it may be transformed into the self of the condensed form of an ant with respect to its *karmic* forces.[20]

The Jaina system blindly argues, that, the nature of self as *anu* is occupying the space proportionate to the body. Moreover, if one accepts the *Jaina's jīva* which is pervading within the space as light rays, then it becomes impermanent and transient because the light rays are nothing but the diffused parts of the light itself and they are having beginning and end. One can add, that, in the rarified place the light particles are lesser in degree and in the condensed place they are greater in degree. Like that, the rarified self is not having insufficient knowledge and the condensed self is not bearing the additional knowledge. So, one cannot accept the *Jaina's* explanation because eventhough the smallest insect has the closed physical parts, it does not have more knowledge. The *Jaina's* explanation of the *jīvas* is not acceptable because of its baseless argument of the condensation and the expansion of the *madhyamaparimāṇa* of the *jīva*.[21]

The Jaina's *karmic* forces are infra-atomic particles of matter activated by mind, body and speech under the influence of desire, aversion and delusion. They are playing a major part to pull back the spiritual quality from the *jīva* and push it towards *kaṣāya*, 'the passion'. The association of the *karmic* force with the *jīva* is inconceivable and incompatible with the dualism of *jīva* and *ajīva*.[22] Eventhough Jaina system considers the *karmic* force as material, it does not come under the category of *ajīva*. This itself shows the obscurity of the spirit and matter. This *karmic* force through the passion results in bondage of the self which causes attachment and carelessness. In this respect, one may distinguish four kinds of *karmic* forces; *mohanīya karma*, 'deluding one' which is having connection in the *saṁsāra* level; *antarya karma* which is entangled in mundane affairs and develops resistance towards the noble endeavours of the self; *jñānāvaranīya karma*, which obscures the right knowledge of the self; *darśanavaranīya karma*, which arrests the right faith in the self.[23]

There may be another division of *jīvas* which mingles with the mundane existence due to the *karmic* forces. They are selves born in hell, selves in animal world, selves in human society and the selves which are born in the divine kingdom. *Jaina's karmic* forces are not like the views of *Sāṅkhya Yoga* and the *Advaita* of Śrī Saṅkara but acting as a real and determining principle of the bondage upon the self. In this respect, it resembles *Nyāya Vaiśeṣika* and *Mīmāṁsā* systems.

The speciality of the *Jaina* system is seen in the fact, that, everything within the solar system from dew-drops to animals are having selves like earth self, fire self and water self, which are gross or subtle and gets birth and rebirth in the *sama* body or other elements. For example, each plant possesses one or many embodied selves where the plants having one self are always gross and survive on its habitual part of the world. They group themselves and live in a colony of many plants which are subtle, invisible and distributed throughout the world and such group is called as *nigoda* in and they are composed of multiple selves. So, the whole universe is made up of many *nigodas* and wherever the selves of plants attained *mokṣa*, 'liberation', these *nigodas* are filling the vacancies by extending the small fraction of the infinitesimal *nigoda* in the place of those liberated from the beginningless past to the present.[24]

Moreover, through the logical analysis of the *syādvāda* and *anekāntavāda*, the *Jaina* system gets the lapses because of the absence of Absolutism. Without this Absolutism, one cannot synthesize the *jīva* and *pudgala*. If one compares it with the *Sāṅkhya*, that, clearly emphasizes the differences of contact between *prakṛti* and *puruṣa*. Though the *Jaina* system of realistic pluralism does not mention the *jīvas* and *pudgala* as the distinctive realities, both are really united. Regarding this concept, there are many conflicts. They are: the *jīva* possesses pure consciousness, pure bliss, pure power and pure faith and which may not have connection with the matter which is unconscious and lifeless; the pure consciousness of self will not mingle with ignorance, passion and the *karmic* forces; and when ignorance and *karmic* forces are having unification with the self, the *mokṣa* may be impossible. Moreover, the system visualizes the union of spirit and matter as real and beginning-less. If it so, the liberation is never possible because a thing which is real and beginningless cannot be removed for ever.

If one includes a single absolute as ultimate reality, all the above said drawbacks will be solved. Then, one can easily infer the ultimate reality as transcending the immanent duality of the *jīvas* and matter. The actual reality is above the *karmic* forces and the unreal manifestation of the plural nature of self with relation to the empirical field.[25] So, from the above critical argument, it is seen, that, it should accept the Absolute, the God as in the *Āstika* systems.

2.1.3. Buddhism

According to Buddhism, everything in the universe is momentary and nothing is permanent so as to have a *svabhāvasaṁyata*, 'substantial base'. So, the self is referred to as baseless, relative and false. Buddhism asserts that the self is in a state of continuous flux of the '*santānā*' or *saṁskārapravīṇa*, 'succession of experiences' or 'aggregate of the unreal five *skandhas*', namely *rūpa*, 'material factors', *vedana*, 'feeling', *saṁjñā*, 'conceiving or generalizing factor', *saṁskāra*, 'volition and other mental forces', and *viñjñāna*, consciousness'.[26] If one thinks the self as true nature, then it would be only a false selfish motive which is ascribed to the substantial reality of constantly flexible impermanent physique or psychic element in the universe.

Generally after Buddha, the techniques were slightly modified and interpreted by his disciples through the four different schools viz., *Vaibhāṣika* and *Sautrāntikā* schools of *Hīnayāna* Buddhism and *Yogāchāras* and *Śūnyavādin* schools of *Mahāyāna* Buddhism. A systematic study of each school with reference to self reveals the actual nature of it.

2.1.3.1. *Hīnayāna Buddhism*

The two schools of *Hīnayāna Buddhism* reject the self substance but accept a series of fleeting ideas as explained in *kṣaṇabhaṅgavāda*, 'theory of continuous moment'. Every aspect of the universe is momentary, impermanent, conditional, dependent, relative, i.e., *pratītyasamutpāda* which is a continuously changing series but changes are linked with each other to form a chain. Within this chain everything is neither being nor not-being but includes ultimate reality as a stream of becoming. Here, it should be noted, that, the chain is not leaving any permanent substance; where as the serious itself seems to be a continuous, which is assumed as such out of wrong perception.

The Greek Philosopher, Hiraclitus supports this concept, that, one cannot bathe twice in the same river because the river is a rapid, cohesive and successive flow of water. The British empiricist Hume argues that he did not catch his self because whenever he tried he stumbled on this or that perception. So, he adds that the self is absolutely unexplainable and unanswerable one but it is simply a collection of different perceptions which move here and there with perpetual flux and movement.[27] William James considers the self as *Hīnayāna* Buddhism under neutral monism and proclaims a system where he states that in a peculiar model aggregation of the stream of conscious states seems to be the self. Here, this aspect may be compared with the flame of a lamp where a series of flames evolve one after another without any break from the first flame. Henry Bergson, the vitalist, considers the unknown nature Élan vital which is passing through the manifested and unmanifested object of beings and non-beings of the universe without any break.[28] Dr. McDougall's animistic notion towards the evolution of anything resembles the *Buddhistic* conception of the self. He observes that within the stream of conscious states at the time of particular unique unification a new character emerges with respect to the subjective environmental status.[29]

Within the stream of consciousness, the cosmic order continues further and further without any maker and beginner. Identity and permanence of states exist only because of the rapid succession. So, one views the stream of consciousness as self. Ultimately *Hīnayāna* Buddhism represents the self as the streaming consciousness of our own ideas and the matter as continuously changing stream of atoms of the four *bhūtas*, i.e., the earth, water, fire and air. Buddhism treats mind and body as a single reality of synonymously moving synthesis with the everchanging empirical consciousness. Within this universe, every individual's activity takes place without the self as an agent; then transmigration means not the migration of self from one birth to next but only its characters, where they are depending upon the impersonal law of *karma* without any assistance of the divine quality. After death within the five *skandhas*, the *saṁskāra*, the changing tendencies of volition and the mental forces' is leading to the next birth as one flame lights the another flame with respect to its accumulated *karmas*. Both past and present life may not be identical like the different flames of the two different lamps. *Hīnayāna* Buddhism treats cognition and memory as recollection of the former moments and the accumulation of the previous knowledge flourishing within certain condition without any agent just as the same fire reaching the particular object in a particular time. With this analogy, one can say, that, the self of a particular individual is the derivation of the accumulative factors within the momentary elements of sensations, images and feelings. So, the self is only a fiction, a mere noumenal existence, a mere description, acquaintance which cannot be grasped by senses or by pure intellect like naming an object. For example, the milk is nothing but a thick fluid of fictitious unification of some colour and taste.[30] Here, *mukti* means negation of rebirth and the annihilation of *upādhāna* by destroying the *avidya*, 'root cause' for our past, present and future life through proper *jñāna* which is behind the five *skandhas*. *Hīnayāna Buddhism* goes into deep towards the conception of the *mukti* as 'blowing out' or 'cessation of all our activities' or 'dissolution of the five *skandhas*'. At the same time, *mukti* may be considered as positive bliss of fearless goal with an indestructible state of the highest bliss which is obtained within the empirical realm. So, *nirvāṇa* is comparable to the extinction of the flame of a lamp after the consumption of its oil as a person attains the state of *mukti* after the consumption of his own desire and passion.

Upto this, both *Vaibhāṣika* and *Sautrāntika* schools of *Hīnayāna Buddhism* agree with each other but between them there are some differences of opinion which may be examined in the following passages.

2.1.3.1.1. *Vaibhāṣika* School

This school is considered to be realistic because the mind and the matter are objectively real and one can get knowledge directly and immediately without any intermediary between the object and his knowledge. The speciality of *Vaibhāṣika* realism is the attribute towards the impermanence of *pratītyasamutpāda*, 'the twelve causal link within the past, present and future'. This *Vaibhāṣika* system deviates from the general concept of the continuous flux to the continuous existence of a thing through past, present and future.[31]

This school asserts that the understanding nature of the world is the unification of the simple and not analysable elements which leads to form concrete objects. This has been not guided by any external agency or fate or God but an unexplainable law of causation. The law of causality within the empirical field is nothing but the outcome of the accumulated *saṃskāra*, 'conditioned elements of ignorance' which is continuing from one birth to next to form *pratītyasamutpāda*, 'existence with paid and sufferings'. Here, one can stop the *pratītyasamutpāda* as emerging out of the *pratisāṁkhya norodha* or *nirvāṇa*, i.e., overthrowing the might causality by means of practicing of *sila*, 'virtues', *samādhi*, 'mediation' and *prajñā*, 'intuitive knowledge'. Like that, one can replace the phenomenal order of pain and misery by noumenal order without the sufferings and its potentialities.[32] In short, both mind and matter are real and the knowledge arises out of direct intact of the both. So, this school deviates from the general conception of the *Buddhistic* doctrines of momentary, substancelessness and the *svalakṣaṇa*, particular it; against the *sāmānya*, 'universality'.

2.1.3.1.2. *Sautrāntikā* School

Sautrāntikā School rejects the *Vaibhāṣika's* attitude towards the performance of the substance in the past, present and future, because of two major reasons. They are as follows: (i) if the same thing exists in the past, present and future, then the temporal distinctions is unreal and meaningless; (ii) This permanence leads *anāthame*, 'tantamount of the rehabilitation' and constant substance with the externalism.[33]

Descartes supports this view. The permanent existence is not absolutely self-evident and demonstratable because the malignant spirit produces the ideas of the object through our mind, which are not real.[34] The assumption of the permanence is only a temporary existence of certain accumulated properties for certain time, which is flashing within our consciousness. But this consciousness is continuously changing. So, from the continuous change of consciousness, it leads to the acquisition of the knowledge of the constant change of the properties of the object and the property itself through a simple inferential enumeration.[35]

Sautrāntikā school introduces the belief in the reality of God as the cause of the effectiveness for the universe in its own ways, where the creatures are neither produced by *Īśvara* nor by *puruṣa* nor by *pradhāna*, neither 'matter' nor, it has been created in its totality by any such single primordial cause. But they are created by a successive series of causes one after the other and they are the result of the successive effects.[36] So, one can understand the aspect of self in *Sautrāntikā* school, that, it accepts the ideas of momentary, absence of substance, *śvalakṣaṇa* and the *dharmas* as in the *Vaibhāṣika* school of *Hīnayāna Buddhism*. It deviates from *Vaibhāṣika* in the realm of indirect knowledge, the impermanent nature of the object in the past, present and future with the acceptance of the basic constant reality as God within the fleeting nature of the phenomenal sphere.

If one observes *Hīnayāna Buddhism*, he may see many inconsistencies within it. Theory of momentary will be applicable only to the empirical realm within which the ethical values and the spiritual experiences are not possible. The theory of momentary as in *Hīnayāna* schools shows absurdity in the field of memory, cognition, desire and conative effect because without a permanent substratum or locus as self, the causal nexus for the above criteria are not possible. Here, cognition is the result of the volitional activities through our desire and conative efforts. The impressions and memory of the psychic states indirectly lead to the permanent state and reject the field of the stream of conscious states. Moreover, even if one accepts the theory of momentary, cognition or perception, the prime cause for all our activities remains unexplained because nothing will happen between the known and the knowing object of the fleeting ideas. So, here one may argue that the self is not the series of changing states but something in addition to the states, i.e., the permanent self with the states comprising of the all series.[37] Without a performer the stream of momentary ideas is not possible. Without an agent or a subject the result of our every activity may not be reaped by anybody. If one accepts the *kṣaṇabhaṅgavāda*, 'state of overcoming the sufferings' by an individual and getting knowledge without a permanent self are not possible, because the synthesizing permanent subject alone can control all the above said activities.

Through perception one cannot perceive the pure self, because there is not such stable data to perceive the qualities of desire, aversion, conative effort, pleasure, pain and even knowledge. Within this, the knowledge may be considered as an object of *Yogaja*, 'extra-ordinary perception of intuitive and immediate one'. The founder of *Vaiśeṣika* philosophy, *Kaṇāda* also asserts that perception fails and inference succeeds when they approach towards the actual nature of self. So, one may come to a conclusion, that perception goes only to a certain extent towards the locus of the self and not the whole.[38] Apart from perception, through inference as a knower of permanence of the substratum of knowledge, one can elucidate the presence of the permanent self with the aid of *sāmanyatodṛṣṭā*. The *sāmanyatodṛṣṭā* inference is based on the uniformity of co-existence and not on the principles of causation.[39] Like that, the internal attributive qualities of desires, aversion, volitional effort, pleasure and pain must have a stable substratum of the self.[40] So, one can say that the actual self may not be perceived but it can be inferred only through our strenuous sense experience.[41]

So, the *Vaiśeṣika* as well as *Sautrāntika* schools of *Hīnayāna Buddhism* have their own drawbacks with respects to the basic view of rejecting the basement for our activities through *kṣaṇabhaṅgavāda*. But in the forthcoming *Mahāyāna Buddhism*, it has been observed that the defects of *Hīnayāna Buddhism* have been removed in the direction of the impermanence with authentic arguments.

2.1.3.2. *Mahāyāna Buddhism*

Great *Buddhistic* follower Aśvaghoṣa modifies the *kṣaṇabhaṅgavāda* and the concept of *nirvāṇa* of *Hīnayāna*

Buddhism to a better one to understand as well as to follow. From the empirical stand point, the reality of the pure spirit pervades as a harmonious whole and as a supreme bliss of *Tathāgatagarbha*, which is having many merits. They are within *saṁsāra* level which undergoes the cycle of births and deaths, sufferings and sorrows, pain and pleasure and young and old age. But from the ultimate stand point the same supreme bliss looks as *nirvāṇa*, 'realizing of positive bliss'.[42] The ultimate reality is neither existence nor non-existence, neither unity nor plurality, neither affirmation nor negation and nor both. It cannot be understood by *buddhi* because it transcends the category of understanding. Moreover, the phenomenal real may not be the same as in the transcendental level. So, the empirical realm consists only of the unreal of the relative real. But due to *avidyā*, 'ignorance' prevailing in us, the universe illumines as many objects like the same clay modifies a variety of pottery.[43] If one acquires true *jñāna* to eliminate the *avidyā*, then he can perceive the ultimate reality of 'absolute calm' and blissful nature within the phenomenal entities of subjective as well as objective entities.

Accepting the above of reality as spiritual, *Mahāyāna Buddhism* is having two different schools namely *Vijñānavāda* and *Śūnyavāda*. *Vijñānavādin* treats the ultimate reality within our consciousness. It comes under subjective idealism because the reality is constituted by the ideas of our own mind.[44] The *Śūnyavādin* describes the ultimate reality of as neither *śūnya* nor *aśūnya* but beyond the categories of our understanding. This system is considered nihilistic absolutism because the ultimate reality is neither material nor spiritual but neutral.[45]

2.1.3.2.1 *Yogācāra* School

The founder of the school is Maitrayanātha; and the followers of *Vijñānavāda* may be termed as *Vijñānavādins* or *Yogācāras*. They treat the self as immutable stone house of the consciousness which forms a permanent background for the continuously changing varieties of feelings and ideas of our mind. They are not real but apparent. The self is characterized by relativity because our ideas are the outcome of the external object upon the *manas* through the *indriyas*.[46] Due to the *avidyā* only the individual thinks that the fraction of our consciousness is without a permanent background. But actually there is a permanent *cittam* of oneness, which is manifesting as various varieties of consciousness. So, behind the five *skandhas*, there is an ever active continuous spiritual energy which may be the part and parcel of the absolute consciousness existing as self which helps us to know the external world.[47] So, one can add that the external world and the phenomenal ego consciousness are the manifestation of the universal consciousness. These subject and object differences are only due to our wrong conception of *avidyā* upon our consciousness. If one transcends the duality through a proper *jñāna*, he can realize the nature of ultimate reality or Pure Consciousness as such; where he may perceive no differences between *saṁsāra* and *nirvāṇa*, the phenomenal and noumenal. So, *nirvāṇa* by *Vijñānavādins* may be considered as the realization of sameness within the universe.[48]

Vijñānavādin distinguishes crude subjectivism or subjective idealism from the realism. They take the self as momentary ideas in a state of constant flux. Eventhough the explanation for reality belongs to phenomenal order, from the actual transcendental standpoint, this process of momentary does not touch the reality because it transcends the duality of subject and object. So, the actual reality is pure consciousness and self-conscious self which is called *alayavijñāna, tathāgatagrapha, cittamatra, vijñāptimātra*.[49] Here, Aśvaghoṣa confesses that the multiplicity of reality is because of the persons' inexplicable *avidyā* which arises out of multiplicity of our empirical centre as mind and the objects.[50]

2.1.3.2.2. *Śūnyavāda* School

Śūnyavādin is called *Mādyamikās*. They follow the middle path between existence and non-existence, affirmation and negation. But at the same time they transcend both extremes. Here the word '*śūnyam*' represents only *avacha* or *anabhilapya*, 'indestructible nature', which is beyond our intellectual capacity to understand. It does not connote 'nothing' or 'empty void' or a 'negative abyss'. Actually this school emphasizes our empirical appearances as *śvabhāvaśūnyam*, 'absence of ultimate reality' and the reality as *prapañcaśūnya*, 'devoid of plurality'. *Śūnyavādins* treat the material and the immaterial substance in double sense as relative and absolute, i.e., *saṁsāra* as well as *nirvāṇa*.[51] Connecting the relativity with absolute one the former represents the plurality without the reality and the latter refers to the reality without plurality. So, *śūnya* is realized as the spiritual experiences.[52] So, ultimate reality transcends the duality of subject, object and the plurality of the phenomenal world.

The *Yogācāra* school considers the consciousness as the ultimate reality with momentarily ever changing ideas but the permanence and the identity are only *vikalpa*, 'superimposition' of the conceptual construction and the changing feature from one identical movement to next.[53] *Nirvāṇa* of *Śūnyavādin* is *anirvādham amutpannam*, 'absence of the essence of all phenomenal existence with ceasing as well as producing states' and *prapañcapravṛtti*, 'extinct phenomenal flow of momentary'. Ordinarily, all are in the state of *saṁsāra*, 'false egoism' by *avidyā* of *rāga*, *dveṣa*, and *moha* and it leads to the desire through *nāmarūpe*, 'five *skandhas* and feelings of senses like a flow of river without any constant base' i.e. existence and non-existence. So according to *śūnyavāda* the *nirvāṇa* is nothing but realizing the *śūnyam* through the middle path of *saṁvṛtisatya*, 'feature of nothing behind the phenomenal entities'.[54]

If one compares the two schools of *Mahāyāna Buddhism*, he may infer both controversial as well as comprehensive approach from the common *Buddhistic* idea towards the reality of *tathata* 'suchness'. The *Vijñānavāda* treats it as a transempirical and undifferentiated reality of subject and object and the *Yogācāras* refers to this as *śūnyata*, 'void'. Both the schools carefully follow the *Buddhistic* concepts of *duḥkha*, 'sufferings', *anitya*, 'impermanence' and *anātman*, 'non-self'. *Vijñānavādin* reaches the above conception by eliminating the subjective as well as objective desires through *vijñāna*, 'consciousness'. So, *Mahāyāna Buddhism* touches the *Buddhistic* heart of *Pudgala nairātmya*, 'insubstantiality of the self' and *dharma nairātmya*, 'insubstantiality of the self' and *dharma nairātmya*, 'object of constantly changing elements' through the elimination of desire by way the contemplation of the *avidyā*.

The total consideration of *Buddhism* towards bondage reveals two kinds namely irremovable sufferings caused by external circumstances like earthquake in certain region of the earth and the internal conditions of *avidyā* which is caused by mental atmosphere such as *sakkaya dithi*, 'dilution of the self', *vicikitsa*, 'doubt', *silabbata paramasa*, 'belief in rites', *kāma*, 'lust', *paṭigha*, 'hatred', *rūparāga*, 'desire for rebirth on earth', *arūparaga*, 'self righteousness' and the tenth criteria of *avijñāna*, 'ignorance'. In addition to the above causes, especially *Buddhism* adds *assavas*, 'impurities' and its *kleśās*, 'affections'.

Mahāyāna Buddhism considers *mokṣa* as the rejection of permanent individuality. *Mokṣa* is analysed into four dimensional views as a state of pure extinction or annihilation, a state of happiness, a state of inconceivable and a state of changeless one. So, negatively the state of *nirvāṇa* is the extinction of the egoism as in *Hīnayāna Buddhism;* but positively it may not be a state of extinction but a way of life with a reconciled way of one's own thinking, feeling and acting.[55]

2.2. *ĀSTIKA* SYSTEMS

2.2.1. Spiritualistic Absolutism

2.2.1.1. Monism

The philosophical treatments upon the reality by *Upaniṣads* belong to 'spiritualistic absolutism', because it treats the spiritual self as the ultimate substance. The transcendental and fundamental principle is immanent connected with the empirical world. According to the *upaniṣads*, the individual self is the product of *avidyā*, which is the combination of the real and the unreal, blend of truth and false, the mixture of the existence and the non-existence and the nearest one towards the absolute. The actual self is pure consciousness, self-shining and self proved and it mingles with the ultimate reality as *sākṣī*, 'witness'. Due to *avidyā* the *indriyas, manas, buddhi*, feeling, willing and emotions are formed and embedded by the actual self to form its individuality. But the true self is above *avidyā*. In *upaniṣads* the word *'ātman'* means life breath. The spiritual self pervades all features within and it may be considered to be the subject to know to experience and to illuminate the objects as such. But actually it wishes to remain immortal in nature. The self forms a basic firm ground for walking, dreaming and dreamless states where the body, dreamy experiences, varied mental states, the present continuum and the stream of consciousness are only the instruments of the self. The actual self is closely connected with the existence of the whole universe through its changes and movements. But it has its superior and transcendental nature which is away from the worldly order.

The *upaniṣads* have declared that, the *ātman* is synonymous with the Brahman in all respects. In *Ṛg Veda*, the term *ātman* has been used in two senses such as the vital breath and the ultimate essence of the universe. Later the *upaniṣads* have treated the Brahman as the ultimate essence of the universe and the *ātman* refers to the innermost essence of man. The innermost essence of the *ātman* represents the various gradations of such as *annamaya ātman*, 'essence of food', *prāṇamaya ātman*, 'essence of vital breath', *manomaya ātman*, 'essence of mind', *vijñānamaya ātman*, 'final essence of the self as pure bliss'.[56] There are many passages in *upaniṣads* which treat the finite self as the reflection of the universe, where the self is found to be the tension point of finite world to become infinite. For example, *Chāndogya upaniṣad* asserts that the self is constituted by fire, water and earth with the principal attitude of infinite.[57] The *upaniṣads* consider the self as the combination of the divine element with *manas* and the *indriyas*.[58] It may be verifiable, that, the presence of ultimate reality within *ātman* through *satyam jñānam anantam*, where *satyam* refers to the certainty of self; *jñānam* points to the spiritual nature and the *anantam* connotes the self's nature of all-inclusiveness.[59]

In *Chāndogya upaniṣads Prajāpati* declares, that, the true self is the ultimate subject, the knower and known, the self-luminous and self-proved, the fundamental postulation of our whole knowledge and the pure consciousness. The self manifests itself as subject and object, the self and the not self. At the same time, the actual self transcends the dual nature.[60] *Yajñavalkya* explains the nature of self in *Bṛahadāraṇyaka upaniṣad*, that, the self cannot be known by others, because it is knower who knows all the object. It cannot reduce itself for known because the knowledge of the knower and the sight of the seer are never destroyable.[61] *Kaṭha upaniṣad* says, that, with the help of self's fire alone, the sun, the moon and the stars are shining.[62] *Muṇḍaka upaniṣad* teaches, that, the nature of self is referring to the immanent nature of fire as its head, the moon and the sun as its eyes, the four quarters of the sky as its ears, the *Vedas* as its speech, the wind as its breath and the universe as its heart.[63] *Kaṭha upaniṣad* also treats it as ultimate reality which explains the *ātman* as Lord traveling on the chariot where the object is road; the body is the chariot; the senses are the horses; the mind is reins; the intellect is the charioteer and the ego is enjoyer. The same *upaniṣad* adds that the external objects, *indriyas, manas, buddhi* are existing for the purpose to serve the self. Because of the above reason the self is identical with this internal object but actually the self transcends them.[64] So, in conclusion, one can admit the *upaniṣadic* treatment of the self is immortal, self-proved and self-luminous. If one transcends the empirical duality of subject-object distinction, he can directly realize the actual nature of self as such.

2.2.1.2 Non-Dualism

Śrī Śaṅkara's *Advaitic* self comes under spiritualistic absolutism, because it treats the Brahman as the spiritualistic element which is forming the basic ground for all other diversified phenomenal objects. The *Advaita* system treats the reality as an undivided spiritual absolutism, which is identical with all substances and devoid of differences. Then the empirical world, the multiplicity, variety and differences are apparently considered as the real but ultimately seems to be the false appearances of the Brahman Himself,[65] because it is devoid of all kinds of differences such as *sajātivabheda*, 'difference from anything of its own', *vijatiyabheda*, 'difference from anything of a different kind' and *svagatabheda* 'difference within itself'.[66]

Śrī Śaṅkara says that the ultimate reality is *svarūpa-jñāna*, 'pure consciousnesses, or the pure self with *nirguṇa*, 'qualityless' and *nirviśeṣa*, 'absence of the categories' of the *buddhi* which combines with *śaktimaya*, '*mūlavidyā*', which is evolving as *saguṇa* or *saviśeṣa* or *Apara* Brahman or *Īśvara* who is acting as creator, preserver and destroyer of the universe. Here, the phenomenal *jīva* is nothing but the real combination of the subjective element i.e., the pure consciousness and the objective element the *ahaṅkāra* with the five *bhūtas* of earth, water, fire, air and ether with the *tejas*, trances. It is considered to be the real agent, the enjoyer of pleasure and pain and the owner of his activities of merits and demerits towards the law of *karma*.

Śrī Śaṅkara considers the self as eternal, all-pervading, self-proved and not derivable and undifferentiated *satcitānanda*, 'pure being, the pure consciousness and the pure bliss'. Pure being refers to the limitless and the infinite existence which is above the level of space and time. Pure consciousness refers to the real feature of *svaprakāśa*, the self is neither the substratum nor the object but itself is self-revealing and the self-luminous. Pure bliss confirms the nature of self and distinguishes it apart from the falsity of *antaḥkaraṇa* as a mere instrument for pleasure and pain; and sufferings and sorrows. The self transcends the pairs of opposites and enjoys the pure freedom and the supreme bliss[67]. So, the self originally does not refer to the mere body, *indriyas* and *manas* but undoubtedly connotes the non-dual universal self, the Brahman.

Due to *avidyā* the individual indulges in false notion of 'I'-ness and 'My'-ness which arise at the time of *manas* or *indriyas* attaching with the fleeting sensations and ideas. Śrī Śaṅkara adds that the self cannot be revealed by others because there is no *vyāpti*, 'invariable concomitance' between the probans and the locus of the probans.[68] Realizing the wrong notion of identifying the rope as snake, shell as silver, through right knowledge which leads to realization of the identity between non due *ātman* and the Brahman. Moreover, the same self due to *avidyā* appears as many empirical selves just as the sun or moon appears as many in ponds. So, according to him, the self is nothing but the Brahman Himself but it has manifested to the world as many with varied *antaḥkaraṇa*.

Regarding bondage, he holds it as unreal and apparent which are caused by apparent concealment of the absoluteness of the *ātman* by the cosmic principle of *māyā*, 'false apprehension of the ultimate reality as many varied unreal objects'. In other words, the absolute nature of self undergoes sufferings in *saṁsāra* level because of its individuality of its *antaḥkaraṇa*. Then liberation means the elimination of the illusory apprehension through negation of the individual self as well as the empirical world and realization of the actual self with the help of proper *jñāna*. Then the self realizes the undifferentiated and non-individual absolute.[69]

2.2.2. Theistic Absolutism

Theistic Absolutism emphasizes more importance to God but the self and the universe are different from Śrī Śaṅkara's spiritualistic absolutism. The empirical world and variety of existence may not be the unreal because God pervades within the finite selves and the external objects. They are not fully equated with God but they are having close relation with Him. This theistic absolutism is developed through the *Vaiṣṇava* tradition which includes four main schools with minute differences among them in the field of relation between Brahman and the empirical world.[70] They are: *Viśiṣṭādvaitavāda*, 'doctrine of the qualified monism' by Śrī Rāmānuja; *Dvaita*, 'doctrine of dualism' by Śrī Madhva; *Dvaitādvaivāda*, 'doctrine of the dual non-dualism' by Śrī Nimbārka; *Śuddhādvaitavāda*, 'doctrine of pure non-dualism' by Śrī Vallabha. The nutshell of their system with reference to the self is studied.

2.2.2.1 Qualified Monism

Śrī Śaṅkara considers that God alone is the real and the empirical objects are unreal through his doctrines of *Saguṇa* and *Nirguṇa Brahman*. But Śrī Rāmānuja treats the Brahman in a different angle as transcendental form of divine and immanent form of the *jīvas* and the *jagat*, i.e. the transcendental non-dual reality immanently pervades within the selves and the worldly objects. Śrī Rāmānuja accepts God, *jīvas* and *jagat* as the real. The self is considered as spiritual, self-luminous and self-conscious substance. The self is *anu*, 'the finite', changeless and it is pervading as an attribute or a mode, or a part of the divine quality. The self is a different entity which is apart from psychophysical complex. It is a real *jñātā*, 'knower', real *karttā*, 'agent' and a real *bhoktā*, 'enjoyer'. It is changeless, perfect and away from birth, death, imperfections, miseries, defects and changeability. In *mukti*, the self gets rid of the *karmic* forces, and becomes pure. Then the purified self leads to *Vaikuṇṭha*, 'spiritual abode of Viṣṇu'. After that, it never returns to the mundane sphere.

Śrī Rāmānuja's conception of the selves is qualitatively alike and quantitatively different from each other. The self is finite in phenomenal order, because of its embodiment of *karmic* forces and it becomes infinite in the noumenal state with immutable and eternal pure consciousness. Infinite and all pervasive knowledge is an essential character of the self which is persisting through the walking, dreaming and the dreamless sleep stages. But due to *avidyā*, the *karmic* forces may obscure the essential knowledge. At the time of *mukti* the obscured self gets away from the *karma* by proper *jñāna* and is restored the original position of *dharmabhūtajñāna*, 'cosmic consciousness, self consciousness and Brahman consciousness'. The liberated self is comprehensive and omniscient and enjoys the *ānanda rūpa*, 'form gives blissful'.[71] Śrī Rāmānuja adds that eventhough the self is independently real it depends upon God as *dhārya* and *dhartā*, 'supported and supporters'; *niyāmya* and *niyānta*, 'controlled and controller'; *śeṣa* and *śeṣī*, 'means and the end'; *prakāra* and *prakārī*, 'mode and the substance'; the *aṁśa* and *aṁśi*, 'part and the whole' and *śarīra* and *śarīrī*, 'body and the self'. He reconciles the human freedom and the Divine Sovereignty. In other words, the God, the author of the law of *karma*, the inner controller and the self-determiner will never interfere with the self's freedom of will at any level.[72]

Śrī Rāmānuja classifies the selves into three kinds. They are: *nitya mukta*, 'ever free selves'. They are existing by the side of Lord Viṣṇu in *Vaikuṇṭha*; *mukta*, 'released selves'. They are free from the worldly activities through proper knowledge and action; *baddha*, 'bonded selves'. They are surviving in the *saṃsāra* state with *karmic* forces.

2.2.2.2. Dualism

Śrī Madhva accepts the three realities, God, selves and matter. He differs from Śrī Śaṅkara's conception of *nirguṇa* and accepts Brahman as *saguṇa* with *bheda*, 'differences within itself'.[73] Regarding *bheda*, Śrī Madhva explains the differences such as the differences between God and self, between God and matter, between self and self, between self and matter and the differences between matter and matter. Eventhough the self and matter are eternal and real they are depending upon God who is absolutely independent and acting as an inner ruler of the self. Due to *karma* the pure consciousness and blissful self gets sufferings and sorrows. The self gets *mukti* when *karmic* forces dissolve by proper knowledge. Like Śrī Rāmānuja, Śrī Madhva also categorises the nature of selves into three kinds such as *nitya mukta*, 'ever blissful', the *mukta*, 'liberated' and *baddha*, 'bounded selves'. The selves are atomic in size; they are acting as real agents and enjoy and they are controlled by God. Śrī Madhva explains the creation as the conjoining factors of stable body into gross body with the embodiment of the selves for the purpose of dissolving the fruits of the past *karmas*.

Eventhough Śrī Madhva's ideas arise from Śrī Rāmānuja, he differs from him in certain respects. They are: (i) His ideas may be regarded as dualism. There is no identity between the existing self and the ultimate reality, i.e., each and every kind of existence is having its own separate and unique feature; (ii) He forcefully rejects the *apṛthaksiddhi*. Instead of the distinction between *dravya* and *avidyā*, he advocates *viśeṣa*, 'real uniqueness' of the attributes among the substances itself. Śrī Madhva adds that eventhough the selves and matters are the parts of God, they are different from each other and from God Himself because of the substantive existence itself; (iii) Unlike Śrī Rāmānuja's qualitative monism with quantitative pluralism, Śrī Madhva advocates that qualitative as well as quantitative pluralism, i.e., 'each and every self has its own individuality'; (iv) In the *mukti* the selves are having individual variations within the realm of knowledge and possessiveness of bliss. But Śrī Rāmānuja rejects the individual variation in *mukti*; (v) Śrī Madhva considers both body and self with respect to God as efficient cause and not as a material cause. God creates the universe through *prakṛti*; (vi) Śrī Rāmānuja's *mukta* resembles God without the powers of creation, preservation and destruction and the immanent quality within the universe. But Śrī Madhva's system emphasizes that even in liberation the selves are considered as inferior to God and they do not enjoy the full bliss. For this, Śrī Madhva describes four stages of liberation during the movement of the self towards God as *sālokya*, 'self residing with God', *sāmīpya*, 'self moving near to God', *sārūpya*, 'self gets the external form as God' and *sāyujya*, 'self enters into the body of God and it partially enjoys the supreme bliss'; (vii) Śrī Madhva supports and believes that there are certain selves like demons, ghosts and the men of evil and hateful nature which are all not in a position to get liberation. But Śrī Rāmānuja rejects this[74].

2.2.2.3. Dualistic Non-Dualism

Śrī Nimbārka accepts the theistic absolutism of Śrī Rāmānuja and Śrī Madhva. He explains that God as the ultimate nature and the *jīvas* and *jagat* are His immanent forms. Śrī Madhva adds, that, Puruṣottama in the divine form is infinite and unconditional, i.e. one without a second within the embodiment of *sat*, 'existence', *cit*, 'consciousness' and *ānanda*, 'bliss'. According to him, the relationship between *jīvas* and *jagat* with God is *Dvaitādvaita*, 'identity and difference'. The identity refers to the self as divine reality and the differences refer to that the self alone suffer by births and deaths and the imperfections and miseries. The identity and differences among the selves and matters are seen because of the *pāratantryasattābhāvaḥ*, 'depending nature upon God'. But God's actual nature is *svātantrasattābhāvaḥ*, 'independent existence apart from the *jīvas* and the *jagat*'. So, to Śrī Nimbārka, *tat tvam asi* means the relationship of God and the self as difference-cum-non-difference like shell-silver because there is resemblance as well as difference in appearance.

While Śrī Nimbārka describes the self as *jñānasvarūpa*, 'nature of knowledge and the substratum' he views it as *dharmidharmabhāva*, 'relation of substantive with the attributive knowledge', i.e. the relation like sun and its light. The self is eternal, real knower, agent, enjoyer, atomic and is many in number. They are supported and controlled by the ultimately independent reality, the God. The self is undergoing sufferings and sorrows, births and deaths with respect to its *avidyā* and *karmic* force. Like Śrī Rāmānuja, he professes that God is the efficient and material cause. As efficient cause, He is responsible for the law of *karma* and as material cause His *cit* and *acit* powers are modified as the universe.

When one compares Śrī Nimbārka's treatment of self with that of Śrī Rāmānuja, the former gives much importance only for the identity or through identity-in-and-through differences or the identity, i.e., qualified by differences. But the latter stresses equal importance to identity as well as differences. Śrī Nimbārka, unlike Śrī Rāmānuja, rejects the self and matter as the attributes of God. Instead of it they are neither like the divinity nor fully constitute the essence of God. In addition they are parts and powers of the ultimate reality.

2.2.2.4. Pure Non-Dualism

If Śrī Śaṅkara's philosophy is *Advaita,* then Śrī Vallabha's is termed as *Śuddhādvaitavāda,* 'pure non-dualism unassisted by *māyā*. He interprets the *jīvas* and *jagat* as real with out the assistance of *māyā* but Śrī Śaṅkara explains the world with the help of the concept of *māyā*. Through this system, he remarks that God out of His will manifests the selves and the matters. In the manifestation He reveals Himself as *satcitānanda,* 'existence, knowledge and the bliss'. God places Himself within *akṛtaparināmavāda,* 'natural evolution of God'. In the evolution He did not undergo any change but He remains between *vivarta,* 'unreal appearance' and *pariṇāma,* 'real changing of reality'.

The *saṁsāra* of the *jīva* represents the presence of *avidyā,* 'ignorance' in the self. He divides ignorance into five divisions such as false identification of the real nature of the self, identifying the body as real, ignorance of the nature of senses, ignorance of vital breaths and falsifying the *antaḥkaraṇas* as the real. To understand Śrī Vallabha's view as such one should compare him with Śrī Rāmānuja, Śrī Madhva and Śrī Nimbārka. Śrī Rāmānuja's self resembles that of Viṣṇu in the *mokṣa* state, Śrī Madhva regards it as differences within the identity and Śrī Nimbārka limited the self's identity as well as the differences within the resemblance of God. But Śrī Vallabha adds that eventhough the self is identical with God, it appears different because the self is nothing but the limited manifestations of the divine parts and the rest is obscured within the self entity.

2.2.3. Realism

This division supports more than one reality which is responsible for the evolution of the universe. The treatment of the self under this division differs from the other groups of spiritualistic absolutism and the theistic absolutism in its manifestation and the characteristic features. This division comes under realism because it accepts self and the eternal world as the real. This division includes *Nyāya Vaiśeṣika* and *Mīmāṁsā* system as pluralistic realism and the *Sāṅkhya* system as dualistic realism. A study of these systems reveals minute differences in the nature of the self with respect to God and the external world.

2.2.3.1. Pluralistic Realism

This system admits the self as neither spirit nor matter. Eventhough the system treats the self and matter as one, the self differs from matter, i.e., the self is substratum and other things are its attributes. So, one cannot put the system under realism metaphysically but it is so epistemologically because the self is immaterial and eternal substance. Being an eternal substance it has numbers and magnitude like other co-eternal atoms and acts as a real substratum for the consciousness of the mental phenomena such as cognition, desire, disposition and violation. These mental phenomena are considered to be the accidental properties of the permanent, unchanging, eternal substance — the self. In other words, the incorporal substance of the self acts as real knower, real enjoyer and an active agent. The self having the connection with the corporal substances as *Vibhu*, 'ubiquitous'. So, the actual self is considered as *jaḍa*, 'unconscious principle' and the accidental property of consciousness need not always be with the self. Instead of it the property may be intermittent.[75]

Nyāya Vaiśeṣika accepts God as co-equal with eternal atoms and the selves, who is acting as mere efficient cause only. The manifestation means the combination of the atoms and the selves as material cause. This is directed by the unseen power of God, who is the author of the law of *karma*. To criticize the *Nyāya Vaiśeṣika's* self, one can say that it may not be possible for the intermittent conscious self to recognize once again. The self as substratum with external qualities may not be acceptable because the self and body are not equal entities and the self is considered as higher level for the connection with the spiritual quality than the body. *Nyāya Vaiśeṣika* explains the self as substance with intermittent consciousness. This is unconceivable because there should be constant consciousness. This consciousness synthesizes the manifold experiences of one's life to form the finite selves as the foundational reality and fragmentary phases of the infinite. *Nyāya Vaiśeṣika* system treats the eternal selves as the co-eternal atoms. This may not be acceptable because the corporal atoms are having definite assignable meaning as persistent substratum of material world with constant quantity and quality. But the selves are constantly changing.[76]

Like *NyāyaVaiśeṣika*, *Mīmāṁsā* system accepts the matter and selves as the real. In the universe the innumerable selves with separate bodies and infinite liberated selves without bodies exist. *Mīmāṁsā* advocates the self as *nitya dravya*, 'eternal substances', *vijapaka*, 'infinite in number', *vibhu*, 'ubiquitous'and *sarvagata*, 'omnipresent' like *Nyāya Vaiśeṣika*. The self may be considered as *jñāta*, 'real knower', *bhokta*, 'enjoyer', *karttā*, 'active agent' and *aṣraya*, 'basic substratum of consciousness', which differs from body, senses, mind and understanding.[77] This system professes that consciousness is the main essence of the self. Śrī Prabhākara considers consciousness as its main substratum but Śrī Kumārila Bhaṭṭa assumes it as the attributive quality of the self.

Śrī Prabhākara confirms that actually the self is *jaḍa* and the consciousness is the accidental quality of the self as in *NyāyaVaiśeṣika* system. The law of *karma*, 'accumulated merits and demerits of the self' decides its cognitions, feelings and volitions. He regards *mokṣa* as the extinction of merits and demerits, then the pure self keeps away from all the qualities including its consciousness and even its bliss. Śrī Kumārila Bhaṭṭa, unlike Śrī Prabhākara, the consciousness is *pariṇāma*, 'the model' or 'an action' or 'process of change in the substratum'. Regarding the main essence of the consciousness, it may change or appear and disappear but it never affects the static and permanent self. Totally one may say that the self is *jaḍa bhodhātmata* or *citacitrūpa* which refers to the self as unconscious substance and as a mode it is consciousness. Both Śrī Prabhākara and Śrī Kumārila Bhaṭṭa accept the state of liberation as pure substance and devoid of its qualities together with consciousness and the bliss[78] through the performance of *kāmya karmas* and *nitya karmas*. But between them there are some sort of differences. Śrī Prabhākara treats *mokṣa* as the absolute cessation of the body which is caused by the disappearance of all *dharma* and *adharma*. The individual who wants to release from the cycle of birth and death has to reduce gradually the accumulated *karmas* in the past through proper *jñāna* aided by self-control and contentment where the *mokṣa* is simply a natural form and the attributeless self having no pain and pleasure. Śrī Kumārila regards the same as positive state within the self and free from all pain and enjoyment. In the *mukti* state the self may be the pure essence and which does not undergo further manifestation.[79]

Mīmāṁsā philosophy rejects the existence of God as creator and destroyer because this system does not support creation and dissolution.[80] But the worldly activities are activated under the unseen metaphysical link of *apūrva*, 'apt and necessary connection between the act and its result'.

Criticizing the *Mīmāṁsā* system one may not digest the speculation regarding the imperceptible antecedent of the fruit and the conscious principle of *apūrva*. Because the multifaceted worldly activities are not possible to be reconciled towards a harmonious result. Hence, Śrī Prabhākara and Śrī Kumārila firmly admit the existence of God as controller to control the universal activities of creation, destruction and preservation.

2.2.3.2. Dualistic Realism

Sāṅkhya accepts the matter and the selves as two different realities of *prakṛti* and *puruṣa*. But *Sāṅkhya* system does not include the conception of the divinity, the God. *Sāṅkhya* regards the *puruṣa* as self as spirit and the subjective knower and co-present and co-eternal with the other reality, *prakṛti*. *Sāṅkhya* treats the *puruṣa*, not as a substance like other two systems of *Nyāya Vaiśeṣika* and *Mīmāṁsā*, but it treats the consciousness itself as its essence having quality which is neither senses nor brain, nor the intellect. So, *puruṣa's* consciousness is transcendental, self-luminous, self-proved. It is the subjective knower, the basic foundation for all knowledge, the neutral seer, the peaceful and eternal with the features of being beyond time, space, changes and activities. In addition the self is the silent witness, the emancipated individual real entity and the prime mover or the first cause of the all cosmic processes. It may be classified as *śuddha*, *baddha* and *mukta* corresponding to pureness, consciousness and freedom.

Sāṅkhya philosophy supports the plurality of *puruṣa*[81] with qualitative monism and quantitative pluralism like *Jainism, Nyāya Vaiśeṣika,* Śrī Rāmānuja and Leibnitz's monadism. This system gives three most important criteria to prove the plurality. They are: (i) Because of the different sensory and motor organs with separate birth and death, the *puruṣa* should be many. (ii) If the *puruṣas* are one, bondage, liberation and the activities of one *puruṣa* should lead to *puruṣas* of the whole universe. (iii) Actually the qualitative *puruṣa* is beyond the nature of *guṇas* and resembles each another but the difference comes because of the difference in occurrence. (iv) For example, in some *puruṣa, sattva* dominates, in some other *rājasa* dominates and the rest *tāmasa guṇa* dominates which result the plurality of the *puruṣa.*[82]

If *Sāṅkhya* treats *puruṣa* and *prakṛti* as independently absolute then these two may not come into contact either in *saṁyogā*, 'real contact' or *saṁyogābhāsa*, 'semblance of contact' or *sānnidhyamātrā*, 'mere presence for the purpose of evolution' because *prakṛti* is considered to be the unintelligible and the *puruṣa* is intelligible and eternal entities. The independent *puruṣa* is always controlling the *prakṛti* and the *guṇa*. *Mukti* means the equilibrium of the *triguṇas* in *prakṛti* and realization of the *puruṣa*. But for *Sāṅkhya, mukti* is impossible because the condition of equilibrium in *prakṛti* is highly restricted by the presence of *puruṣa* over the equilibrium of the *prakṛti* which leads to continuous evolution only. So, there will be no place for dissolution, i.e. the state of *mukti*. This system draws back the ultimate transcendental *puruṣa* into the level of empirical ego. But it is actually not so because the eternal, passive, indifferent and inactive *puruṣa* is not acting as an enjoyer of the *prakṛti*, the object to be the enjoyed. Moreover, there may not be the existence of many *puruṣas* in the universe. Instead of it, there should be only one *puruṣa* alone in the transcendental level. Then if one accepts one eternal *puruṣa*, applying the same logic, he can also derive and prove the existence of one *prakṛti,* instead of many. So, discussing the above aspect one can easily disprove the quantitative plurality of *puruṣas* as well as the *prakṛti.* In addition regarding *mukti, Sāṅkhya* treats it as a negative cessation of the three *guṇas* which result in the pain and not the state of positive bliss because this system considers the bliss as the product of *sattva guṇa.* The explanation of bliss may be possible in the empirical level but not in the transcendental level. In the transcendental level the bliss differs from that of empirical level. So, the system reveals many inconsistencies about the self which have been rectified in the treatment of the self in the *Bhagavad Gītā.*

2.3. METAPHYSICS OF SELF IN BHAGAVAD GĪTĀ AND ITS PLACE IN INDIAN PHILOSOPHY

The essence of the Indian metaphysical treatment of the self is explored in the *Bhagavad Gītā* with omission and commission. The *Gītā* explains the nature of self, which positively resembles each and every system of Indian Philosophy and negatively omits the inconsistent ideas. To substantiate the above view, a comparative account of the Indian Philosophical system with the *Gītā* will be helpful to evaluate the outstanding and a reconciled description of the self in the *Gītā.*

Eventhough the general concept of the *Bhagavad Gītā's* treatment of the self comes under the orthodox systems and it also includes the salient principles of the heterodox systems. The *Gītā* essentially differs from the *Cārvāka's* idea. In that the *Gītā* explains the self with respect to the human values of *dharmas* but *Cārvāka* denies the above principle. The *Gītā's* self is quite opposite to *Jaina's jīvas* of the condensation and expansion, *madhyamaparimāṇa.* The treatment of the *nirvāṇa* of the *Bhagavad Gītā* resembles *Buddhism.* The former explains the *nirvāna* as the spiritual integration of self and the latter differs from the former and describes it as absolute stoppage of births and deaths and sufferings and sorrows. The *Gītā* also differs from *Buddhism,* where *Buddhism* describes the insubstantiality of the self in a different degree within its four schools. But the *Gītā* views the self as the eternal spiritual substance co-equal with the supreme spiritual reality, the God.

In the orthodox treatments the *Gītā* stands supreme because its teachings give much importance to the spiritual nature of the self. The spiritual leads to practical salvation through mental poise and freedom from the sufferings. The metaphysical teaching of the *Gītā* comprises all the specific and detailed relevances which are included within the realm of all other orthodox systems with the specific improvement in all sides over the other systems. Coming closer the *Gītā* can be said to preach the spiritualistic absolutism because its explanation of the self resembles that of the *Upaniṣads.* Later the *Upaniṣadic* treatment of monism has been developed by Śrī Śaṅkara within his commentary.[83] One can also treat the *Bhagavad Gītā's* self under theistic absolutism because Śrī Rāmānuja and his followers commented and treated the same in their concept of *Vasudevas sarvam.* When one compares *Nyāya Vaiśeṣika* and *Mīmāṁsā's* pluralistic realism with the *Gītā,* both are entirely different from each other because the former treats the self in a defective and inconsistent way as eternal *jaḍa* with the accidental property of consciousness. But the *Gītā* rectifies the defects as eternal and spiritual substance with the constant consciousness as its main essence. The *Gītā* can also be placed under dualistic realism because the *Bhagavad Gītā* systhesizes the twenty-five categories of the traditional *Sāṅkhya* treatment and it also admits the twenty-sixth category of Lord Kṛṣṇa described as Puruṣottama. The *Bhagavad Gītā* can also be related in the traditional *Yoga* system where the *Gītā* treats God as the basic principle of the spiritual integration and reduces the eight successive steps into three kinds of *yogas* into *karma, bhakti* and *jñāna.* The classical *Yoga* emphasizes that after attaining the eighth step of *samādhi,* he himself becomes *kevala,* 'absolute'. But the *Gītā* goes one step up, and affirms the spiritual communion of the self with the God Himself.[84]

A thorough and a comprehensive study of the nature of self as treated in the *Gītā* and Indian Philosophy shows that the *Gītā* is distinguished from all other systems, especially from *Vedas, Upaniṣads* and *Buddhism* on the one hand and *Sāṅkhya* and *Yoga* system on the other hand.[85] Here no one can deny, that the *Bhagavad Gītā* has more proximity with traditional *Sāṅkhya* and *Yoga* system than the other systems in the metaphysical nature of self and this is to be verifiable through a systematic comparative study. Eventhough the *Bhagavad Gītā* uses *Sāṅkhya* terminologies of *puruṣa* and *prakṛti* with its three *guṇas* of *sattva, rājas* and *tāmas.* It not only rejects the independent nature of the *puruṣa* and *prakṛti,* but also adds the existence of an *Uttamapuruṣa* and the dependence of the *Sāṅkhya's* dualistic reality with the proper explanation.

REFERENCES

1. Rajagopalan, T.S., *The Life Immortal,* p. 23.
2. Hiriyanna, *Outlines of Indian Philosophy,* p. 16.
3. Runes, Dagobert, D. (ed.), *The Dictionary of Philosophy,* p. 222.
4. Hasting, James, (Ed.), *Encyclopaedia of Religion and Ethics,* Vol. 9, p. 570.
5. Hiriyanna, *op. cit.,* pp. 20-21.
6. Radhakrishnan, S., *Indian Philosophy,* Vol. II, p. 28.
7. *Ibid.,* p. 25.
8. Hasting, James, (Ed.), *op.cit.,* Vol. II, p. 745.
9. Balbir Singh, *The Conceptual Frame Work of Indian Philosophy,* p. 106.
10. Joshi, Shanti, *The Message of Sankara,* pp. 16-17.

11. Banerjee, Nikunja Vihiri, *The Spirit of Indian Philosophy*, p. 137.
12. *Ibid.*, p. 136.
13. Hiriyanna, *op.cit.*, p. 191.
14. Radhakrishnan, S., *op.cit.*, Vol. I, p. 309.
15. Banerjee, Nikunja Vihiri, *op. cit.*, p. 191.
16. Radhakrishnan, S., *op. cit.*, Vol. I, p. 311.
17. Chaudhuri, Anil Kumar Ray, *Self and Falsity in Advaita Vedanta*, p. 11.
18. Banerjee, Nikunja Vihari, *op.cit.*, pp. 191-192.
19. Hiriyanna, *op. cit.*, p. 158.
20. Chaudhuri, Anil Kumar Ray, *op.cit.*, p. 13.
21. *Ibid.*, p. 14.
22. Banerjee, Nikunja Vihari, *op.cit.*, p. 192.
23. *Ibid.*, p. 336.
24. Radhakrishnan, S., *op.cit.*, Vol. I, p. 322 and Dasgupta, S., *History of Indian Philosophy*, Vol. I, p. 190.
25. Sharma, Chandradhar, *op.cit.*, pp. 67-68.
26. Banerjee, Nikunja Vihari, *op.cit.*, p. 161.
27. Banerjee, Nikunja Vihari, *Kant's Philosophy of Self*, p. 46.
28. *Encyclopaedia Americana*, The International Reference Work, Vol. 25, p. 27.
29. Laird, John, *The Idea of the Soul*, p. 100.
30. Dasgupta, S., *op. cit.*, Vol. I, p. 118.
31. *Ibid.*, p. 117.
32. Banerjee, Nikunja Vihari, *op.cit.*, p. 64.
33. *Ibid.*, p. 24.
34. Radhakrishnan, S., *op.cit.*, Vol. I, p. 620.
35. *Ibid.*, p. 621.
36. *Ibid.*, p. 623.
37. Chaudhuri, Anil Kumar Ray, *op.cit.*, pp. 15-16.
38. *Ibid.*, p. 197.
39. Sharma, Chandradha, *op.cit.*, p. 200.
40. Chaudhuri, Anil Kumar Ray, *op.cit.*, pp. 18-19.
41. *Ibid.*, pp. 19-20.

42. Sharma, Chandradhar, *op.cit.*, p. 109.
43. *Ibid.*
44. Banerjee, Nikunja Vihari, *op.cit.*, p. 197.
45. *Ibid.*, p. 204.
46. *Ibid.*, p. 199.
47. Radhakrishnan, S., *op.cit.*, Vol. I, pp. 629-631.
48. Sharma, Chandradhar, *op.cit.*, p. 109.
49. *Ibid.*, p. 121.
50. Banerjee, Nikunja Vihari, *op.cit.*, p. 198.
51. *Ibid.*, p. 228.
52. Sharma, Chandrahar, *op.cit.*, pp. 86-87.
53. Dasgupta, S, *op.cit.*, Vol. I, p. 142.
54. *Ibid.*, p. 144.
55. Banerjee, Nikunja Vihari, *op.cit.*, pp. 350-351.
56. *TU*, II.7.
57. *ChU*, 11.3 & 4.
58. *ChU*, 8.12.
59. Hiriyanna, *op.cit.*, p. 57.
60. *ChU*. 8.3-12.
61. *BU*, IV.36.
62. *KU*, II.2.5.
63. *MU*, II.1.4.
64. *KU*, 2.3-4.
65. Banerjee, Nikunja Vihari, *op.cit.*, pp. 205-206.
66. *Ibid.*, p. 224.
67. Chaudhuri, Anil Kumar Ray, *op.cit.*, pp. 65-101.
68. *Ibid.*, p. 99.
69. Banerjee, Nikunja Vihari, *op.cit.*, p. 334.
70. Radhakrishnan, S., *op.cit.*, Vol. II, p. 692.
71. Hiriyanna, *op.cit.*, pp. 388-389.
72. Radhakrishnan, S., *op.cit.*, Vol. II, p. 695.
73. Banerjee, Nikunja Vihari, *op.cit.*, p. 214.
74. Sharma, Chandradhar, *op.cit.*, p. 375.
75. Radhakrishnan, S., *op.cit.*, Vol. II, p. 149.
76. Chaudhuri, Anil Kumar Ray, *op.cit.*, p. 24.

77. Banerjee, Nikunja Vihari, *op.cit.*, p. 172.
78. Chaudhuri, Anil Kumar Ray, *op.cit.*, pp. 38-39 and Radhakrishnan, S., *op.cit.*, Vol. II, pp. 408-413.
79. Radhakrishnan, S., *op.cit.*, Vol. II, pp. 423-424.
80. Dasgupta, S., *op.cit.*, Vol.I, p. 403.
81. *Sam.Ka*, 18.
82. Balbir Singh, *op.cit.*, p. 97.
83. *Philosophy East and West, A Quarterly of Asian and Comparative Thought,* Vol. XXIX, No. 4, p. 506.
84. *BG*, 6.47.
85. Radhakrishnan, S., *op.cit.*, Vol. II, p. 575.

CHAPTER-3

RELATIONSHIP OF THE BHAGAVAD GĪTĀ WITH SĀṄKHYA, PATAÑJALI'S YOGA, JAINISM AND BUDDHISM

In the second chapter, the fact has been verified that the philosophical essence of the it is a mixture of Indian traditional systems because it includes the theistic and speculative terms and the principles from the *Vedas, Upaniṣads, Sāṅkhya, Yoga,* Jainism and Buddhism. In the introduction, efforts have been taken to reveal the relationship of the *Gītā* with the *Vedas* and *Upaniṣads*. So, putting asides the *Vedas* and *Upaniṣads* a critical study is helpful to understand the *Gītā's* affinity with other systems, which are having the commentaries and terminologies affinities.

There are three kinds of views about the affinities of the *Gītā* with *Sāṅkhya* and *Yoga* Philosophy. They are: (i) Garb argues that the philosophy of the *Gītā* is constituted by *Sāṅkhya* and *Yoga* with the *Vedānta* philosophy.[1] (ii) S.C. Roy rejects Garbe's view because the term *Sāṅkhya* used in the *Gītā* is different from its original system of Kapila. Instead of Garbe's view, Roy says that the *Gītā* depends upon the *Upaniṣads* especially upon *Śvetāśvatara Upaniṣad*. According to Roy the influence of the *Sāṅkhya* upon the *Gītā* should derive its principles from the common source of *Upaniṣads*. For this, Roy refers to Deussen's work, where Deussen traced step by step the dualistic doctrine of *Sāṅkhya* and the evolution of the doctrines of *guṇas* and *mukti* from the common source of

Upaniṣads. In short, one can say that the *Sāṅkhya* philosophy gets its philosophical background from the theistic *Upaniṣads* especially from the *Śvetāśvatara Upaniṣad*. Then it influences the *Mahābhārata* and the *Gītā* with the speculative aspect.[2] (iii) There is another view that primarily the *Gītā* is theistic in character where Kṛṣṇa speaks of Himself. Later it has been adapted in the pantheistic sense where Lord Kṛṣṇa speaks to Arjuna, who is identified as Kṛṣṇa Himself. In other words, the ancient poems of Kṛṣṇa with *Sāṅkhya Yoga* has been modified with the addition of *Vedāntic* philosophy.[3]

On the other hand, Tilak also analyses the same problem and expounds three possibilities. They are: (i) The *Upaniṣads* and *Sāṅkhya* philosophy grew side by side where the *Gītā* gets its principles from both. (ii) First the *Upaniṣads* borrowed its doctrines from the *Sāṅkhya*. Then the borrowed principles are used in the *Gītā*. (iii) Kapila would have developed his *Sāṅkhya* system with his own principles and selected ideas from the *Upaniṣads*. So, *Sāṅkhya* principles within the *Bhagavad Gītā* are derived from the *Upaniṣads*.[4] With this background let the discussion to specify the affinities of the *Gītā* with specified system.

3.1. THE BHAGAVAD GĪTĀ AND SĀṄKHYA PHILOSOPHY

S. Radhakrishnan says that, the *Gītā* accepts the psychological features of the self and the order of creation but rejects the metaphysical implication of the *Sāṅkhya* philosophy.[5] In other words, the *Gītā* resembles the *Sāṅkhya's prakṛti* with its three *guṇas* and the principles of *puruṣa* and the ideas of *kaivalya*, 'liberation'. In addition to *Sāṅkhya's* principle, the *Gītā* recognizes the existence of *Uttamapuruṣa*, 'supreme *puruṣa*'.

3.1.1. *Prakṛti* and its three *Guṇas*

Prakṛti according to *Sāṅkhya* means the unmanifested, ubiquitous, undecaying and unconscious principle which stands at the ultimate cause and the background of the universe.[6] The term *'mahad brahma'* of the *Gītā* refers to *Sāṅkhya's* principle as *prakṛti*. In the *Gītā*, *prakṛti* acts as female and *Puruṣottama Puruṣa* acts as male and charges His spiritual energy upon the material basis for manifestation of all creatures.[7] *Prakṛti* is made up of three *guṇas*. *Guṇas* are considered to be the infra-atomic quanta of real rather the forces than substances in a state of continuous flux. This varying permutation of combinations of the *guṇas* result in all sorts of collocation which are manifested in the worldly objects.[8] *Sattva guṇa* means the real existence which is acting as a medium for the reflection of the manifested objects within the realm of our consciousness. The presence of *sattva guṇa* represents goodness, luminosity of light in our consciousness, reflection of power, upward movement towards the spiritual state, pleasure, happiness, contentment, bliss, *laghu*, 'buoyant' and *prakāśā*, 'illumination'. The presence of *rājasa guṇa* represents foulness and dynamic principle of motion. It has the tendency of overcoming resistance to our conscious work. The occurrence of *rājasa guṇa* enhances pain, restless activity, feverish effort, *chala*-'mobile', wild and stimulations. The *tāmasa guṇa* considers as darkness which is the principle of inertia and produces apathy and indifference, ignorance, sloth, confusion, bewilderment, passivity and negativity.[9]

The *Bhagavad Gītā* also attributes the three *guṇas* and the immortal nature of the self pertaining to the corporeal body. The *Bhagavad Gītā* says, *'sattva, rajas, tamas,* these *guṇas,* O mighty-armed, born of *prakṛti,* bind fast in the body the embodied, the indestructible'.[10] To give importance to *guṇas,* the *Gītā* states that there is no creature either on earth or among Gods who is all free from the three *guṇas*.[11] In this aspect, the *Gītā* differs from *Sāṅkhya* philosophy, where the former system says, that, the *guṇas* are automatically come out from *prakṛti*[12]. But to the *Gītā* the *guṇas* are produced by *prakṛti* through the fertilization of God's energy.[13] The *Bhagavad Gītā* says, that, *sattva guṇa* binds the self with the *jñāna saṅgena,* 'knowledge' and *sukha saṅgena*, 'pleasure through its nature of purity'[14] and get rid of the ego-sense. In this way, the *sattva guṇa* lays a path for the true *jñāna* relating to *buddhi* and distinguishes the self from the pure conscious of the *ātman* and it finally leads to *mokṣa*. On the other hand, *rājasa guṇa* initiates *tṛṣṇāsaṅgasamudbhavam*, 'desire and attachment and is fastened together with the egoistic thinking through the action'. Even though the self is not acting as agent, *rājasa guṇa* terminates the original self into the idea of 'I am the doer', the basic notion towards the egoism which makes a gap between the self and the state of liberation.[15] *Tāmasa guṇa*, the quality of dullness or ignorance deludes the self into negligence or carelessness, indolence or illness and sleep or lethargic nature.[16] Like the *Sāṅkhya* system, the *Gītā* also conceives the nature of the existing objects with the occurrence of the above said three qualities differing in contents and time with respect to its environment. Thus at certain times *sattva guṇa* dominates over *rājasa* and *tāmasa guṇas* where the knowledge rises into its loftier height through all the states of sense gates.[17] If *rājasa guṇa* predominates over the *sattva* and *tāmasa guṇas*, the mind will be submerged with the tendency for different kinds of activities and the passion seeking life with disquiet and ambition.[18] If the temperament of *tāmasa guṇa* predominates, the effects of the other two *guṇas* are suppressed through its unlighted errors, unwillingness towards action, fecklessness, dilutions and false beliefs.[19]

3.1.2. *Puruṣa*

Sāṅkhya system considers the *puruṣa* as conscious and inactive principle in all individuals. It is termed as spirit, the subject and the knower. *Puruṣa* refers to neither to the body nor senses nor brain nor *manas* nor *ahaṅkāra* and nor *buddhi*. It is the essence of transcendental consciousness, 'ultimate knower' and the silent witness which is beyond time and space and change and action. Moreover, it is self-luminous, self-proved, uncaused, eternal, immutable and all-pervading indubitable real and it is set against the unconscious active *prakṛti*.[20]

Like *prakṛti*, the *Bhagavad Gītā* divides *puruṣa* into two kinds as lower *puruṣa* and higher *puruṣa*. The lower *puruṣa* always mingles with the *prakṛti* and in the various activities of the *guṇas*. So, the lower *puruṣa* is different from different bodies with respect to the *guṇas*. On the other hand, the higher *puruṣa* exists in an unattached and unaffected state which is apart from the activities of *guṇas*. So, the lower *puruṣa* being with the *prakṛti* enjoys the modes of the three *guṇas* and gets attached to it. So, the lower *puruṣa* leads to the next birth whether good or bad with respect to its past *karmas*.[21] Instead of the lower *puruṣa*, the higher *puruṣa* being detached with the *prakṛti* acts as passive perceiver, the on which permits, the supporter, the enjoyer and the Great Lord.[22] Here, the higher *puruṣa* is considered to be the *Paramātman*, 'supreme self' because it is different from our psychological organs and its actual nature is immortal by transcending the conscious level through the detachment of *prakṛti* and its three *guṇas*.[23] The lower *puruṣa* is considered to be the *kṣarapuruṣa*, because it is changeable with respect to *guṇas*; and the higher *puruṣa* is called as *akṣarapuruṣa* because it is unchangeable and beyond the nature of *guṇas*. So, the *prakṛti* makes a ground for all causes and effects and it possesses the fundamental principle of our dynamic operations, motivations and the actions within which the *puruṣa* consolidates all the above said experiences and the sorrows and joy of the *prakṛti*.[24]

Sāṅkhya philosophy accepts *kṣara* and *akṣara* nature of *puruṣa*. The *Gītā* adds one more *puruṣa* which is above the level of *akṣarapuruṣa* namely Puruṣottama or God. So, in the *Gītā* the mere term *puruṣa* refers to the Puruṣottama, the Lord Kṛṣṇa; *akṣarapuruṣa* refers to the Brahman,'highest self' and the *kṣarapuruṣa* represents the lower nature of self.[25] But in *Sāṅkhya*, there is no distinction as in the *Gītā*. In *Sāṅkhya* the *kṣara* and *akṣarapuruṣas* represent only the lower and higher nature of self and it totally rejects the existence of Puruṣottama, 'God'. The *Bhagavad Gītā* distinguishes the nature of higher self and the lower self. The higher self is comparable with *Paramātma puruṣa* which is all pervasive and exists within the individual as an entity untouchable through the experiences of joy, sorrow and the attachment of the worldly objects. Against the highest self, the lower self is getting connection with the experiences and the activities of the three *guṇas*.[26]

3.1.3. *Kṣetra* and *Kṣetrajña*

The *Bhagavad Gītā* refers to the psychophysical complex as *Kṣetra* and the force which controls the *Kṣetra* as *Kṣetrajña*. Here *Kṣetra* and *Kṣetrajña* are nothing but the *prakṛti* and *puruṣa*.[27] It is difficult to know the *prakṛti* by itself before the stimulation of God's energy. The categories are not considered as the *prakṛti* because they are the products formulated only after the initiation of God's energy over *prakṛti*. For *prakṛti*, the *Gītā* emphasizes two ways of explanation. They are: (i) It is product of *prakṛti*, over that the *guṇas* are mingling as knowable, enjoyable, emotional and moral or immoral qualities. (ii) It is considered to be lower nature of God because it is acting as mother where God as father changes His energy. However, it is difficult to consider the categories as the lower *prakṛti* of God because the *Gītā* does not include any passage to refer to the categories as *Sāṅkhya* philosophy. So, all the categories are considered to be the ultimate principle and they are having intimate connection with God and co-exist with Him. In other words, the *Kṣetra* or *apara prakṛti*, 'lower nature of God' refers to the categories and the *Kṣetrajña* or *para prakṛti* or *puruṣa*, 'higher nature of God' who controls the power of life.[28] In comparison with the *Sāṅkhya* philosophy, *Sāṅkhya* combines the lower and higher *prakṛti* as one and eschews the idea of God. So, *Sāṅkhya* philosophy says that the *guṇas* are produced not only the basic stuff of our experiences but also the psychophysical complex.[29] The difference between the *Sāṅkhya* and the *Bhagavad Gītā* reveals that *Sāṅkhya* treats the *guṇas* not the product of *prakṛti* but, they themselves constitute the *prakṛti* at the time of equilibrium. But the *Gītā* states that the *guṇas* as the product of the *prakṛti* that produces by the limitation of God's energy and they will never constitute *prakṛti* at the time of equilibrium.

3.1.4. *Avyakta*

Upaniṣads do not analyse the self as *avykta* or unmanifested. Instead of it, they treat the self as pure consciousness and the self manifested. Even, all the *Vedāntic* works understand the self as *anubhūti svabhāva* being immediately intuited.[30] But the *Gītā* refers to *avyakta* self as unmanifested, unthinkable, changeless and deathless nature of self and it does not mean the pure consciousness. The *Bhagavad Gītā* explains the consciousness as *cetana*, 'consciousness'[31] which is having connection with changeable *kṣetra* and not with *Kṣetrajña*. Here, one can expect a clarification that if consciousness has no connection with *Kṣetrajña* then how the self will know the *Kṣetra*. The *Gītā* states that the self can be recognized as *Kṣetrajña* only with respect to *Kṣetra* where the self becomes the principles of consciousness, i.e. the '*Kṣetra*' bears the *cetana* and with the association of the self it becomes '*Kṣetrajña*'.[32] The *Gītā* explains the *puruṣa* as *jīvabhūta*, 'the life principle' in which it upholds the whole universe. The *Gītā* missed to explain the particular way in which the *puruṣa* upholds the world. But *Sāṅkhya* philosophy distinctly described the *ātman* as the life principle and holds the principles of *buddhi*, *manas* and *indriyas* on one side and the other principles such as good, bad, pleasure, pain, bondage, liberation and the worldly process on the other side. *Sāṅkhya* philosophy treats the *puruṣa* as *cetenadhātṛ*, 'upholder of consciousness'. It arises at the time of joint operation of *manas*, *indriyas*; and the worldly object. But the *Bhagavad Gītā* considers the same problem in a critical way, i.e., *puruṣa* is not *cetanadhātu* but *cetana* or consciousness and it has constituted by *Kṣetra* over which the *puruṣa* presides. In another way also one can derive a relation between *Sāṅkhya's* view and the *Gītā*, *Sāṅkhya* philosophy advocate '*satkāryavāda*'. It means that the fruits of action are only the effect of the unfolding evolution, where the effect is nothing but the outcome of what was already potentially present in the cause.[33] *Sāṅkhya's* theory of causation is not parallel to that of the *Gītā* because *Sāṅkhya* gives no importance to effect, i.e. the effect is not a new one but what was already potentially present in the cause. The *Gītā* accepts the *satkāryavāda* through the exploration of the immortality of the self or the self as effect which is nothing but the causal form of God Himself. This view is illustrated through the *Gītā's* explanation of the self as, "Of the unreal no being there is; there is no non-being of the real".[34] The *Gītā* too deals with *asatkāryavāda* which includes importance to the effects and produces by the collection of various causes. In other words, the effect of the cosmos is the result of the inter-related and interdependent *prakṛti, puruṣa* and the God's simulative energy.[35]

3.1.5. The Evolutes

A study upon the evolution of the categories through the combination of *puruṣa* with *prakṛti* reveals the many more views about the relationship between them. Before manifestation, the psychophysical complex exists in an unmanifested form. Then the eternal inactive *puruṣa* initiates the *prakṛti* for manifestation. Here *puruṣa* only influences the activity of *prakṛti* like a magnet placed very near to iron. Due to attraction the magnet does not lose its own state. Like that, due to the *prakṛti's* activity, the *puruṣa* never changes its feature and it acts as mere on-looker of the evolution.[36]

The *Gītā* accepts the *Sāṅkhya's* evolutionary process[37] with the twenty-five categories. In addition, it adds one more category to the above *prakṛti* and its evolution of *Sāṅkhya* philosophy. In other words, the *Bhagavad Gītā* adds twenty-sixth category the Lord Kṛṣṇa, along with the twenty-five categories of *Sāṅkhya* philosophy as Puruṣottama. The *Yogasūtra* explains the Lord as a special type of spiritual monad which is omniscience and ancient and untouched by time and *karma*.[38] In addition the *Gītā* by having understood the

Sāṅkhya's material nature of the universe and *puruṣas*, it adds one more special significance to the Puruṣottama, i.e. the spiritual monads are not independent entities but they are minute parts[39] and germs of God.[40]

Even though, the *Sāṅkhya* and the *Gītā* explain the self as qualityless, inactive and apathetic,[41] they differ in the description of *mukti*. *Sāṅkhya* points out, that, *mukti* is just like the separation of the outer skin of grass from its internal stock, the *prakṛti* has to separate itself from the *puruṣa*.[42] But in the *Bhagavad Gītā* the individual's attitude and the grace of the Lord are playing a major role for *mukti*. *Sāṅkhya*[43] and the *Gītā*[44] state, that, if the individual does not transcends the *prakṛti* and *guṇas* in his life he will never escape from birth and death. For instance, during his life, if *sattva guṇa* predominates he will be born in the heavenly realm; if *rājasa guṇa* predominates he will be born in human sphere and if *tāmasa guṇa* predominates he will be in animal kingdom. But both accept that when the aspirant transcends the all *guṇas* he will be always in perfect state.

3.2. THE BHAGAVAD GĪTĀ COMPARED WITH PATAÑJALI'S YOGA

The general meaning of the term *yoga* is derived from the three roots, namely *yujir yoga*, *yuj samadhan* and *yuj saṁyamane*. The root *'yujir'* means to join; the root *'yuj'* means the cessation of mental states or the state of one point and the *'yuj'* within the *yuj saṁyamane* refers to the sense of control over the five *indriyas*, the five sense organs. Patañjali, in his *Yoga Sūtra* uses the term *'yoga'* as *cittavṛttinirodha*, 'cessation of one's mental states'. The *Gītā* does not follow Patañjali's *Yoga* system. Instead, the *Gītā* proclaims various unconnected views without any interrelation among them.[45] The *Gītā* uses the root *yuj* in a positive as well as negative sense. Positively *yuj* means to join with something; negatively it represents a control or restriction of the obstacles within to join the supreme state. Ernest Wood expresses the varied definitions and descriptions of the term *'yoga'* of the *Bhagavad Gītā*.[46] They are: 'equilibrium in success and failure', 'skilful living activity', 'an ancient science revived by Lord Kṛṣṇa', 'supreme secret of life', 'a producer of the greatest felicity', 'serenity', 'non-attachment', 'destroyer of pain', 'separation of pain', 'effected by self-control', 'used for concentration', 'attained by contemplation', and 'to practice for self-purification'.

Unlike Patañjali, the *Bhagavad Gītā* formulates the following methods to attain the yogic state[47] : *Sāṅkhya yoga*, '*yoga* by science'; *buddhi yoga*, '*yoga* by wisdom'; *ātma yoga*, '*yoga* of the self'; *karma yoga*, '*yoga* by action'; and *saṁnyāsa yoga*, '*yoga* by renunciation'. In the second chapter the *Gītā*, Lord Kṛṣṇa discusses with Arjuna the permanent nature of self, impermanent nature of body, the actual feature of the self while undergoing transmigration and the temporal nature of pleasure and pain to the self. These explanations are scientifically accepted and represented as *Sāṅkhya Yoga*. Mere getting *Sāṅkhya Yoga* is inadequate knowledge. So, one should have a knowledge to apply this to the benefit of his continuing life. The *Gītā* refers to this attitude as *buddhi* or wisdom. So, attainment of the intimate association with the particular type of constant endeavour upon our wisdom is viewed as *buddhi yoga*. The *Gītā* also explains *yoga* as fixing our *manas* upon our self which is called *ātma yoga*. Similarly, if one associates himself with his own duties, he may be termed as *karma yogin*. The *Gītā* adds one more *yoga* namely *saṁnyāsa yoga*. It means the renunciation of the fruits of our activities. So, all types of *yoga* represent the sense of fixing to a particular state where the process of fixing implies disjunction or the dissociation with the desires, pleasures and towards the fruits of our activities. The *Gītā* says, 'Do thou, O Pāṇḍava, know Yoga to be that which they call renunciation; no one, verily becomes *Yogin* who has not renounced thoughts'.[48]

The cessation of the desires of the fruits of action is called *yoga* because unless one attains that attitude one should not get the higher mental plane. If one wants to become a *Yogin*, he should get success over his sensuous attachment towards his sense objects. With this, he also gives up all his desires towards his fruits of action. If a person attains this highest step, he will succeed in elevating his self to the highest plane. In that state he completely gets rid off all the motives of his self interest, pleasure and enjoyment. Within this sphere, one can be aware of two kinds of self namely *ātman*, the lower self and *Paramātman*, the higher self *Ātman* always indulges in psychological and prudential conditions of self-interest and pleasure. Naturally, the self exists as friend and foe to himself. If he includes himself with the lowest temptations of sensual pleasures his self becomes his self becomes his enemy and takes downward step to evil. Instead of the downward path, if he understands his sense of duty, he raises himself from the downward step to upward through the destruction of the basic attitude of attachment with the sensual pleasure. So, if the self gets upward step the self becomes his friend but if he takes the downward step the same self becomes his enemy. The *Bhagavad Gītā* adds, 'Let a man raise himself by himself, let him not lower himself; for, he alone is the friend of himself, he alone is the enemy of himself'.[49] While uplifting the *ātman* to *Paramātman* level the individual has to pass through many stages. They are: (i) He has to perform his duties, which has prescribed by *śāstras.* (ii) He has to dissociate himself from his selfish motives and enjoyment. (iii) He has to get success to overcome all the drawbacks and attain higher state of self.

The *Bhagavad Gītā* says, that, even after attaining the higher level the person should directly continue his duty with his duty consciousness alone. During the process he is joined with the higher self or God. So, any person who attains the state of *Paramātman* or even union with *Paramātman* he will be considered as a true philosopher; he realizes intuitively and mingle with the truth; he has the unshakable attitude in every walk of life, he gives equal importance to gold and stone because of his conquest over his own senses and he looks alike the friend and foe as one.[50] Thus, the above discussion reveals that the *Bhagavad Gītā* derives *yoga* from the root *yuj* which means joining with the higher plane of *Paramātman* level.[51] When one compares the *Gītā's Yoga* systems with Patañjali's *Yoga* the former recommends the middle path and the later favours the complete stoppage of our mental as well as physical functions. The *Gītā's* middle path helps the *yogī* to get union with the *Paramātman* through meditation and self control and leads his life with freedom from the mental tendencies of desire and longing for the possession[52]. While doing *yoga,* the *Yogī* should seat himself upon the firm and clean ground which is neither too high nor too low and that seat is made of three layers of *kuśa* grass, a leopard skin and a soft linen.[53] He controls his senses and he should concentrate his mind upon God. Through the union with God he can easily purify his life.[54]

Both the *Bhagavad Gītā* and Patañjali use the term, *'yoga'* in the basic sense of association. But the *Gītā* takes further step to reach the state of higher self or get union with God through the detachment towards the fruits of our action. In this respect, the *Gītā* declares *yogaḥ karmasu kaụsalam,*[55] 'real art of performing one's duties with unattached sentiments', which indirectly paves the way for the performance of the real *yoga*. So, in addition to Patañjali's meaning of *yoga* as association, the *Gītā* adds better meanings[56] which are considered to be the evolution of higher and higher ideas in all sorts of way.[57] Moreover, Patañjali's yoga system suggests that the last state of *samādhi* represents the total isolation of the self from the worldly nature and even from God.[58] Here the *Gītā's* usage of *yoga* differs from the traditional *Yoga* because it makes an improvement of using our internal sense organs and worldly attitude. The *Gītā* transcends one's self interest to a wider and higher vision within the nature and a close link with God. At this stage a *Yogin* perceives God in all things and all things in God where the *Yogin* has the same perception towards both low and high, virtues and sins and gets supreme realization of equanimity among the inequality of race, creed, position, virtue and vice, higher thing and lower thing. So, the *Gītā* suggests a proper channel to acquire a supreme bliss and sub line ecstasy where the *Yogin* does not feel any sufferings or sorrows.[59]

3.3. THE BHAGAVAD GĪTĀ AND JAINISM

Unlike the *Bhagavad Gītā's* affinity with traditional *Sāṅkhya,* Patañjali's *yoga* and Buddhism, there is no clear cut metaphysics link between the *Gītā* and the Jaina system.

In spite of the criteria, the following views reveal the philosophical views of agreements. (i) The *Gītā* considers the embodied self as a spiritual eternal part of the Ultimate Reality which co-exists within the individual body. In Jaina system, the self is as everlasting, uncreated, eternal conscious spirit, the *Jīva,* which is associated with the *jīva,* the unconscious non-spirit. But in liberation the self is equated with Godhood. (ii) Jainism expounds the self as Infinite Faith, Infinite Knowledge, Infinite Bliss and Infinite power. The self is *jñātā,* 'knower', *kartā,* 'agent" and *bhoktā,* 'enjoyer'. The *Gītā* accepts the above explanation with one difference. That is, the absolute spiritual self acts as a mere witness and the *guṇas* alone bear the responsibility of the worldly activities. (iii) The Jaina system includes the *jīvas* into *astikāyadravya* because of its principle of *madhyamaparimāṇa,* 'condensation and ratification of the consciousness of the self with respect to the body', and pervades within the space as light particles. The *Gītā* rejects the above said principles, but accepts the divinity which pervades within the universe as His lower and Higher nature. (iv) The law of *karma* in Jainism is due to desire, aversion and delusion may be comparable with *Gītā.* (v) Jainism views about the selves in hell, selves in animal world, selves, in human beings and they are having some sort of co-ordination with the *Gītā's* explanation of the status of next birth with respect to the preponderance of the *guṇas* in the present birth.

(vi) A close examination of *jīvas* and *pudgala* results in a resemblance of the *puruṣa* and *prakṛti* of the *Gītā*.

Just as agreement, there are contradictory views between them. They are: (i) Jaina system maintains the plurality of selves and they are qualitatively same and quantitatively different and they are differentiated as *mukta* and *baddha*. But in the *Gītā* the theistic absolutists alone follow the principle of pluralism and the differences of selves in accordance with the law of *karmas*. There are no differences as *mukta, baddha, trasa, sthāvara* as in the *Gītā* but Jaina system accepts them. (ii) Jaina system says, that, the *karmic* forces are as infra-atomic particles. But in the *Gītā* it is a metaphysical concept which works within the selves. (iii) Jaina system explains the *karma* as *mohanīya karma, antarīya karma, jñānāvaraṇīya karma* and *darśanavaraṇīya karma*. But there is no such division in the *Gītā*. (iv) *Mukti* in Jainism assumes that by negating and destroying the *karmic* forces, the individuals can attain the *kevala jñāna* of infinite perception, infinite power and bliss. But the *Gītā* declares that by weakening the *karmic* forces through *yogas* and the right action one can rise from lower state to higher state and finally he can achieve the *mukti* state. By understanding the comprehensive understanding, one can easily understand the affinity between the two; more specifically it could be elucidated that these are some allied thinking regarding the inner nature of the self.

3.4. THE BHAGAVAD GĪTĀ AND BUDDHISM

Like *Sāṅkhya* and *Yoga* philosophy, the *Bhagavad Gītā* has a firm connection with the Buddhism in the philosophical adherence of the *nirvāṇa* [60] and the performance of *yoga*.[61] Even though a comprehensive study reveals a controversial outlook towards the connection; the *Gītā* sparingly uses the technical words of Buddhism with certain modifications of its own. The technical terms used by *Bhagavad Gītā* from Buddhistic philosophy may be listed and explained.

(i) *Anityā*[62]

Anityā, 'impermanent', which is a typical Buddhistic word. In Buddhism, the senses are attached to its objects, because of the *māra*, 'Buddhistic devil' which operates between the links. So, the person has to destroy the devil and get *nibbana* or *nirvāṇa* or from *saṁsāra* or *anicca*, the impermanent.[63] Like Buddhism, the *Bhagavad Gītā* also uses this term in order to cassette the link between the senses and the objects of the senses.

(ii) *Āhāra*[64]

When explaining the *sthitaprajña*, the *Gītā* uses the terms, *nirāhārasya*, 'person who does not eat'. This term is absent in the *Upaniṣads*, *Sāṅkhya* and *Yoga* system, but occurs in Buddhistic Pāli canon as *āhāra*, where it represents only the bodily food but also the food of the senses through *phassāhāro* and *vijñāna*,'contact of mind and will, and of the consciousness'.[65]

(iii) *Rāgadveṣau* and *Saṁmohaḥ*[66]

For *sthitaprajña*, the *Bhagavad Gītā* also uses these words as '*rāgadveṣau* and *saṁmohaḥ*', 'passion and hate' and 'bewilderment' or 'the confusion' respectively. According to Buddhism it represents *tanha*, 'cravings' or 'strong desire', which should be denounced from one's mind for the purpose of attaining the *nirvāṇa* state.[67]

(iv) *Nirmaṁ Nirahaṅkāraḥ*[68]

The term '*nirmaṁ nirahaṅkāraḥ*' refers to the mentality of the *sthitaprajña*, 'person who refuses to think as 'this is mine' or 'this I am' which resembles the *ahaṅkāra-mamakāra* of the Pali canon; and it refers to the illusory appearances of body or *manas* or *indriyas* or feeling or perception or consciousness or anything. Here, the *Gītā* refers to the Buddhistic refusal of a thing, which exists in our present time and space, called as 'I' or 'mine' or 'the self'. So, while attaining the state of *sthitaprajña* for the first time within Hinduism, the *Bhagavad Gītā* alone takes the direct idea or *nirmaṁ nirahaṅkāraḥ* from the Buddhistic Pāli canon.[69]

(v) *Brahma-nirvāṇa*[70]

The *Gītā's* term *brahmanirvāṇa* does not directly occur in Pāli canon but it has derived from the two Buddhistic terms such as *brahma-bhūta,* which refers: to Brahman and *nirvāṇa. Brahma bhūta* has been derived from a phrase of Pāli canon as *nicchāto nibbuto sīto bhūto sukha patisamvediī brahmabhūtena attenā,* 'without craving, appeared, cooled and experiencing joy with his self become Brahman'.[71] The *Gītā* takes the Pāli term *brahmabhūta* with respect to the nature of self, i.e., the self is existing in a condition which is unconditioned by space, time and causation. The next term *nirvāṇa* is a Buddhistic one because through the *Gītā* only the Hinduism adopts the ideology of *nirvāṇa.* According to Buddhism, *nirvāṇa* means the blowing out of the lamp or fire of existence which actually refers to the cessation of sensation or extinction of becoming, craving and pain or getting peace through the *Vairāgya,* 'detachment from' or *nibbidā,* 'disgust' or *nirodhā,* 'bringing to an end' of our phenomenal existence by *upāsana,* 'tranquilising of senses', *abhinna,* 'wisdom' and *sambodhi,* 'enlightenment'. *Nirvāṇa* is not only the extinction of our life, but also a state of liberation, the spiritual freedom in the transcendental sphere, where the reason, the wisdom and the *aśvas* of passion, hatred and delusion are absent. With reference to the *sthitaprajña,* the word *brahma* and *nirvāṇa* connote the *yoga* of sameness and one's skill in works. This means the complete detachment from our senses through absorption of the *manas* into *budhi, budhi* into self.

(vi) *Naiṣkarmyaṁ*[72]

The term *naiṣkarmyaṁ* means the freedom from the bond of work. This also comes from the Buddhistic Pāli canon, *nekkhamma.* It means self abnegation, detachment, passionless and freedom from desire.[73] The *Gītā* uses this term not as *akarman*[74] or worklessness but as a man who sees worklessness in work itself and work in worklessness.[75] So, *'naiṣkarmyaṁ'* means doing one's duty and eliminates the desire or passion towards the fruits of his performed duty.

(vii) *Duḥkha*[76]

It also comes from Buddhism and it refers to *annica*, 'the transient'. Here, the *Gītā* takes the principle that while performing *nirvāṇa*, the person should transcend the contact of our senses with the worldly activities. Our senses should withdraw its forces from their objects and set free the contemplative *buddhi* as *nirvāṇa*.[77]

(viii) *Nirvāṇa-cetasā*[78]

The *Gītā* takes the phrase as 'with mind dismayed' or 'transient', where the text says that during the realisation, the person should be away from the worldly problem.[79]

(ix) *Bhagavan*

The term is assigned to Puruṣottama Kṛṣṇa and Mahāpuruṣa Buddha. The similarity of the concept of *avatāra* and the devotional attitude towards Kṛṣṇa and Buddha show the influence of Buddhism upon the *Gītā*.[80] In addition to the Buddhistic terms, *Bhagavad Gītā* also directly adheres to the Buddhistic ideologies to emphasize a person, who is undergoing certain firm and hard practice to attain the still state of *nirvāṇa*. They are: (i) When explaining the nature of *sthitaprajña* the *Gītā* says, 'The dangerous senses, O son of Kuntī, forcibly carry away the mind of a wise man, even while striving (to control them)'.[81] This idea which is connected with *nirvāṇa* aptly resembles the Buddhistic Pāli canon, where Buddhism reveals, that, the *nirvāṇa* can be achieved only through annihilation of the force of contact between the senses and its objects. Buddhism adds that the contact between them is not because of the senses or its object but because of the *candraga*, the mutual attractive force of the both.[82] (ii) At the time of practicing the *yoga*, for the first time Lord Kṛṣṇa explains Himself as *matparaḥ,* 'object of meditation to perform the *yoga* by one-pointed concentration'. *Bhagavad Gītā* says, 'Restraining them all, a man should remain steadfast, intent on Me. His knowledge is steady whose senses are under control'.[83] The one pointed concentration essentially resembles the Buddhism in the process of detachment from one's own mind from the worldly object. In the *Gītā,* the atheistic view of concentration upon an object in Buddhism, has been transformed into the theistic concentration upon God, who is either personal or impersonal. (iii) When explaining the peaceful intellectual nature of the *sthitaprajña* the *Gītā* proclaims, 'He attains peace, into whom all desires enter as waters enter the ocean, which filled from all sides, remains unaltered: but not he who desires objects'.[84] Here the explanation and example given for the ocean are also seen in Buddhism.[85] (iv) In the third chapter, the process for destroying the *kāma* to attain *nirvāṇa* the *Gītā* says, "It is desire, it is wrath, born of the energy of *rajas,* all devouring, all sinful: that, known thou, is the foe here".[86] The total condemnation of the desire represents the influence of Buddhistic idea.[87] (v) In the fifth chapter, when explaining the characteristic features of purified self the *Bhagavad Gītā* says, "He who does actions, offering them to Brahmin, abandoning attachment, is not tainted by sin, as a lotus leaf by water".[88] (vi) The same metaphorical explanation of lotus petal within the water is present in the Buddhist scripture.[89] (vii) While describing the correct approach of the wise man the *Gītā* says, 'For, those delights which are born of contacts are only generators of pain, having a beginning and an end. O Son of Kuntī; a wise man rejoices not in time'.[90] The treatment of delights as pain by the *Gītā* is also derived from the Buddhistic ideology.[91] (viii) The *Gītā* explains the performance of a person to attain the *nirvāṇa* state through the yogic practice as, '*Yoga* is not possible for him who eats too much, nor for him who does not eat at all, nor for him who is addicted to too much sleep, not for him who is (ever) wakeful. O Arjuna, to him whose food and recreation are moderate, whose exertion in action is moderate, whose sleep and waking are moderate to him accrues *yoga*, which is destruction of pain'.[92] Here the *Gītā* recommends a reconciled notion of life within every activity and it aptly resembles the middle path of Buddhism in every aspect.[93] (ix) While explaining the goal of spiritual exercises, the *Gītā* says, "This severance from union with pain, be it known, is called union (*Yoga*).[94] This definition of *Yoga* refers to the Buddhist standpoint towards the *nirvāṇa* state. Buddha refers to the senses as *māra* or devil. When this *māra* comes into contact with the sense object there result the case for bondage and went it withdraws from its objects then the *buddhi* becomes free. Here, Buddhism and the *Gītā* accepts the cessation of the senses from its object as *nirvāṇa*.[95] (x) The *Bhagavad Gītā* teaches that by utilizing *śraddhā*, 'faith', *Ceṣṭā*, 'effort', *smṛti*, 'remembrance' *samādhi*, 'concentration; and *jñāna* or the *prajña*, 'wisdom'; one can attain the highest goal. It aptly resembles the *Buddhistic panea balani*, 'five pears or faculties'.[96]

3.5. A CRITICAL APPROACH UPON THE AFFINITIES OF THE BHAGAVAD GĪTĀ AND BUDDHISM

Even though the *Bhagavad Gītā* denies some of its principle from *Sāṅkhya* philosophy through *guṇas, prakṛti* and its derivatives it uses the term *Sāṅkhya* into his sense of the philosophical wisdom or the way of getting *jñāna*. One can get this view from the verse as, 'Now listen to wisdom concerning *yoga*, which possessing thou shall cost off the bond of action'.[97] In the above verse, the term *Sāṅkhya* refers to the immorality of the self because the previous verses of the same chapter[98] deal with the same problem. For self-realisation the *Gītā* says as, 'By meditation some behold the self in the self by the self others by *Sāṅkhya yoga*, and others by *Karma yoga*'.[99] Where the term *sāṅkhyena yogena* refers to the path of self realization. But in the preceding verse the *Gītā* regards that if a man knows the proper nature of *puruṣa* and *prakṛti*, he will never be born again.[100] So, through a comprehensive view, one can certainly assert, that, the term '*Sāṅkhya*' refers to the knowledge of wisdom. In the third chapter, the *Bhagavad Gītā* proclaims as *jñāna yogena sāṅkhyānaṃ, karma yogena yoginām,*[101] which means for the men of theory the spiritual exercise of wisdom and for men of action the spiritual exercise of wisdom and for men of action the spiritual exercise through work. Since the term *yoga* refers to the association the phrase *Sāṅkhya yogena* which refers to the association with *Sāṅkhya*. So, the term *Sāṅkhya* has been used in two ways which are as follows: (i) The distinction between the path of *Sāṅkhya* or wisdom and the path of *yoga* or the path of performing the regular duties. (ii) *Bhagavad Gītā* uses the term to explain the proper way of union with God through proper *jñāna*.[102] It says as, 'That state which is reached by *Sāṅkhyas* is reached by *Yogins* also. He sees, who sees *Sāṅkhya* and *Yoga* as one.'[103].

Here, the *Bhagavad Gītā* treats the *Sāṅkhya* as wisdom as well as the renunciation of action in so far as it is bound with the person. The *Gītā* refers to the *yoga* as the performance of duty without minding the result. So, the term *Sāṅkhya* and *Yoga* of the *Gītā* refers to the *yoga* as the performance of duty without minding the result. So, the term *Sāṅkhya* and *Yoga* of the *Bhagavad Gītā* mean the same. In other words, *Sāṅkhya* leads to the pure contemplation leading to intuitive apprehension of reality and *yoga* leads to an active life without ambition. Then the *yogin* reaches the contemplative nature which results in the realization of God.[104] The *Bhagavad Gītā* also uses the term '*sāṅkhya*' in a different sense as 'true knowledge, and renunciation'. Combining these two views, the *Bhagavad Gītā* refers to *karma yoga* as the performance of one's duties with true knowledge and with the attitude of a *tyāga*.

According to *Sāṅkhya* philosophy, *puruṣas* are many. They are in different environment, differences in life and death, and variations in pleasures and pains. So, *Sāṅkhya* philosophy avers that the whole world has been constituted by many *puruṣas* united with *prakṛti*. The *Bhagavad Gītā* compromises the above said dualism of *prakṛti* and *puruṣa* through the monistic *Parabrahman*. In other words the *Bhagavad Gītā* utilizes the dualistic term *prakṛti* and *puruṣa* as synonymous within the field of *Kṣetra* and *Kṣetrajña*.

Sāṅkhya philosophy explains *triguṇātīta* as a person who transcends the three *guṇas*. Even though he transcends the level of *guṇas*, the *sattva guṇa* is preponderant with the special quality of reason. Here reason means the qualities of *jñāna*, 'realization', *vairāgya*, 'asceticism' and *aiśvarya* 'power'. The same explanation also occurs in the *Bhagavad Gītā* as, "That by which a man sees the one Indestructible Reality in all beings, in separate with the separated, that knowledge know thou as *sāttvic*".[105] In the *nirvāṇa* state, the *Gītā* differs from the *Sāṅkhya*. Fourteenth chapter of the *Bhagavad Gītā* explains the *siddha* or the released state as the transcending force of *māyā* through proper *jñāna* and the realization of *Paramātman*. But *Sāṅkhya* philosophy describes *mukti* state as the isolation of the *puruṣa* from the three aspects of the *prakṛti*.

A study of Buddhism and the *Gītā* reveals the truth, that, in no way the *Bhagavad Gītā's* ideas are connected with the Buddhism. For example, the practice of *Yoga* in Buddhism the *Yogin* concentrates his mind upon the particular object with the right endeavour for the purpose of shifting and changing the person's mind. For that the *Yogin* has to do the following practices: (i) The person has to disregard the appetitive desires for food, drinks but he has to take the food as unavoidable evil till the disappearance of all the sorrows and sufferings. (ii) He has to train his mind to look upon his fellow beings as nothing but the conglomeration of four elements, namely earth, water, fire and wind. (iii) The person has to pass through various pacificator processes like thinking about the virtues of Buddha, *śīla*, 'sense control', *cāgānussati* , 'to offer gifts', *maraṇānussati*, 'nature of death' and *upāsaṇānussati*, 'extinction of the phenomenal order'.

In addition to the above, the *Yogin* has to think and practice *passāsa*, 'inhale' and *assāya*, 'exhale of his breath'. Thus the *Yogin* should concentrate his mind on *jñāna* or meditative realm and finally pulls back his mind away from the bodily elements. Buddhism explains the meditation as *brahmavihāra* and systematizes it into four fold order. They are: (i) Through *mattā* 'universal friendship', the *yogin* thinks about the way of avoiding the death and misery. (ii) Through *karuṇā*, 'grace' he can understand the equality of the other beings with himself. (iii) Through *muditā* 'mental attitude' of the happiness of all. (iv) Through *upekṣā* 'thinking' about his own unattached and unconnected nature among his own friends, foes and all other human beings. After crossing the four folded order, the person may reach indifference between happiness and misery, and the indifference of happiness of himself and the same condition of others. Thus, the person reaches *nibbāṇa* or *cetovimuthi* 'final release through the four-folded order' within the first stage of concentration.[106]

Buddha was all compassion to every kind of being animate as well as inanimate. So, Buddhism teaches that compassion should be an essential quality. It produces the feeling of oneness and that is what any form of *yogas* aims at. While explaining *Yoga*, the Lord in the *Bhagavad Gītā* advocates the compassion as realising Brahman within the selves of all beings[107]. This is not different from what Buddha told regarding the ultimate end of *Yoga*.

REFERENCES

1. Roy, S.C., *The Bhagavad Gītā and the Modern Scholars*, p. 36.
2. *Ibid.*, p. 40.
3. Hasting, James (Ed.), *Encyclopaedia of Religion and Ethics*, Vol. 2, p. 536.

4. Tilak, Bal Gangadhar, *Gītārahasya*, p. 203.
5. Radhakrishnan, S., *Indian Philosophy*, Vol. I, p. 528.
6. *Sam. ka*, 15.
7. *BG*, 14. 3.
8. Chakravarti, Pulinbihari, *Origin and Development of the Sāṅkhya Systems of Thought*, p. 209.
9. *Ibid.*, p. 154.
10. *sattvaṁ rajas tama iti guṇāḥ prakṛtisaṁbhavāḥ/ nibbadhnanti mahābāho dehe dehinaṃ avyayaṃ// — BG.14.5*
11. *Ibid.*, 18.40.
12. *Sam. ka.* 61.
13. *BG*, 14.4.
14. *Ibid.*
15. *Ibid.*, 14. 7.
16. *Ibid.*, 14. 8.
17. *Ibid.*, 14. 11.
18. *Ibid.*, 14.12.
19. *Ibid.*, 14.13.
20. *Sam. ka*, 19.
21. *BG*, 13.12.
22. *Ibid.*, 13.22.
23. Radhakrishnan, S., *The Bhagavad Gītā*, p. 209.
24. *BG*, 13.20.
25. Modi, P.M., *Akṣara*, pp. 17-18.
26. Dasgupta, Surendranath, *A History of Indian Philosophy*, Vol. II, p. 466.
27. *Ibid.*, p. 464.
28. Vedakar, D.D., *Bhagavad Gītā*, pp. 46-47.
29. Dasgupta, Surendranath. *op. cit.*, Vol. II, p. 465.
30. *Ibid.*, p. 471.
31. *BG*, 13.6.
32. Dasgupta, Surendranath, *op. cit.*, Vol. II, p. 471.
33. *Sam. ka*, 8.
34. *BG*, 2.16.
35. *Ca. sa*, IV.1.54.
36. *Sam. ka*, 21, 57, and 59.
37. *Ibid.*, 3.
38. *Yoga sūtras*, 1.24-26.

39. *BG*, 15.7.
40. *Ibid.*, 14. 3.
41. *Ibid.*, 13.31-32.
42. *Sam.ka*, 13.34.
43. *Ibid.*, 44, 54.
44. *yaṁ saṁnyāsaṃ iti prāhur yogaṁ taṁ viddi, pāṇḍava/ an hy asaṁnyasta-saṅkalpo yogī bhavati kaścana//* —*BG*, 14.18.
45. *Yoga sūtra*, 1.1.
46. Ernest Wood, *Yoga*, p. 216.
47. *Ibid.*
48. *yāṁ saṁyāsaṃ iti prāhur yogaṁ taṁ viddhi pāṇḍava/ na hy asaṁnyastansaṅkalpo yogī bhavati kaścana//* —BG, 6.2
49. *uddared ātmanā atmānaṁ mātnānaṃ avasādayet/ ātmaiva hyātmano bandhur ātmaiva ripur ātmanaḥ//* —*Ibid.*, 6.5
50. *Ibid.*, 6.7-9.
51. Dasgupta, Surendranath, *op.cit.*, Vol. II, p. 446.
52. *BG*, 6.10.
53. *Ibid.*, 6.11.
54. *Ibid.*, 6.12.
55. *Ibid.*, 2.50.
56. *Ibid.*, 2.53; 6.7; 12.9; 17.11.
57. Dasgupta, Surendranath, *op.cit.*, Vol. II, p. 452.
58. Zaehner, R.C., *The Bhagavad Gita*, p. 141.
59. Dasgupta, Surendranath, *op.cit.*, Vol. II, p. 453.
60. Hasting, James. (Ed.), *op.cit.*, Vol. 2. p. 538.
61. Dasgupta, Surendranath, *op.cit.*, Vol. II, p. 459.
62. *BG*, 2. 14.
63. *Sam.ni*, IV. 178.
64. *BG*, 2.59.
65. *Sam. ni*, V. 102.
66. *BG*, 2.63, 64; 3.34.
67. *Sam. ni*, IV. 251, 297.
68. *BG*, 2.71.
69. *Maj.ni*, iii. 19, 32 and *Sam.ni*, 11. 252, 275, iii. 80, 236.
70. *BG*, 2.72; 5.24.
71. *Di.ni*, iii.84, 233; *Maj. ni*, i. 341, 412, 412, i.iii, ii. 159; iii.195; S, 561; *Sam.ni*, 94; *Am.ni*, v. 226.

72. *BG*, 3.4.
73. *Di.ni*, iii.275.
74. *BG*, 3.4.
75. *Ibid.*, 4.18.
76. *Ibid.*, 2.14; 6.23.
77. *Su*, 54; *Di.ni*, ii.100; iii.58.
78. *BG*, 2.23.
79. *Sam.ni*, ii. 172; iii. 45; iv. 9.
80. Upadhyaya, Kashi Nath, *Early Buddhism and the Bhagavad Gītā*, p. 97.
81. *yatato hyapi kaunteya puruṣasya vipaścitaḥ/ indriyāṇi pramāthīni harabti prasabhaṁ manaḥ// —BG*, 2.60.
82. Upadhyaya, Kashi Nath, *op.cit.*, p.97.
83. *tāni sarvāṇi saṁyamya yukta āsīta matparaḥ/ vaśe hi yasyendriyāṇi tasya prajñā pratiṣṭhitā// —BG*, 2.61
84. *āpūryamāṇaṃ acalapratiṣaṁ samudraṃ āpaḥ praviśanti yadvat / tadvat kāmā yaṁ praviśanti sarve sa śāntiṃ āpnoti na kāmakāmi// —Ibid.*, 2.70
85. *Sam.ni*, iv. 376-377.
86. *kāma eṣa krodha eṣa rajoguṇasamudbhavaḥ// mahāśano mahāpāpmā viddhyenaṃ iha vairiṇaṃ// —BG*, 3.37.
87. Zaehner, R.C., *The Bhagavad Gita*, p. 176.
88. *brahmaṇy ādhāya karmāṇi saṅgaṁ tyaktvā karoti yaḥ/ liopyate na sa pāpena padmapattraṃ ivambhasā// —BG*, 5.10.
89. *Sam.ni*, iii.140.
90. *ye hi saṁsparśajā bhogā duḥkhayonya eva te/ ādyantavantaḥ kaunteya na teṣu ramate budhaḥ —BG*, 5. 22
91. *Sam.ni*. iv, 207.
92. *nātyaśnatas tu yogo asti na caikāntaṃ anaśnataḥ / /*
    na cātisvapnaśīlasya jāgrato naiva cārjuna//
    yuktāhāraviharsya yuktaceṣṭasya karmasu/
    yuktasvapnāvabodhasya yogo bhavati duḥkhahā// —BG, 6.16-17.
93. Sharma, Chandradhar, *A Critical Survey of Indian Philosophy*, p. 72.
94. *taṁ vidyād duḥkhasaṁyogaviyogaṁ yogasaṁjñitaṃ/ —BG*, 6.23.
95. *Sam.ni*, iv. 39, 92 and 128.

96. Upadhyaya, Kashinath, *op.cit.*, p. 196.
97. *buddhyo yukto yayā pārtha karmabandhaṁ prahāsyasi//* —BG, 2. 39.
98. *Ibid.*, 2.38.
99. *dhyānenāmani paśyanti kecid ātmānaṃ ātmanā/*
    anye sāṅkhyena yogena karmayogena cāpare// —*Ibid.*, 13.24.
100. *Ibid.*, 13.23.
101. *Ibid.*, 3.3
102. Dasgupata, Surendranath, *op.cit.*, Vol. II, p. 457.
103. *yat saṅkhyāiḥ prāpyate sthānaṁ tad yogair api gamyate/*
    ekaṁ sāṅkhyaṁ ca yogaṁ ca yaḥ paśyati sa paśyati// —BG. 5.5
104. Zaechner, R.C., *The Bhagavad Gita*, p. 203.
105. *sarvabhūteṣu yenaikaṁ bhāvaṃ avyayaṃ īkṣate/*
    avibhaktaṁ vibhakteṣu taj jñānaṁ viddhi sāttvikaṃ —BG.18.20.
106. Dasgupta, Surendranath, *op.cit.*, Vol.II, pp. 459-460.
107. *BG*, 6. 29-32.

CHAPTER-4

METAPHYSICS OF SELF IN THE BHAGAVAD GĪTĀ

The previous three chapters have properly assessed and highlighted the place of the *Bhagavad Gītā* in the treatment of the self within the overall context of Indian Philosophy. In continuation, a metaphysical analysis will help to realize the essential nature of the self in detail.

4.1. MANIFESTATION OF THE SELF FROM SŪKṢMA TO STHŪLA STATE

Among the *śruti* and *smṛti* of Indian Philosophy, the *Bhagavad Gītā* gives a clear-cut explanation to the spiritual self about its *sūkṣma* state of the *sthūla* state. Even though *Vedas* and *Upaniṣads* offer different information for the manifestation of the *sthūla* self, they are all vague and confused with polytheistic and mythological conceptions. Clearing the confusion created by *Vedas* and *Upaniṣads,* the *Bhagavad Gītā* describes the change of its form from *sūkṣma* to *sthūla* state with proper reasons. For the proper explanation a systematic and comparative discussion may be added to the above conception.

4.1.1. *Vedic* Views

Ṛg Veda contains four different views of the manifestation of the *sthūla* state. They are as follows: (i) *Viśvakarman,* 'Lord of All-Maker' who bears eyes and limbs on all sides and constructs the heaven and the earth through His mighty power without any assistance from anybody. (ii) *Prajāpati*, 'Lord of Creatures' who creates *Hiraṇyagarbha* and from which the earth and the heaven are evolved. (iii) *Aspati*, 'Lord of Prayer' who makes everything like a smith. (iv) *Puruṣa Sūkta*, 'famous Hymn of Man' explains, that, while sacrificing the thousand member parts of a giant, the parts are modified into the different parts of the world and human beings. At that time the moon arises from the mind; the sun mingles from his eye and Gods starts from his mouth. During the period, *Brāhmaṇas* emerge from his mouth, *Kṣatriyas* from his arms, *Vaiśyas* from his thighs and the *Śūdras* from his feet. In short, the *Vedas* assumes, that, the existing *sat*, 'real' emerges from the non-existing *asat*, 'unreal', i.e., something comes out from nothing.[1]

4.1.2. *Upaniṣadic Views*

Upaniṣads explain, that, there is something and from that alone the whole universe might emerge out.[2] There are three views and they are: (i) In the beginning there are *Svayambhu*, 'Self-existent Being' who is omnipresent with many parts. In course of time *Svayambhu* creates water where He places His seed, then it becomes as *Hiraṇyagarbha*, 'golden egg'. This golden egg turns into two halves, out of which one, 'silver' is modified as earth and second, 'gold' is formed as sky.[3] (ii) In the beginning the water exists with the potential power for manifestation and from which all the evolving forces emerged. Where the divine Brahman comes out and produced the *Prajāpati*, 'Lord of manifestation'. From *Prajāpati* the Gods, matter and life, men, women and the demons are manifested. During manifestation of the selves, the water becomes as egg. Then it enters into hearts and governs the whole organism of the living beings. During differentiation the undifferentiated Self divided into paired things as man and woman and got *nāma rūpa*.[4] (iii) Based on the firm principle of an unifying knot within the diversified objects of the universe, *Upaniṣad* confirms that from the basic neutral force of Brahman, 'Holy Power', the animate, inanimate and the spiritual self originated.[5] This above said view could be confirmed through the following views: (a) The term comes from *'brah̩'* which means to grow or to increase. This is expressed to indicate the power of strength, force, energy, a mysterious power and a holy potentiality. The analysis of the meaning of Brahman shows the transition of the primeval power which pervades within all objects. (b) The ancient saints and sages realized the diversified objects as themselves and they merged their selves within all Gods. (c) Materially the Brahman is breath, speech, eye, ear, mind, foot and heart. Metaphysically the Brahman is matter, life, *manas, buddhi* and bliss.[6] (d) Our human body is the existing place of and the space outside from him and minute space of heart are considered to be the modified form of Himself.[7] (e) Brahman is compared to imperishable, eternal, all pervasive and the basic life of all creatures. The origin of everything from the can be competed to the spider and the extension of its thread and to herbs, arising out of the earth and hairs coming out from the body.[8] (f) Brahman is clearly brought out as front, behind, right and left, below and above of the whole universe and the selves.[9] (g) The whole universe evolves from Brahman and dissolves within Himself. The unborn, eternal and the Supreme Brahman mediates through the world that exists as selves.[10] (h) The Supreme Brahman is concealed by *māyā* and He appears as diversified manifestation of many and the changing shape where *māyā* refers to the deceit of the juggler and illumination of the rope to the snake or the pearl to the silver.[11]

4.1.3. Biblical views

According to Bible, in the beginning there was desert without rain and plants where the trees, rivers and the garden were formed. After that man evolved from the basic matter as doll. Then the God, the Jehovah or Yahweh blew into His nose to breath the self into him. In Bible the process of manifestation bears two views and they are: (i) God creates the man, trees, rivers and the garden out of his creative words.

(ii) The Divine Wisdom of God acts as an agents for manifestation.[12]

4.1.4. Islamic View

In Islam, Allah creates the self from nothing and He is also having the power to separate it from the body at the time of sleep, dream and death. Islam accepts the existence of the self after death. For this the Quran says, that, when the pious died, Allah brings his self to Him and at the time of judgment. He unites the same self with its risen bodies.[13] The old traditional ideas also support the above views, that, before importing Adam's self and the individual selves, Allah stored all the selves within His shrine which is attached in His throne. At the time of creation He transmitted it into the human embryos. Islam accepts the manifestation of non-human self such as sprits, animals, demons and angels.[14]

One may not accept the Christian views because the manifestation of water, earth, trees, four rivers and men all occurred within seven days and it is a logical inconsistency. Manifestation out of wisdom also may not be acceptable because wisdom is only a moral quality. Moreover, the formation of earth out of the combination and the process of spiritual brooding in the water are not possible, Islamic views too are unacceptable because the self is considered in the Islam as breath. It is also thought as purified by the same self through the right action of its ear and eye and they seemed to be the logical irrelevance. Though *Vedas* and *Upaniṣads* are rationalistic, they are mythological because the process of manifestation carries the mythological value but not the philosophical interest. But the *Gītā* explains the manifestation of the self from the supreme external divinity and its re-union with the same without any doubt.

4.1.5. The *Bhagavad Gītā's* view

From the unmanifested sphere, manifestation of the contingent beings is evolved out of the combined copulative activity of Lord Kṛṣṇa Himself as father and the Great Brahmā as mother.[15] The manifested objects have been classified into the cosmic and the individual stands for *puruṣa*. With respect to God, *prakṛti* and *puruṣa* can be referred to as lower and higher nature. The lower nature is the earth, water, fire, air, space, *manas, buddhi* and egoism and the higher nature is the self.

The animate and the inanimate beings are evolved from Kṛṣṇa's divine creative power of *māyā* which is composed of three *guṇas*: *sattva, rājas* and *tāmasa*.[16] This *māyā* is equalized with the *prakṛti* and the material nature of the universe. The *Gītā* considers this *māyā* as the real and divine because it depends upon God. At the same time it distracts man's attitude. This *māyā* stands between the individual self and God and obscures the proper *jñāna*. In other words, the presence of *māyā* is responsible for the self to distract the development of the higher nature of the self.[17] If one transcends the lower nature of the self through the proper *jñāna*, he can understand that the *māyā* as positive element for the manifestation and the negative energy to suppress the actual *jñāna* of self as divine being. Thus the *māyā* derives its combination from the *puruṣa śakti* and *prakṛti*. It is considered as divine *māyā* or *Yoga māyā*.[18] The *Gītā* explains the manifested and the unmanifested duration as night and the day of the Brahma, i.e., a thousand *mahāyuga* represent a 'day' and the same time as 'night'. One *mahāyuga* represents 43, 20,000 earthly years.[19] The *karmic* forces evolve at the time of manifestation and its shrinks and returns to the unmanifested level along with the manifested objects. Again, it flourishes when the next manifestation starts under the control of God.[20] The thirteenth chapter of the *Gītā* describes cosmic material nature and the knower of same through *Kṣetra* and *Kṣetrajña*. With respect to man, his body is made by *prakṛti* and witnessed by *puruṣa*. With respect to the whole universe it is also made by *prakṛti* and supervised and controlled by the Supreme Puruṣottama, the highest state of *puruṣa*. When a particular individual realize himself he perceive the non-difference between the Universal Form and the individual form where the particular *puruṣa* becomes Puruṣottama. Then, he is recognized as *Mahākṣetra*, 'the Great knower of the field' or *Sarvakṣetrajña*, 'knower of all fields'.[21]

The connection of the Universal Self and the individual self has been described by Lord Kṛṣṇa as 'A ray of Myself, the eternal *Jīva* in the world of *Jīvas*, attracts the senses, with *manas* the sixth, abiding in *prakṛti*'.[22] The *Bhagavad Gītā* adds that the Highest Self or the God indwells within the Universe through the extension of His lower nature of *prakṛti* with its three *guṇas*. He transcend sits own nature and exists within the timeless and space less centre. Like this the self who is mingling within the individual body does not have any close connection with the *prakṛti* or *buddhi* or *ahaṅkāra*. If one knows the actual nature of *puruṣa* and *prakṛti*, he gets *mukti*. Then the individual self will never enter into the next birth.[23] From this differentiation and the combination of *puruṣa* and *prakṛti* with the universal and the individual form, one can easily understand that a thing which exists in the universe is the derivation of both under the control of Lord Kṛṣṇa.[24]

The *Bhagavad Gītā* explains the Universal Form of the Ultimate Reality as cosmic fig-tree at the *saṁsāra* level.[25] Within the cosmic process of *sasṁāra*, the external minute part of god has been caught up and enmeshed. This firm-rooted *aśvatha*, 'fig-tree' represents Lord Kṛṣṇa as the basic support and the foundation of the whole universe,[26] the imperishable, unmanifested, indeterminate and unthinkable God within the worldly level as *māyā* is composed of three *guṇas*.[27] So, he who trusts himself in God can pass beyond the *māyā* through his proper *jñāna*.[28]

The *Upaniṣadas* and the *Bhagavad Gītā* refer to the self as a soul which is nothing but the psychological complex, i.e. the *indriyas*, *manas* and *buddhi*.[29] The *Bhagavad Gītā* also explains that the self is not an entity to act but the individual's action in the world is only the conglomeration of the three constituents of *sattva, rājasa* and *tāmasa guṇas*.[30] These *guṇas* are bound by the self within the body without any changes of its essence. So, the embodied self is subjected to bondage within the worldly realm and maintains its original standpoint of immortality.[31]

To understand this, Arjuna wants to know the explanation of the terms called *brahma, adhyātma, ādhibhūta, ādhidaivam, adhiyajña* and *karma* from Lord Kṛṣṇa.[32] If one understands the above terms, he can easily understand the metaphysical view about the manifestation of the individual self from the Ultimate Reality.[33] Here, the term, *'brahma'* represents the indestructible Supreme Being within the manifested and the unmanifested realms of animate and the inanimate objects.[34] *Upaniṣads* also points out Brahma as the immortal and imperishable *Pradhāna* from which the perishable things are being involved.[35] The term *ādhyātma* refers to the existence of the Brahman within the individual during his worldly existence. *Ādhibhūta* connotes the mode of destruction of the living and non-living objects of the Universe. *Ādhidaivam* means the living principle of God as the lower and higher nature, i.e. the *prakṛti* and *puruṣa*. *Ādhiyajña* expresses the activities of the individual's performance as sacrifice to the divine God.[36] *Karma* represents the initiating centre for the cause of manifestation of the self from the Brahman.

This explanation reveals that, Lord Kṛṣṇa Himself pervades within the individual self as *ahaṃ*. In other words, the individual self is the derivation of cosmic nature of the Ultimate Reality. Along with this the mental qualities are also derived from the ultimate divine centre.[37] Eventhough Arjuna refuses to fight but finally he has to fight because the situation and the actual nature of his own *svabhāva*. The confusion in the lower nature can be arrested and ordered to fight by the higher nature which is activated by the Divine.[38]

4.2. UNMANIFESTED NATURE OR SŪKṢMA STATE OF THE SELF

In the unmanifested state the primal stuff of *puruṣa* and *prakṛti* remains constant without any action. The manifested objects use nothing and maintain the characteristics of being eternal, all-pervasive and inactive and rely on its own state. In other words the productive and the dynamic quantitative as well as qualitative objects remain constant.[39] The *Bhagavad Gītā* says that beyond the unmanifested state there is Supreme Puruṣottama to govern the whole states of manifested and the unmanifested.[40] The unmanifested state becomes manifested level because of the active *sattva, rājasa* and *tāmasa guṇas* under the guidance of Puruṣottama.[41] Lord Kṛṣṇa as the efficient cause initiates the material cause-the *prakṛti* through His *yogamāyā*.[42]

The ultimate transcendental timeless spiritual God discerns as self and controls the human activities i.e., the Lord's higher nature of *puruṣa* controls His lower nature the *prakṛti*.[43] The material nature is nothing but the three constituents of *guṇas*. They are considered to be the causality of all manifestations where the *puruṣa* only experiences the activities. The whole universe has been constituted by the combination of the selves and the matter.[44] Thus in the unmanifested *sūkṣma* state; the spiritual *puruṣa* and material *prakṛti* with its three *guṇas* are kept intact without any active participation for manifestation and controlled by Puruṣottama.

4.3. MANIFESTED NATURE OR STHŪLA STATE OF THE SELF

Under the control of the Puruṣottama, the manifestation starts from the unmanifested realm. The manifested objects represent the primal matter and the eleven senses namely the five internal, the five external *indriyas* and the *manas*.[45] The *Gītā* explains the union of the two extreme principles of *puruṣa* and *prakṛti* within the manifested level.

The *Bhagavad Gītā* adds that the combination of *puruṣa* and the *prakṛti* under the guidance of Lord Kṛṣṇa, where He connects the law of *karma* with the appropriate self.[46] Thus, the *puruṣa* and *prakṛti* have emerged out from the unmanifested state to the manifested level under the control of Lord Kṛṣṇa. In other words, Lord Kṛṣṇa Himself appears as *prakṛti*, 'lower nature' and as *puruṣa*, 'higher nature' and initiates the manifested state as father who feeds the seed upon His own female form of the creator, 'Great Brahmā'.

4.4. MATERIAL NATURE ACTING AS AN AGENT

The earlier part reveals that the manifested spiritual entities and the material objects have emerged from the unmanifested centre. In this respect, one should understand that, whether the actual transcendental self acts as agent to the worldly activities or some other forces other than the self performs the same. In detail, one can analyze the self in two views. They are: (i) Within the immanently order, the timeless Eternal Being emerges from the transcendental to this world through the series of time and space by the process of becoming. (ii) In the transcendental order even though the eternal spiritual self comes into contact with the worldly order through its *ahaṅkāra*, *buddhi* and *manas*, the same self maintains its original eternal state.

According to the *Gītā*, the *prakṛti* is the unity of three *guṇas* in the equilibrium state and the change of the same state through *puruṣa* results in the manifestation. So, one can say that the manifested objects are only the changing modality of the *guṇas*. In short, the *guṇas* alone can be regarded as agent for the activities of the worldly order. A deep analysis of the *guṇas* may reveal that the eternal and all-pervasive self does not change its original nature when it co-exists with the *buddhi*, *ahaṅkāra* and *manas*. The *Gītā* points out that the foolish alone can think that the self is the authoritative one for the worldly activities.[47] The sense of 'I'-ness is only a kind of sense experience within the psychic complex and it arises, when the internal senses come into contact with the external object. If the contact disconnects the experiences may not arise. For example, the pleasure and pain of the individual's experience are only sense-experiences, which emerge out of the contact between psychosomatic organisms with the material nature of the external objects. If there is no connection or if the individual disconnects the contact the particular individual may not experience pleasure or pain.[48] From this, one can understand, that, the actual self does not experience the worldly activities but the psychosomatic organism alone acts towards the particular object.

Prakṛti is considered to be the basic root cause, *'pradhānā'*. It is subtle, imperceptible, unintelligible and unconscious principle. Within the unmanifested, the entire world is implicitly present within the bosom of the *prakṛti*. During manifestation the world evolves from the *prakṛti*.[49] This ever active *prakṛti* is nothing but the unity of three *guṇas*. Eventhough these *guṇas* are subtle in nature, these can be realized through their effects like pleasure, pain and the undifferentiated nature. For example, the *sattva guṇa* may be inferred through the manifested objects within the realm of consciousness, it is goodness that produces pleasure, it can be represented as light and bright, buoyant and illuminative and this is the power of reflection, upward movements, happiness contentment and bliss.[50] The *rājasa guṇa* can be described as foulness and the basic principle for motion or creation. This *rājasa guṇa* is responsible for the experience of pain, restless activity, feverish efforts, will, stimulation especially the *chala*, 'mobile' and *upastambhaka*, 'effects of stimulation'.[51] The *tāmasa guṇa* is the basic principle for inert and it produces apathy, indifference, ignorance, sloth, confusion, bewilderment, passivity and negativity. Especially this *tāmasa guṇa* can be visualized as the quality of enveloping the right sense of our mental activity.[52] Though these *guṇas* are conflicting in nature, they are co-operative with one another to form the *prakṛti* like the three opposed things of oil, wick and the flame of the lamp and they are co-operatively produce.

Considering all factors one can accept that each and every activity of the universe and the individual is derived from the *prakṛti*, i.e., they are formulated and governed by the three ultimate constituents namely the *guṇas*. Here *puruṣa* does not act but experiences the whole activities.[53] So, from the above statements it is seen that a person within the still state of Brahman or liberation should realize that within the microcosm of the individual and the macrocosm of the whole universe, the *puruṣa*, 'individual self' and Puruṣottama, 'Universal Self' are acting as mere witnesses i.e., the *guṇas* act as true agents for the worldly activities.

4.5. ETERNAL NATURE OF SELF IS ACTING AS NO AGENT

The actual self within the body is called as *dehi* or the embodied self. The owner of the body is God and not that of the individual where the embodied self does not act as cause for any work.[54] The physical body is a temporal station for the individual which is nothing but the lower nature of the Lord Kṛṣṇa.[55] Here the embodied self is only a guest who comes to the body without any date of arrival and goes out without any fixed time. To understand the actual nature of this body one should understand that his body is not a permanent station and he should also know that the embodied self is derived from the higher nature of Lord Kṛṣṇa Himself.[56]

The *Bhagavad Gītā* emphasizes that egoism stands as the authority of one's own work and the attachment towards the fruit of the action leads to happiness or pain of his own state. Moreover, the particular individual should assume the Lord as the responsible authority for pleasure and pain. If it is not so the reason may be due to the delusion arising out of *avidyā*. Particularly if the individual understand that the work done by him is directed from God Himself and the fruit of the particular activity may not go to the individual. If a person understands the three following views such as the embodied self acting as no agent; the eternal self having no response for the worldly action and the self's detachment towards the fruits of action he can realize the all-pervasiveness of Lord Kṛṣṇa. In addition the particular individual will know the fact that the individual activities and the universal activities are organized and controlled by *guṇas*.[57]

Eventhough the all-pervading Lord exists within the embodied self as a part of Him, He does not receive the result of good or bad activities of the individual. The *Gītā* puts the goodness or badness as the apparent by-product of the *avidyā*.[58] In other words, the individual self neither initiates the work nor accepts the fruits of the same work but all these are considered to be the Brahman. So, all the diversities of the activities are merged and unified within the Ultimate Reality.[59]

4.6. RELATIONSHIP BETWEEN KṢETRA AND KṢETRAJÑA

The last part states that the actual self has no connection with the external world. But it has been discussed that the spiritual self bond within the material body is controlled by the Lord Kṛṣṇa through His lower and the Higher Nature. So, a deep analysis of the discrimination between the *Kṣetra* and the *Kṣetrajña* will be helpful to understand the relationship between the self and the material body.

The *Gītā* describes the *Kṣetra* as body or field and the *Kṣetrajñā* as the knower of the field. The explanation of the *Kṣetra* and *Kṣetrajñā* of the *Gītā* resembles the traditional *Sāṅkhya's* description of the *prakṛti* or *Kṣetra* as unconscious centre. But the *puruṣa* or *Kṣetrajña* is the active conscious principle and it acts as a witness or the knower of the *prakṛti* or *Kṣetra*. *Upaniṣads*[60] also treat the same problem like *Gītā*, where *prakṛti* or *Kṣetra* extended into various diversified objects with respect to the individual as well as the universal[61]: (i) *Mahābhūtas* - five elements of earth, water, fire, air and ether. (ii) *Ahaṅkāra* - the medium for the individual differentiation. (iii) *Buddhi* - the centre within which the individual acquires the capacity of grasping, knowing and the knowledge. (iv) *Avyakta* - the primordial *prakṛti.* (v) The eleven senses - the five external senses, five internal senses and *manas.* (vi) The five objects of senses such as sound, touch, colour, taste, and smell. (vii) *Icchā* - the characteristics of longing, wish and desire for enjoyment. (viii) *Dveṣa* - the special feature of having enmity towards somebody. (ix) *Sukha* - the feeling which gives delight to the sense-organs. (x) *Duḥkha* - the feeling which gives pain to the sense-organs. (xi) *Saṅghaṭa* - the relationship between the body and the senses. (xii) *Cetana* - the individual's consciousness, movement and effort or conscious effort. (xiii) *Dhṛti* - the individual's capacity of sustaining, the supporting and holding all.

The *Bhagavad Gītā* reconciles the *prakṛti* and *kṣetra,* where the former refers to the instrument to form the body and the whole universe and the latter refers to the entire body of an individual and the universe.[62] *Bhagavad Gītā* explains the various aspects of both by using various terms. They are: (i) *Saguṇa* - the *prakṛti* constituted by three *guṇas.* (ii) *Tamas* - the specialized feature of *avidya,* 'darkness' and the inability to grasp the attitude of *jñāna.* (iii) *Jaḍa* - the immovable or the matter. (iv) *Kṣara* - the original nature of destructibility. (v) *Sthūla* - the *Kṣetra* in gross form. (vi) *Vyakta* - the state of visibility. (vii) *Prakṛti,* i.e., the *'pra'* represents the special and *'kṛti'* refers to the activity. So, the term connotes the primordial matter's activity for every action of the individual body as well as the universe. (viii) *Bhūtas* - the objects arise from the *prakṛti.* (ix) *Deha* - the individual being arises from the accumulation of the *mahābhūtas.* (x) *Kṣetra* - the total field of the individual and the universe.

Thus, if one understands the actual nature of the *Kṣetra*, 'field', he may sow the best seed upon it to get the choicest fruit. In other words by knowing the above, the individual can understand his original duty with respect to his predominated *guṇas* to reach the *mukti* state. In other words, even the *tāmasa guṇa* may be diverted into *sattva* through austerities and faithful adherence to *yāma* and *niyama*, 'control of body and *manas* by yogic practices and meditation'.[63] In other words, *Kṣetrajñā* means the subject who has discovered the treasure of Brahman world or hidden hoard of gold which is housed within the heart of the individual[64]: (i) *Nirguṇa* - the witnesser of *Kṣetra* or *guṇas*. (ii) *Jyotiḥ* - the lustre, i.e., the perfected light through which the individual finds his path towards liberation. (iii) *Cetena* - consciousness, by which the individual acquires knowledge. (iv) *Akṣara* - the indestructible or subtle, unmanifested and the all-pervasive nature. (v) *Sūkṣma* - the subtle nature of the *Kṣetrajña*. (vi) *Avyakta* - the unmanifested state of the *Kṣetrajña* or the spiritual self in the subtle state which witnesses the bodily activities. (vii) *Puruṣa* - the term can be split as *'puri'* and *'vas'* which means one who indwells within the field. (viii) *Ātma* - one who moves all over and watches the field. This can be mentioned as *'ahaṃ'*, which refers to the supreme perfect being. (ix) *Dehi* - the individual being arises from the accumulation of the *mahābhūtas*. (x) *Kṣetri* - Both terms denote the individual who is a master in his own *Kṣetra*.

In a modified form, one can assess the supreme knowledge as the understanding capacity of the Ultimate Reality or God as knower of every field through the individual selves as well as the material nature of the Universe.[65] From this stand point, one can say, that, the Ultimate Reality, the *Paramātma* exists within the individual body. Otherwise, if the embodied self removes its *ahaṅkāra*, he may be called as the highest person. In short, the false identification of *ātma* within our body is subject to limitation. When the self transcends the *ahaṅkāra* and the material body, the self becomes as universal in form where the *ātma* can be perceived as *Paramātma*. This fact could be explained through all pervasive ether which is shut up in a room or a jar as so termed as ether in the room or other in the jar. But after removing the limiting instruments the ether within the room and ether with the jar are identified as one. Arguing thus, the *Bhagavad Gītā* equates the *ātma* and the *Paramātma*, 'Spectator and Permitter, Supporter, Enjoyer, the Great Lord and also spoken of as the Supreme Self, (is) the *Puruṣa* Supreme in this body'.[66] Thus, the above distinguished knowledge of the *Kṣetra* and *Kṣetrajña* reveals the all pervasiveness of the Universal *Paramātma* within the individual *ātma*. This knowledge also indirectly enables us to cultivate our field or *Kṣetra* in such a way to realise his self.

4.7. RELATIONSHIP BETWEEN THE SELF AND BUDDHI

Upto this, the spiritual self from the material body haye been differentiated. Apart from this, as an advance step towards the problem, a detailed study may be made to differentiate the self from the body. *Buddhi* is the second evolutes after *mahat*. Eventhough *buddhi* is considered to be the highest faculty of material nature the actual nature of this seems to be a bridge between the pure spiritual self and other psychophysical complex of *manas*.[67] Like the other psychophysical complex *buddhi* also has a firm connection with the three *guṇas*. As usual, if the *ātman* fails to develop the controlling capacity of the *buddhi* upon the *guṇas*, the *buddhi* will always get attachment with the phenomenal order. Then the way towards the realization of the actual nature of the self will be closed by the activity of the *buddhi*. From this, one can easily understand that, through the control of the *buddhi*, the same individual can easily become aware of the eternal nature of the self.

In the last chapter, the *Bhagavad Gītā* clearly explains the three kinds of *buddhi*. They are: (i) *Sattva Buddhi* - helps for right path towards the highest position where the individual knows what can be done and what cannot be done, what to fear and for what not to fear, what causes bondage and what does not cause bondage and to know what is wrong knowledge which drawbacks the individual as degraded.[68] Then, the individual realizes the right path to liberation. (ii) *Rājasa buddhi* - causes misery and creates contrary ideas by wrong activity where the individual does not distinguish the *dharma* from *adharma*.[69] (iii) *Tāmasa buddhi* - leads to absence of knowledge itself and degradation in every possible way, where the individual has no knowledge of *dharma*. He acquires incorrect and contrary views towards the reality.[70]

The above classification of the *buddhi* with respect to three *guṇas* emphasizes the view that if one rightly controls it he can realize his self. To realize the divinity one should cultivate the *buddhi* through by controlling the *guṇas*.[71] The *Gītā* suggests two ways to control the activities of the *guṇas* for realizing the self through *buddhi*. They are: (i) the integration or control of the total personalities of the individual upon the *buddhi*, so that the particular individual can get rid of the bondage. (ii) The *Gītā* emphasizes the spiritual exercise for the purpose of separating and realising the actual nature of the self by *buddhi* through eliminating the experiences like passion and hate.[72]

Through the spiritual exercise, the individual can attain *samādhi* by controlling and concentrating his personality upon the *buddhi*.[73] Then if the individual lives in a way prescribed by the *Gītā*, he will reach the ultimate state of.[74] If the individual follows the prescribed spiritual exercise with loyalty and devotion and deviate from the *guṇas* the athlete will never miss to become.[75] In short, the *buddhi* is the organ of the integration where the total human personality of the individual lies in the highest grade. So, it has become clear that *buddhi* acts in a triple way with the human personality. They are: (i) It acts as a bridge between the materialistic psychophysical complex and the spiritualistic subjective self. (ii) By controlling the effects of *guṇas* and *buddhi* spiritualizes the material body. (iii) By controlling the *buddhi* through spiritual exercise one can realize the self, the highest state of self-realization can be attained through the control of *buddhi.*

4.8. RELATIONSHIP BETWEEN THE SELF WITH MANAS AS WELL AS INDRIYAS

With the psychic centre the *indriyas* and the *manas* play major role to the self through *buddhi*. For this the *Gītā* stipulates that the activity of the *indriyas* and the *manas* should be controlled step by step through *yogic* exercise. The *Gītā* gives the reason for controlling the *indriyas* and the *manas*[76]; where the attachment of the *indriyas* with *manas* results in the active participation of the individual through the worldly activities. If the individual performs the worldly activities the law of *karma* joins the self. Then the self-realization may not possible.[77] So, if the individual detaches his *indriyas* from the worldly activities and disciplines the *manas* he moves towards the self realization by the active participation of the *buddhi.*[78]

While explaining the importance of the control of *indriyas,* the *Gītā* never misses to analyze the drawbacks of the attachment, within the worldly order. When the *indriyas* get attachment the *buddhi* is destroyed and the individual gets into a peaceless state. The peaceless *manas* wipes away the wisdom of the same individual. Then the individual never reaches the state of self realization.[79] The *indriyas* and the *manas* are considered to be the lower nature of the Lord Kṛṣṇa and they depend upon the *guṇas*. Since the *indriyas* and the *manas* are working under the control of the three *guṇas,* one should control all the activities or change it into the sattvic activity. Then, it will pave the way for visualizing the self through *buddhi*. For this, through the spiritual exercise the individual should clean the senses and mind by detachment from the worldly activities.[80]

When explaining the performance of the spiritual exercise, the *Bhagavad Gītā* puts forth a series of means. They are the individual should integrate himself in a lonely place with the attitude of detachment from the worldly affairs through the concentration of his *manas* and the *indriyas* by concentrating upon a single object; while concentrating he should keep his body, head and neck in a straight line and fix his eyes on the tip of the nose without seeing here and there; at the time of the *yogic* practice the *Yogi* should not eat too much; he should not sleep or keep awake too much; he should never undergo any kind of recreation and he should control his thought like a lamp within a windless place.[81] During the practice, the individual has to concentrate upon the self. So, if the person practices it he will see the self.[82]

In the final stage of controlling our *indriyas,* the *manas* acquires the realised state by conjoining the self with the Ultimate Reality. In short, (i) Attachment of *indriyas* and *manas* with the phenomenal activities results in keeping one away from the realisation of the self. (ii) Instead of attachment, through detachment one can cut off the connection of the *indriyas* from the worldly affairs; so that, the whole personality of the individual can be concentrated upon the *manas* and he attains self-realisation through *buddhi.*

4.9. RELATIONSHIP BETWEEN THE SELF AND THE WORLDLY ACTIVITIES

Human personality can be divided into two ways as inward and outward personalities. The former represents the inward analysis through the series of *indriyas* to *manas, manas* to *buddhi* and *buddhi* to the self. The latter represents the outward analysis through the *indriyas* and its activities within the worldly order. Within the external activities the *antaḥkaraṇa* is connected with the control of the *indriyas* through which one can realise the actual nature of the self. In short through the realisation of the *manas* by *indriyas* and *buddhi* by *manas* one can attain self-realisation. On the other hand, through outward analysis, i.e., through the proper external activities of the *indriyas* and *manas,* he can purify the *buddhi.* Through this, the same individual reaches self realisation. In other words, if the individual performs worldly activities without any attachment towards the fruit of work he can reach the self realisation.[83] In comparison, the approach of the self through the desireless activity of the *indriyas* is considered as easy one and open to all because without the external action no one can lead one's life.[84] On the other hand, if the same individual gets attachment with the fruits he becomes as hounded self.[85] So, it will be worthwhile to discuss the realisation of the same self through outward personality, i.e., realisation of the self through the individual's activities.

As already seen, the embodied self is only the effect of the combination of the manifested objects of the *prakṛti* with the implication of the *puruṣa,* under the control of the Puruṣottama. This combination has taken place through the active condition of the *guṇas*, i.e., the empirical self is the product of the action with respect to the *guṇas*. In this way, one can also explain the whole cosmic process as the result of the conjugation of the causes undertaken by the universal *prakṛti* with that of *puruṣa*. In short, one can infer that the divine and eternal inactive spiritual self appears within the worldly order as false active embodied self because of the ever active *guṇas* of *prakṛti*. The effect of the action is also applicable to the universe. Here, even Lord Kṛṣṇa also undergoes the action without gap. If the activities of God get a gap the regularized order of the phenomenal activities would lead to ruin and confusion. So, the whole universe will collapse.[86]

Understanding the universal nature of action activated by the *guṇas*, the individual should follow the same, then only his *jñāna* may fall in right place.[87] Otherwise, the same individual forgets the above truth because of the action stimulated by his desire and he himself becomes as enemy of his own.[88] In other words, the false attachment of the self with desire stimulates the action which is crude and disquiet.[89]

To sum up, there are two immanent principles which pervade within the universe, i.e., the *guṇas* and the actions. They are discerned from the transcendental Ultimate Reality[90] through worldly order as various categories with respect to the law of *karma*.

To consider the universal activities as the outcome of the *māyā* the Divine embodiment of the Universe or the immanent feature of the Ultimate Reality is treated as *Yogamāyā*. The same *māyā* with respect to the individual can be identified as *ātmamāyā* or the *avidyāmāyā*.

The above study shows that the action is inseparably associated with the athletes. Human beings are intimately in co-existence with action and they should attain perfection through the same action. Regarding the way of action, the *Bhagavad Gītā* advises the person to perform his activity in a spirit of detachment from the fruits of his action[91]. The action advised by the *Bhagavad Gītā* as *niṣkāmyakarmayoga* may be analysed as follows: (i) Man is always performing the action. (ii) The fruit of the action is not related to him. (iii) He should never desire for the fruit of the action. (iv) He should not be away from the action.

If he performs in this manner he will reach the state of sameness-and-indifference or liberation.[92] While explaining the situation, the *Bhagavad Gītā* describes two kinds of people as hypocrite and the superior. The hypocrite controls his *indriyas* from the activity but his *manas* thinks about the same result of the activity. So, he gets delusion and failure in self-realisation.[93] But the superior detaches his *indriyas* from its object and practices the spiritual exercise and realises his self.[94] This dedication casts off the thought from the ego-centre to free it from desire[95] which finally leads to self-realisation.[96] The *Bhagavad Gītā* describes the actual nature of action as the individual perceives action within the inaction and inaction within the action.[97] In that way, if the person ploughs his *manas* and realizes the desireless and motiveless action, he will get real *jñāna*, 'wisdom'. Thus if a person realises his self the result of action will never distract him from the *jñāna*.[98] The *Bhagavad Gītā* explains sacrifice as the result of action and paves way to understand the Ultimate Reality through self-realisation.[99]

Through this way the person annihilates the *ahaṅkāra* which leads to realisation of self. It means, that, the sacrifice of our work leads to the wisdom or the realisation of because both sacrifice and action are nothing but Brahman and Brahman is derived from the Ultimate Imperishable Reality.[100] The sacrifice of the work leads to wisdom as fire reduces the fuel to ashes.[101] After realisation the performances of the external worldly activities does not defile the actual self.[102] Here, the self resembles the mirror with the dust which accumulates on it. After removing the dust from the mirror, it regains the actual state. Like that, the actual self after breaking the contact of senses with its object becomes pure.[103]

So, the value of *niṣkāmyakarma* has been elevated to highest level, where the *Bhagavad Gītā* recommends that the individual should dedicate all his desireless action to the Divinity with the self subjugation to attain the peace.[104] In short, understanding the nature of action initiated by *guṇas* enables the self to renounce the fruits of the action and perform the spiritual exercise. In other words, through *niṣkāymakarma yoga* an athlete can realise the actual nature of the self by understanding the influence of *guṇas* upon actions.[105]

4.10. TRANSMISSION OF THE SELF

Upto this attempt is made to distinguish the spiritual element from the material body. Here, efforts may be undertaken to argue the self as a transmigrating entity. For this one should be aware of three categories. They are: (i) Individual self clothed within the body exists in the past and when the body is left behind it will continue to exist.[106] (ii) The embodied bodies are the stationary place of the self for its realisation.[107] (iii) The self passes through the material bodies within the series of time and space.[108]

To understand transmigration one should know the process of manifestation. For this the *Bhagavad Gītā* says, 'Beings have their beginning unseen, their middle seen, and their end unseen again. Why any lamentation regarding them?'.[109] Before manifestation all the animate and inanimate beings are indistinct and formless. After manifestation all diversified beings get distinctive forms. During manifested state the constant births and deaths take place until they return to their unmanifested states.[110] During transmigration the self throw out the bodies like the old clothes and enters into new one. The embodied self perceives the fruits of action performed in this birth and the previous births along with its will, *manas* and *buddhi* throughout the journey within the time series.[111] For transmigration the *Bhagavad Gītā* advocates two contradictory principles. They are: (i) The Eternal Self is not involved in transmigration.[112] (ii) The embodied self during *saṁsāra* state undergoes birth and death along with the psychosomatic organism until its ultimate perfection.[113]

Reconciliation of both may result in the births and deaths of the human bodies.[114] In other words; the spiritual self undergoes birth and death due to its law of *karma* within the time and special series until its perfection. To know the reason for transmigration, the *Gītā* says, that, the self involves itself within the mundane existence because of its *guṇas*.[115] The presence of the *guṇas* within *prakṛti* with its subtle essence of *mahat, ahaṅkāra, tanmātra* and *mahābhūtas* the particular individual is bearing the responsibility for births and deaths.[116]

The self with *sattva guṇa* bears good knowledge, cleanliness, harmless, enlightenment, strength and guiding mentality with sound health, diseaselessness *indriyas* and unperturbed sleep. This makes the pure consciousness or the luminocity of *prakāśa*. During transmigration, the above features pass from this birth by *sūkṣma* and *kāraṇa* bodies to the next birth where the same self gets birth among the excellent-pure-harmless wise people like *Devas*. The particular individual with *rājasic guṇa* of action, vigour and passion within the present birth performs his activities with the selfish desire for sensual pleasant objects with greed, unrest, pain and want of restraint. They result in unconquered thirst over the unattainable thing and the attachment towards the attained objects. Here, the individual with the *rājasic* self is involved continuous dreams of disturbed sleep. During transmigration these characteristics are carried on from the present birth to the next, where the self gets the body among those attached to action. The self with *tāmasic guṇa* results in ignorance, darkness and others up the vigilance of understanding. The delusion and non-discrimination cloud the knowledge and push the individual towards laziness, devoid of intelligence and the non-performance of necessary duties. During transmigration the above characters are continued to the next. Then, the particular individual gets birth among the ignorant beings indulging in doing error, sloth and slip upto the depth of ignorance, i.e., he will born within the wombs of cattle.[117] During transmigration, the accumulated knowledge in the previous births are carried into the next birth. Otherwise, those who are practicing the *yoga* but failed to attain realisation will be born into the house of pure and health where he can proceed further step towards the final goal.[118] The *Bhagavad Gītā* recommends the self realisation within the worldly activities where the aspirant should use the gross world and embodied body through self-control.[119]

Along with the reason the *Gītā* suggests various channels to arrest transmigration. They are: (i) *Yogayukta* - the principle of *karma yoga* to perform the athlete's duties with disinterested action towards the fruit of actions he should maintain equanimity and indifference in mind and skill in action.[120] (ii) *Vijitātma* - who conquered himself and *jitendriya* who conquered the *indriyas* are considered to be the *yoga yukta*. Normally, the ordinary self clings to the worldly object with desire, anger, greed, infatuation, pride and jealousy. So, the self leads to the lower level. If the same level rises above the level through the principles of *'yoga yukta'*, the same self gets purification through conquering the *indriyas, manas* and *buddhi*. (iii) *Sarvabhūtātmabhūta* - helps the individual to attain Brahman state where he understands all selves as his own and even Brahman Himself.[121]

To attain the supreme peace in the Brahman state, the *Bhagavad Gītā* lays down the correct practices of *yoga*. They are: (i) He should isolate himself in a holy place where he should be steadily concentrated upon his *buddhi*.[122] (ii) He should be away from desire for enjoyment of worldly object. (iii) He should control his *indriyas, manas* and *buddhi* by performing good deeds and avoid the evil acts. (iv) While concentration, he should place himself upon a steadied seat made up of sacred grass, the *darba*, deer-skin and a piece of cloth. (v) Upon the seat he should control his physical acts and concentrating his mind upon one point.[123] (vi) While concentrating upon the mind, the athlete should position his trunk, neck and head in a straight line and fix his gaze upon the tip of the nose without any motion.[124] He should be away from mental disturbance where his breathing of heart alone should continue. If so, he will experience, the inner light which is burning within his own material body. Then the disturbance like fear, disparity and the evil impressions would have left from the *manas*.[125] (vii) The *yogic* practices push the mind towards the Divine realm where the individual attains the state of liberation and the highest spiritual qualities.[126] In other words, the manifested spiritual self enters into the unmanifested state.

For the aspirant, who has no faith in the *yoga* or even not practicing the *yoga* or failed in his *yogic* practices or partial practices of *yoga*,[127] the *Bhagavad Gītā* treats them as follows: (i) If the athlete does auspicious deed, it continues to the next birth.[128] (ii) Eventhough the gross body and subtle body destroyed within the birth, the destination of the athlete's action remain within the casual body till the time of spiritual perfection.[129] (iii) In the series of births, the casual body with its residue of the activities remains uninterrupted. Through the practice of purity in thoughts, words and deeds the athlete removes the impurities to acquire the self purification.[130]

A close observation of the transmigrating process shows that the specific spiritual element is the fraction of Ultimate Reality, i.e., the Self. The *Bhagavad Gītā* supports the idea that the eternal part of God in course of time reunites repeatedly with the psychophysical complex till the union of the self with God.[131]

4.11. THE SELF AS SPIRITUAL ENTITY

Indian philosophy asserts that the self is spiritual and emerges from the Supreme Spiritual Ultimate Reality. The spiritual Reality enters into the empirical level through the cosmic process as individual self, i.e., when the Reality enters into space and time, it gets union with the prescribed psychophysical complex and becomes as self. The *Gītā* explains the embodied self as spiritual and immortal. Within the unmanifested stage, the self exists with the Divine essence and while manifestation, it enters into the embodied bodies.[132] When explaining the spiritual self, the *Gītā* explains it through the explanation to *sat* and *asat*.[133] The *sat* represents the eternal being which is beyond time and space as '*ātman*–Brahman' and the *asat* refers to the material body. Apart from this explanation, the *Gītā* describes the connection through the medium of creatorship, the perfect and the presence of manifestation. Within the process of creation, the text supports, that, the *asat* is emerged from the *sat* and where *sat* exists before the manifested objects like the potter before the pot.[134] Here, the manifestation and the destruction will ever be repeated; and by analysing the same with the help of the anecdote, it is inferred that the creator is eternal, immortal, uniform and infinite. From this one can also infer that all the object manifested by the Perfect Creator should be perfect for ever and they may not need any alteration. Eventhough, the inanimate material objects emerged from the spiritual centre, both will be never separated but the former is controlled by the latter. From this analysis, it is inferred that, Ultimate Reality which pervaded within the material objects is eternal, indestructible and not diminishable.[135]

The second chapter of the text explains the qualities of the self in detail. The uniform, eternal and spiritual self perpetuate its immortal nature through the births and deaths of the material bodies.[136] The immortal self casting off the useless body and enters into the new ones like wearing the new and the better garments after throwing the old.[137] The actual self is *avināśī,* 'indestructible', *nitya*, 'eternal', *aja*, 'unborn', *avyaya,* 'not diminishable', *sarvagata*, 'all pervasive', *acala*, 'immovable', *sanātana*, 'ancient', *avyakta*, 'unmanifest', *acintya*, 'unthinkable' and *vikārya*, 'immutable'.[138] In short, the individual selves are nothing but the units of the Universal Self.[139] A close observation of the *Prasthānatrayam* verifies the above statement that there is no difference between Universal Self and the individual self. This can be realised in the state of sound sleep. Within the waking state, the individual experiences the duality. But in dream state he undergoes the experience of duality where the unreal appears as the real. But within the dreamless state, the individual experiences no such duality where the individual self is mingling with the Universal Self.[140]

By analyzing the opposite pairs, one can also realise the eternal nature of the self. The pairs of opposite depend upon the mental condition. If the individual perceives the favourable sensual contact he will get pleasure and if not, he will get pain. If the individual maintains the equanimity, the mind does not ruffle by the effects of the opposite pairs.[141] Then, the individual controls his *indriyas* from the external influence. So, at the end he will realise the eternal immortal nature of the self[142] by turning his *antaḥkaraṇa* inwardly.[143]

4.12. NATURE OF THE LOWER SELF

Upon this, a synthetic approach about the general metaphysical features of the self is discussed. Hereafter, the two levels of the self may be analyzed, i.e., the lower self and the higher self. Between these two states there are vast differences. The study of these differences may be helpful to synchronize the salient features of various paths known as *karma, jñāna, bhakti* and *prāpti mārgas*. Through these paths, the lower state entangled with the worldly object is elevated to the higher state. Moreover, this analysis may be helpful to understand the changing attitude of the *puruṣa* within the products of the *prakṛti*.

The *Bhagavad Gītā* considers that the active nature of the *guṇas* is to push the self into the lower level and influence the individual to do action within the worldly order.[144] Then the self will be within the *saṁsāra* state, where the self bears the endless thoughts and fails to discriminate the desire, power and pleasure.[145] Due to this attachment, the lower self suffers from the peaceless state of desire, wrath, delusion, absence of memory, powerless intelligence, the inability of sense-organs and the discrimination of the right and wrong action.[146] Then, the lower self is away from the happiness and the state of tranquility in contemplation.[147] The *Gītā* brands the lower person as the ignorant because of his attachment towards the fruits of his actions.[148]

The lower self may not understand the existence of the Ultimate Reality in the animate and the inanimate beings.[149] This spiritual ignorance takes place because of the ostentation, arrogance, anger and self conceit, i.e., the *avidya*.[150] The *Bhagavad Gītā* treats the athletes with lower nature as the persons who have *rājasic* and *tāmasic* faith upon God. The aspirants with the *rajāsic* faith practice the penance for the sake of increasing his sensual pleasure with lust and possession which are not sanctioned within the scripture.[151] Without understanding the existence of God within him, the person bearing *tāmasic* faith weakens his *indriyas*.[152] As for food, the *rājasic* persons use the same as bitter, sour, excessively hot and rough tasted.[153] Persons with *tāmasic guṇa* take tasteless food which is unfit for sacrifice. Persons with *rājasa guṇa* worship for himself and the fruit of his action.[154] The athletes who possess *tāmasic* influence worship the God contrary to usual ordinance prescribed by the ritualistic scriptures. As for the austerity performed by physique, by speech and by mental, the lower self with *rājasic* and *tāmasic guṇas* differ from the higher self with *sattva guṇa*.[155] A person with *rājasa guṇa* performs the austerity in a foolish manner because he tortures himself through the same practicies.[156]

The *Bhagavad Gītā* differentiates the lower nature from the higher nature through renunciation of the fruits of actions with firmness and enjoyment by performing the prescribed duties of the four castes with respect to the *guṇas*.[157] The lower self with *rājasic* and *tāmasic guṇas* act against the *niṣkāmakarma yoga* with the *sāttvic guṇa*. The *rājasic* aspirant never abandons the fruits of his activity because of the pain and fear of the physical suffering.[158] The *tāmasic* renunciation of action with ignorance is also not preferable because it will never lead to self-realisation.[159]

As for the action, the *Bhagavad Gītā* refers to the trials as knower, object of knowledge and the knowledge, i.e., the agent, activity and the instrument. The trial can be even categorized into three with respect to the *rājasic* and *tāmasic guṇa* as lower and the *sattva guṇa* as higher.[160] The *rājasic* knowledge refers to the apprehension of different views about the single objects.[161] The *tāmasic* knowledge refers to the wrong knowledge of the object.[162] *Rājasic* action expresses the firm attachment towards the fruits of the actions with *ahaṅkāra*.[163] *Tāmasic* action reveals the delusion without care about the result of the action and the self-realisation.[164] The *rājasic* agent represents the desire towards the fruits of the action with greed, cruelty and impurity which results in disease, anxiety, violence and restless fickle mind. *Tāmasic* agent refers to the nasty habit of unbalance, vulgar or uncultured *buddhi*, obstinate, deceptive in his powers, malicious, indolent to action, desponding spirit and procrastination with the sluggishness.[165]

The lower state of *rājasic buddhi* wrongly understands the *dharma* as *adharma*.[166] The *tāmasic buddhi* is always covered with darkness which results in the observation towards the *dharma* as *adharma* and the *adharma* as *dharma*.[167] *Rājasic* firmness is described as the attachment towards the *dharma, artha, kāma* with the desire of the fruits of the same on its specific occasions without minding the *mokṣa*. *Tāmasic* firmness is stupid, sleepy, fearful, depression and the arrogance. The analysis of the pleasure imbued with the different *guṇas* is helpful to know the lower state of *rājasic* and *tāmasic* self than the higher state of *sāttvic* self. Here, the *rājasic* pleasure arises out of the contact with sense-organs which first yields joyness like a nector but at the end results in the bad effects like poison.[168] In other words, the *rājasic* pleasure is momentary and deteriorates the aspirant's strength, vigour, colour, wisdom, *buddhi*, wealth and energy because of the *adharma* which results. *Tāmasic* pleasure with wrong action deluding the self in the enjoyment increases sleep, indolence and negligence.

4.13. THE PATHS FROM LOWER SELF TO HIGHER SELF

To get perfection in conscious endeavour with spiritual divinity and supreme satisfaction in self, the *Bhagavad Gītā* formulates the comprehensive *yogic* disciplines as *jñāna yoga*, 'path of knowledge' towards the Reality; *karma yoga*, 'path of action' to discipline the human will for the divine purposes and the *bhakti yoga*, 'path of devotional love and adoration' to merge with the Reality through passion.

Among these, *jñāna yoga* helps the persons with the reflective, emotional and active mind to reach the spiritual realm. In it knowledge, love and action are intertwined with the *sat*, 'reality', *cit* - 'truth' and *ānanda*, 'bliss' of the Supreme Reality. Through this the *rājasa* and *tāmasa guṇas* are transformed into *sattva guṇa*. Through the *yogas* the *puruṣa* within the *prakṛti* separates itself and conjoins with the Puruṣottama.[169] As far as the transformation of the consciousness is concerned, if it continues its connection with the outer world through *indriyas* the self leads to lower state. But when it turns inward through the *yogas*, the consciousness acquires the introspective apprehension of the self and it subjectively unites with the Ultimate Reality. Through the *karma yoga* the athlete detaches desire from the fruits of his action and dedicates it to God. Through this *niṣkāmyakarma yoga* he understands the self by separating it from the worldly order. The *prakṛti* alone acts as true agent and the eternal self as an observer. This is obtained by the control of *indriyas, manas* and *buddhi* and suppressing the *ahaṅkāra*. In other words, through *karma yoga* the *akṣara*, 'Reality within the self' is realised by the same self through the *kṣara*, 'mutable facets' of the *prakṛti* such as *buddhi, manas, indriyas* and the external worldly activities. *Bhakti yoga* develops because of the distinction between the creature and creator and the God's grace over the self. *Bhakti yoga* inspires devotion and self-surrender through adoring His qualities, singing His praises and doing services to Him. While practicing *Bhakti yoga*, God eliminates the aspirant's incomplete knowledge and error through His infinite grace and purity; so that, the self detaches itself from the worldly pleasure and joins the blissful divine realm. *Bhakti yoga* requires indominant *śraddhā*, 'faith' in God through which the *bhakta* moves towards the ecstatic state, where the Absolute absorbs him; so that, he forgets himself, where the state of *aparokṣanubhava*, 'separate individuality' is destroyed and it merges with the Ultimate. Then God becomes the controlling and Ruling Person of the aspirant's mind where the self acts for the glory of the Supreme.

The athlete may not get the God's grace merely out of his sheer love and faith or through the emotional piety. For that the aspirant must simply surrender himself to the feet of Almighty in a humble way and directly reveal his ignorance and shallowness. This is called *prāpti yoga* in the *Gītā*. In other words, *bhakti* has been exemplified as *markatanyāya*, 'young one itself has to cling to its mother monkey', i.e., the self has to enter into the graceful feet of the God. *Prāpti* has been amplified through the anecdote of *mārjaranyāya,* 'cat itself carries away its offspring in her mouth', i.e., the Supreme bears the responsibility to offer His grace to the meek self for its upliftment.

4.13.1 *Karma Yoga*

In *Karma yoga* the *Bhagavad Gītā* reconciles *pravṛtti,* 'attainment of wisdom by action' and *nivaṛtti,* 'attainment of the same by renunciation of action'[170] action refers to the act of worship of *Yajñā* and it has to be performed within the previous birth for destroying the sins committed by the aspirant. So, that results in the attainment of knowledge[171] in this birth. The *Gītā* recommends the *karma yoga* to all because every individual within this universe has been constrained to action.[172] While practicing the same *mārgas* the athletes have to give up the attachment of the *indriyas* with its object by understanding the value of the action than inaction because even for our bodily maintenance the action is required.[173] Here, one can doubt that the performance of action may lead to bondage because of its *apūrva* conjoined with it. But the *Gītā* explains that the action performed with the detached *manas* towards the result and the action for the sake of sacrifices the effect of *apūrva.*[174] The *Upaniṣads* also refers to the same point namely sacrifice to God helps the individual to nullify the implication of *apūrva.*[175]

The aspirant should nourish God through sacrifice and gift and eat the remnant of sacrificial food as amrita or ambrosia then he will get sinless enjoyment.[176] The *Gītā* recommends the sacrificial act because the all pervading eternal Brahman rests in the sacrifice. In other words, sacrifices help to rain; from rain the food is produced and the food formed the living being's blood and men. Moreover, the sacrifice comes out from action and this action has come out from for the purpose of moral and physical necessity.[177]

Upaniṣads also views the same idea that Brahman produces food and from that the whole creatures maintain their living.[178] So, the *Gītā* synthesizes that the whole universal existence and states that actions are derived from and consists of the sacrifice and which leads to acquisition of the knowledge of the Brahman and His part as his self.[179] After getting the true knowledge he gets satisfaction. He also gets the unaffecting nature towards gain or loss and the independent status from his interested and uninterested external object.[180] Then he devoted his fruits of the actions to the welfare of the society.[181] While performing the *karma yoga,* the ignorant misses to understand the three *guṇas* over the *indriyas* to worldly order and result in the attachment and condemns the self from its realisation. But the wise with knowledge understand the *guṇas* and transform them into *sāttvic* action towards self-realisation.[182]

The wise thing about their self and renounces action to the Divine with the understanding that they are against for God where they are freed from desire, from the fruits of the object and *ahaṅkāra.*[183] With the above perspectives, they always think about the teachings of God without pride and prejudice but with full of faith.[184] At the same time if the aspirant who forgets the above teachings of the Lord out of the deluded knowledge due to misuse the *indriyas* he is led to destruction.[185]

The *Gītā* considers desire as the chief cause for delusion of the self. The desire seated upon the *indriyas, manas* and *buddhi* deludes the self like the fire surrounded by smoke, mirror by dust and the fetus by womb.[186] Understanding the drawbacks of the desire, the aspirant should practice the *karma yoga* to restrain the *indriyas* through *jñāna* acquired by the *śruti* and from the *Ācāryas* and *vijñāna,* 'knowledge gained from the personal experience'.[187] After elimination of the desire, the *manas* and *buddhi* will be purified.[188]

4.13.2. *Jñāna Yoga*

The *jñāna yoga* is a direct means to the *mokṣa* where the passion, fear and anger are destroyed and the individual self is purified by the wisdom which is attained by the *tapas*.[189] Before trying to understand the *jñāna yoga* the aspirant should know the meanings of manifestation of the universe. Even though Lord Kṛṣṇa is considered to be the Supreme Entity over the animate and inanimate beings, He descends to the world for the purpose of eliminating the *adharma* and inaugurating a new world with *dharma* through His *yoga māyā*, i.e., the universe out of the *sattva, rājas* and the *tāmas guṇas* with action. So, *jñāna yogin* should understand the above principle and merge with the Supreme Reality after leaving this body.[190]

The *Jñāna Yogin* performs his *karmas* to maintain his body without the desire for fruits of his actions and self-control. The result of action will never bind him because he has realised the connection between the action and himself, i.e., the individual is as an instrument before the Ultimate Reality. *Jñāna Yogin* should understand the implication of action within inaction and vice versa. In detail, the self is actionless as explained by *śruti* and *smṛti* but due to habit the *manas* connects the action with the self. So, even the wise are deluded because of the above mistake of inaction for action.[191] So, the *Gītā* explains the meaning of action and inaction to remove the false idea of the self's imagination as authority of the action and its fruits. In other words, if the self realises the inaction in action it obtains the right knowledge that the self as actionless and immutable.[192] If the aspirant performs his action with the knowledge of self-control, he is desireless, purposeless, possession less and is satisfied with what he has acquired by chance. If he is balanced within the opposite of pairs and is free from envy, he will never come into contact with the sin because he may not be bound with its result.[193]

As for *karma yoga* the *Gītā* recommends the sacrifice for realisation of the self. In sacrifice the realised person sees the instrument through which the oblation takes place, i.e., things poured into the fire is nothing but, where Brahman is not an external existence but the self itself who is acting as agent for the offerings. The results of sacrifice and the goal are also considered to be the Brahman Himself.[194] Through the same sacrificial action, *Jñāna Yogin* removes the duality and perceives the Brahman everywhere where his action is being melted away and the inactive self has been enlightened by the *sattva guṇa*.[195] The *Upaniṣads* also stress that, the idea of the Brahman is fixed upon action and its accessories like the idea of Viṣṇu is fixed upon the idol or the Brahman is fixed by a name.[196] The *Bhagavad Gītā* recommends the wisdom-sacrifice as superior one because material sacrifice yields only the material effects but wisdom sacrifice leads to *mokṣa*.[197] Even though, the *Bhagavad Gītā* recommends the wisdom sacrifice as supreme, one should understand the following sacrifices because he can perceive the speciality of the wisdom sacrifice: (i) The *āhuti* of the *yajñā* is the self poured by the self itself into Brahman.[198] In the *yajña*, the self renounces all actions and is identified with Brahman. (ii) Aspirants offer the sensual acts as hearing, seeing, tasting to the fires of restraint, '*saṁyama*' with respect to the different individual's *indriyas*.[199] (iii) To get the discriminative knowledge, the aspirants are performing the sacrifice by dissolving the functions of *indriyas* and the functions of *prāṇa*, 'vital air' through the true concentration of his *manas* upon the self.[200] (iv) To become the true *Jñāna Yogin*, some are sacrificing their wealth and the austerity to the deserving people; some are performing the severe practice of *prāṇāyāma*, 'restraining of the vital breaths' and *pratyāhāra*, 'detachment of *manas*' from the external objects through mental concentration; others are repeating the *Vedic* texts with the prescribed rules and others are studying the *śāstras*.[201] (v) Aspirants become the *Jñāna Yogin* by practicing the *prāṇa*, 'inward breath' and *apāna*, 'outward breath'.[202] (vi) Rest of the *Yogins* are eating the prescribed food which is the remnant of the sacrifice as *amṛta*. They merge the life-breath with the life-breath itself. Then his accumulated sins have destroyed and he will attain *mokṣa*[203] where he understands his deed, speech and action. Then he raised himself from the state of *saṁsāra*.[204] So, finally the aspirants get self-realisation where the *dharma* and *adharma* will never bind him within the world because the fire of wisdom has reduced his fruits of action into ashes.[205]

4.13.3. *Bhakti Yoga*

Bhakti yoga is the individual's surrender to God without expecting any reward. While the *Gītā* prescribes *dhyāna, 'yoga* of meditation' by concentration of *manas* and *buddhi* and constraining the *indriyas* by *niṣkāmyakarma*, they require knowledge to practice the same for transforming his *rājasic* and *tāmasic guṇas* to *sattva*.[206] But the aspirants who are unable to discriminate their selves due to the lack of proper knowledge they practicing the *bhaktiyoga* to attain *mokṣa*.[207]

When the *Yogin's antaḥkaraṇa* detached themselves from the *indriyas* and surrenders to the Lord's feet with faith they attain the balanced state by discarding the *karma* and *krodha*.[208] He contemplates on the Ultimate Reality with ineffable joy and unites his consciousness to the Divine Light. Thus, he attains the *nirvāṇa* by eliminating his sins and doubts through self-control and devotes himself to the welfare of the society.[209]

The *Gītā* describes two types of *bhakti* as worship to the *akṣara* Brahman devoid of all *upādhis* known as *nirguṇa bhakti* and the worship to *kṣara* Brahman with *upādhis* of the *sattva guṇa* known as *saguṇa bhakti*. Through *nirguṇa bhakti* the *yogins* abandons his desire towards the fruits of his actions and directly mediates on the *akṣara* Brahman. Through *saguṇa bhakti*, the *Yogin* fails to follow the Brahman without *upādhis*. So, he worships with faith and devotion and cross the *saṁsāra* state by renouncing the fruits of his actions to the feet of the Lord where he contemplates on His supremacy within his *buddhi*. [210]

For those who fail to practice the *bhakti yoga* the *Gītā* gives two other ways as *abhyāsa yoga*, 'concentration upon the

Universal Form' and *niṣkāmyakarma yoga*, 'desireless action and devoted to the fruits of his action to the Lord.[211] Through the *abhyāsa yoga*, 'the concentration of the *manas* upon the external object' the *antaḥkaraṇa* leads to control of *buddhi* which helps to realise the Brahman.[212] The *niṣkāmyakarma yoga* has to do actions on behalf of Lord Himself because the self is nothing but the *Vāsudevaḥ* and the actions are resulting factors of the *guṇas*, i.e., the lower state of Brahman. Where the *Yogin* attains purity in *manas* and steadfastness in *buddhi* which results in *mokṣa* through perfect knowledge.[213] Eventhough, some perform injustice to them the *bhakti yogins* show friendliness and compassion to them. They are freed from *ahaṅkāra* and the worldly attachment and maintain the poised states within the opposite pairs. They always maintain endurance contentment, balanced mind, self control, passive state of firm conviction and their *buddhi* are always thinking of the Ultimate Reality. They never disturb the world, the world also never affects them and they are always freed from their mind from joy, envy, fear and sorrow. They are perfect in words, acts and deeds, clever in action, impartial to all and they renounce the fruits of all actions for the sake of Lord. They neither rejoice for the attainment of the desirable objects nor grieve for anything nor desire for the worldly objects but they renounce the goodness and evil effects of their activities to God. They always maintain silence within themselves, content with anything, homeless and they are having steady mindedness and bear indomitable faith upon the Supreme Brahman.[214] While explaining *bhakti yoga*, the *Gītā* does not fail to explain the *prāpti yoga* to contemplate the Ultimate Reality through supreme *bhakti* and *niṣkāmyakarma yoga*. If the aspirant himself surrenders everything to the feet of Ultimate Reality through absolute devotion, the gap between the individual and the absolute will be reduced to one, so that the *yogins* think that their actions are not activated by themselves but by Lord Himself.[215] Thus the *Bhagavad Gītā* describes that the *bhakti* and *prāpti yoga* helped the individual to obtain the true knowledge of the Reality through devotional attachment of the individual with Absolute.[216]

4.14. NATURE OF THE HIGHER SELF

The last part of the *Gītā* deals with the lower nature of the self and the various means for self-realisation. As a continuum an elaborate view about the nature of pure self and its relations with the Ultimate Reality may be discussed. For this the problem may be approached from three angles namely the nature of self, its activity in the worldly order and the negative qualities from which the self should be away.

To understand the actual self, one should follow the qualities of *ahiṁsā*, 'absence of injury', *satya*, the truth, *asteya*, 'the absence of theft' and *sucita*, 'purity'. There are two kinds of self as the carnal self should be subdued by the spiritual self by the above ways. Then the pure self reaches its original state. On the other hand, if the carnal self overcomes the spiritual self the self will not attain its pure state because the carnal self connects the effects of *guṇas*[217] and to the psychophysical complex through desire, anger and greed.[218] They destroy the carnal self by the past *karmas* through the transmigrating process.[219] Normally, the *ātma* is considered to be the atomic which is having all the worldly possessions. But the same *ātma* can be attained to the highest state of *Paramātma*, which is all pervading and all-encompassing. For that the individual should conquer his own self by the spiritual self which is free from misery and passion. So, in order to attain the supreme state the *Gītā* formulates the following mediums: (i) the individual self should conquer his own self, '*jīvātmā*'. (ii) the individual self should be happy within himself '*ātmatṛptaḥ*'. (iii) the same self should be satisfied with his own knowledge and realization, i.e., the *jñānavijñāna-tṛptātmā*. (iv) the same self should be in equanimity, '*samabhāva*'. (v) the self should be away from the desire for fruits of his own action, '*nirāṣiḥ*'. (vi) the self should be viewing everything in comparison with one's self, '*atmopamya*'.

Jitātma conquers all the temptations and gets delight within himself which is against the *Parajitātma* who is mentally wandering everywhere and getting satisfaction from the external objects. To become *jitātma,* the *ātma* requires many steps such as self dependence and control over its *indriyas, manas, buddhi* and *ahaṅkāra*. For this the athlete should steady his *indriya* and *manas* in his words, deeds and acts. Then the individual should have infinite courage over the *buddhi* by eliminating its desire and fear. The unrefined self is fickle which is experiencing the object of the *indriyas* and resulting the law of *karma*. Instead of the external contact, if the self gets the highest bliss from its own self, the atomic nature of *ātma* attains the all-pervading *jītātma*.[220]

Eventhough the higher self has no *guṇas*, the *Gītā* recommends the presence of *sattva guṇa*.[221], The higher self preserves the steadfastness with purity where the *vāsanā* of the past birth have weakened.[222] If the self matured with accomplishment of reasons the worship,[223] then it arrests the *jñāna* out of sense-object contact and maintains the steady wisdom like the tortoise which withdraws its limbs from all sides.[224] So, it enjoys the supreme peace and happiness through self-control and abandons the desires without selfishness[225] where the self maintains the state upto *nirvāṇa* and enjoys with the Ultimate Reality.[226]

The *Gītā* advises the higher self to do action without expecting reward. To understand the active nature of the universe, the *Gītā* stresses that action is superior to inaction.[227] But he should perform the same with the detached mentality to isolate the self from the worldly order through control of the psychophysical organism. Then the self-knowledge.[228] The higher self performs his action and renounces the desire for its fruit. Then the fruit of the action does not affect him but he will be liberated from the action bounded.[229]

The higher self overcomes the desire by understanding the self from the psychosomatic organism.[230] Like fire reduces the fuel to ashes, the acquired wisdom eradicates the results of the actions.[231] Then the highest self perceives the Ultimate Reality from the cow, elephant, dog and the out-caste or the dog-eater.[232] The higher self detaches the sense object contact and finds joy and peace within Him.[233] At the time the sins and the doubts are destroyed. Then he works for the sake of the welfare of the society.[234] The highest self understands the *Kṣetrajña* as God in his *Kṣetra*. To understand this, he should be followed certain virtue to realise the *Kṣetrajñā* in Him. He should follow the faith service to the elders. He should be cultured steadfastness inaction and self-control. For this the *Gītā* advices the highest self even without affection for his son and wife. On the way he can maintain the balanced state within the desirable and the undesirable objects. The highest aspirant constantly thinks about the self-knowledge in the Ultimate Reality through identity and the perfect devotion with him.[235] After that the individual perceives the God in everything irrespective of beings within the universe.[236]

The *Gītā* considers that the highest self is having the *sattva guṇa* and bears the faith, worship, austerity and offering fights to God[237] in accordance to the same *guṇa*. The characteristic of the higher self with *sattva guṇa* is as follows: (i) The *sāttvic* aspirant takes food which increases his life, energy, strength, health, joy and cheerfulness.[238] (ii) The *sāttvic* aspirant practices the austerity which is prescribed by scriptural laws.[239] (iii) The *sāttvic* person bears knowledge which represents the identification of the Ultimate Reality within the living and non-living objects like the same gold in the different ornaments.[240] (iv) The *sāttvic* action represents the detached attitude towards the fruits of the same without the feelings of love or hatred.[241] (v) The *sāttvic* agent maintains the balanced state indifferent to success and failure because he performs his action with the help of the *śāstra* as the supreme authority.[242] (vi) The *sāttvic* person reconciles *pravṛtti*, 'path of *karma*, and *nivṛtti*, 'path of inaction' in his *niṣkāmyakarma yoga*.[243] (vii) For *sāttvic dhṛti*, the *Gītā* says that the individual maintains the *samādhi* state of *manas* in critical situation.[244]

For the *sāttvic* pleasure, the *Gītā* recommends the painful sensation at first. But finally the same situation should leads to beneficial one to the individual.[245]

The *Gītā* recommends that the perfect self should understand the *jñānavijñānatṛptātmā*, 'importance of knowledge and realisation' because then only the actual self gets satisfaction and conquers his *indriyas*.[246] The study of the *Kṣetrajña* is termed as *jñāna*. The mere study of science, i.e., '*vijñāna*' is only partial because it deals with the physical study of *ahaṅkāra, manas* and *buddhi* fill the gap left by the *vijñāna*. So, the study of perfect self is possible through *jñānavijñānatṛptātma*, where the *ātmā* becomes *Paramātmā*.

Regarding the balanced approach of the supreme *manas* the *Gītā* utters, 'The *Yogin* whose self is satisfied with knowledge and wisdom, who remains unshaken, who has conquered the senses, he is said to be a saint, for whom a lump of earth, a stone and gold are equal'.[247] Here, the balanced state does not mean the failure to understanding the preciousness of gold as different from the stone. But the actual realisation shows, that gold and stone are nothing but the modification of the basic primordial matter the *prakṛti*. The *Gītā* states, "In a *brāhmaṇa* endued with wisdom and humility, in a cow, in an elephant, as also in a dog and in a dog-eater, the wise see the same".[248] Based on this verse, the balanced state includes that the actual self does not change with respect to the forms of the objects and temptations. In other words the self should have *samabuddhi* or *samadharśana*, 'the seeing of the *Paramātma* in each and every beings'.[249]

Generally, persons are attached to the good or evil qualities. The perfect self should not deviate towards the evil nature because it will lead to lower state. For that the *Gītā* prescribes many ways. They are: (i) *same kṛtvā* - the aspirant approaches the opposite pairs like pleasure and pain with the even mind.[250] (ii) *samaḥ siddhāv asiddhau* - the individual has to feel as same both the victory and defeat.[251] (iii) *saye sthitiḥ* - if individual attains the state of equality he can conquer his birth.[252] (iv) *samaṁ pasyati* - the perfect self sees pleasure of his own as that of others and he one realise the actual meaning of evenness everywhere.[253] (v) *ahaṁ samaḥ* - the perfect self experiences the presence of Brahman in all animate and the inanimate objects.[254] (vi) *samaḥ* - the person who realises the even mindedness in friends and foe.[255] (vii) *samaṁ paramesvaraṁ pasyati* - the perfect self realises the presence of the indestructible highest lord in all beings.[256] (viii) *sarveṣu bhūteṣu samaḥ brahmabhūtaḥ* - when the perfect self perceives evenness it becomes the Brahman.[257] (ix) *samas cittatva* - the athlete should be even-hearted towards the desirable and undesirable activities.[258] (x) *samadarśanaḥ* - the highest self should perceive his own self in the all beings and his own self in all other selves.[259]

The *Gītā* explains the various process and the way of practicing for the attainment of the highest self, While explaining the perfect self, the *Gītā* appreciates the desirelessness towards the fruits of individual's actions. For that the perfect self divert his fruits of his actions to the goodness of the society. Moreover, if he directs the mental force towards the fruits[260] of the actions the body, *indriyas, manas* and *buddhi* are brought under the control of the individual. Thus the perfect self through the desire less activities and dedication to the society gets the state of Brahman.

The *Gītā* adds the *ātmopamya*, 'supreme state of realising the other selves as his own'.[261] Otherwise, it can be referred as *ātmavadbhāva*, 'he who realise everything'. It results in supreme happiness within this world and seeks Supreme God in the *mokṣa*.[262] Eventhough, the individual sees, feels and speaks the self as wonder strange and marvelous entity, he fails to reach the supreme position because of his doubt and vacillation. So, a very few alone in many thousands attain the perfection through self-discipline, steadfastness and non-attachment.[263] One among many thousands follows the way of cultivating his *buddhi* within the spiritual realm by passing away from the worldly enjoyment like opposite pairs, the taste of power, practicing the *Vedic* principle, following the spiritual exercise, passing away the embodiment of the *guṇas,* firmness in the purity and practicing *niṣkāmakarma yoga.*[264]

The perfect self should understand that pleasure and pain, joy and sorrow, success and failure, heat and cold are the results of the contact between the *indriyas* and the external objects. The mental condition arising from the contact may result in happiness, or it may result sorrows. So, the absence of the contact results in no feelings at all to the *manas.* Moreover, within the worldly order one cannot escape from this contact. For that, the *Gītā* lays down the methods as sensing the opposite pair as alike. If the individual self gets the capacity it can be considered as immortal.[265] The perfect self ultimately realises that the basic material nature of the universe and the spiritual residue of the animate and the inanimate objects are indestructible and eternal, i.e. the material universe with all living beings emerge from the pure *sat,* the unmanifested supreme quality.[266]

To the perfect self the *Gītā* prescribes three main paths as possession of pure reason within the *buddhi,* possession of perfect knowledge and the desireless activities.[267] The athletes should have valid reason and balanced *mind,* so that, he could dedicate himself to the service of humanity irrespective of caste, creed, race and colour. The possession of perfect knowledge refers to the capacity of conquering his own mind through renouncing the fruits of his activities in order to get rid of his bondage. Regarding the destruction of the bondage, the *Bhagavad Gītā* suggests three kind of *tyāgas* one due to ignorance arising form *tāmasic* quality; the second *tyāga* due to feat of painfulness of body arising out of *rājasic* quality and the third *tyāga* due to the discriminative knowledge coming out of sātvic quality.[268] *Tyāga* by *tāmasic guṇa* is inferior because there is no purity, good conduct and truth. *Tyāga* by *rājasic guṇa* is mid way because the resulting activity does not bring the athlete to *mokṣa.* But *tyāga* by *sāttvic guṇa* is preferable the athlete can sacrifice the fruits of his actions with disinterestedness devoid of avarice. Then, he gets freedom from bondage which will lead the self to the supreme state of Brahman. In addition, if he destroys his desire, he will never undergo re-birth and merges with the Universal Self. This limitlessness results in the supreme state of Brahman without sufferings and sorrows where he acquires balanced mind with controlled *indriyas* and he dedicates the fruits of his activities to welfare of the society. For this the *Bhagavad Gītā* formulates ways as eradicating the delusion from *buddhi;* removing fecklessness and making *buddhi* to contemplate anything to achieve the final state of Brahman.[269] To acquire steady knowledge the perfect self follows serenity contemplation, self-satisfaction, disinterested actions, steady mind both in pleasure and pain, detachment and fearlessness.[270] If so, he may not get annoyance at any extreme and depressed state. A close observation shows that the desireless self exists within the ecstasy of supreme happiness and finally results in *mokṣa*.[271] The *Bhagavad Gītā* states, that, if the athlete is satisfied and contended in his self he may not to do any other work. At the same time the self interested athlete may not incur sin from his work because of its purity of *indriyas, manas* and *buddhi.*

The *Gītā* explains the negative result of the contact between the *indriyas* and the external objects. The *Gītā* points out the degradation of the eternal self through sensual pleasures and the sublimation of the self control. The athlete gets desire by thinking about the object. The desire results in anger. From anger the delusion emerges. Delusion follows the failure of the memory. Then this memory completely destroys the total personality of the individual.[272] So, the perfect self should not follow the sense objects because it results in demerits to the self.[273] If the athlete understands the drawbacks of the sense-object contact he will control his self by controlling his own *antaḥkaraṇa* and becomes devoid of love or hatred towards its object. Then, he gets the supreme state of pure heart and steady *manas* without any sort of miseries. Peace and balanced mind steadies his will upon the Lord and frees him from the sorrows.[274] The *Bhagavad Gītā* explains, that, the athlete who missed his control over sense objects contact may not get wisdom or knowledge about the self.[275]

So, if the athlete lives his life by renouncing desire, steadies his life through detachment, selflessness and the sensation of vanity he will reach the supreme state of peace, i.e. the end of *saṁsāra* state[276] where the usual worldly activities or the result of the sense object contact or the desire of the athlete's activities may not disturb the pure self like ocean, i.e. eventhough many rivers enter the ocean it never changes its nature.[277] The *Bhagavad Gītā* compares the perfect self with the Supreme Reality i.e. the *ātmā* with *Paramātmā*, i.e., *nara* with Nārāyaṇa.[278] The *Gītā* understands the inevitable nature of the action which is caused by the *guṇas* present within the *prakṛti*.[279] Within the natural action the perfect self has to realise itself. The perfect self performs the worldly activities without thinking about the result, i.e. the perfect self commands the mind to avoid thinking of the results. The *Bhagavad Gītā* criticizes the aspirant who is interested in the taste of sense object contact through the mind. He is considered to be a hypocrite.[280] The *Bhagavad Gītā* also explains that if the individual who controls his *indriyas* who indulges in disinterested action there will be no attachment with the fruits of action.

The athlete should practice the detached attitude towards the objects. If not, he should perform the action and give away the fruits for the benefit of the humanity.[281] The *Bhagavad Gītā* explains the same that he should act and sacrifice the result to the feet of God. In that way, the *Bhagavad Gītā* recommends *Sāṅkhya Yoga* and *niṣkāmyakarma yoga* to attain spiritual good.[282] If the athlete performs the action with *Sāṅkhya* knowledge, the perfect self is elevated to the spiritual level. While explaining the *niṣkāmyakarma yoga* the *Bhagavad Gītā* describes the balanced mind towards the pairs of opposite and the way to free from bonds of the action.[283] The *Bhagavad Gītā* systematizes the following characteristic features of the *Niṣkāmyakarma Yogin*: (i) The athlete who performs the action may not be hated by others. (ii) He may not desire anything because he has renounced the results for the benefit of the others. (iii) He will look alike on the opposite pairs like pleasure-pain, gain-loss, friend-foe, high-low and happiness-misery. (iv) He will never incur sin because he neither wishes to enjoy nor abandonment of the sense-object contact.[284] The *Gītā* advises the perfect self to maintain state of perfection in his various activities and to elevate himself towards the Ultimate Reality in the following ways: (i) *Adveṣa* - the individual should not hate to others. (ii) *Maitri* - the tendency of friendship to all. (iii) *Karuṇā* - the presence of kindness helps the athlete to get friendship. (iv) *Nirmanaḥ* - the absence of *ahaṅkāra*. (v) *Aniketaḥ* - the perfect self has no shelter of its own. The *Gītā* supports the principle of non-ownership of anything because the presence of this will lead to attachment, attachment will lead to worldly pleasure then the individual will never realise his own perfect state and Ultimate Reality. (vi) *Nirahaṁkāraḥ* - the absence of egoism in the individual keeps him away from finding fault with others. (vii) *Satatam santuṣṭaḥ, santusṣṭaḥ yene kenacit* - one should be content with the acquired property with which he should be satisfied. (viii) *Anapekṣaḥ*, the perfect self should be free from the expectation of the worldly pleasure.

To control the expectation of pleasure, the *Bhagavad Gītā* formulates the following views: (i) *yatātma* - The individual should control his self from the sense-object contact because the absence of self control results in the increasing the longing for pleasures and possible evils to the society. (ii) *Samabhāvaḥ*- the perfect self should practice the balanced mind within the favourable and the unfavourable situation. (iii) *Dṛḍhaniścaya*- the perfect self acquires a firm resolve in his dealings to the world. (iv) *Harṣa amarśa bhaya udvegair vimuktaḥ* - the perfect self should be free from joy, anger, fear and disgust. (v) *Śubha aśubha parityāgi* - the athlete should abandon the auspicious and the inauspicious action. Here a view should be considered. One may know the negative outcome of the inauspicious action, but he should also avoid the auspicious action. For example, too much attraction towards the master of *yoga* also results in misery because of the attraction to the auspicious act. So, the perfect self should not incur in attraction to both extremes. Understanding the whole situation the *Gītā* advocates, that, he has to give up all sorts of desire in his undertakings to lead a superior state of eminence without caring for enjoyment and sufferings.

According to the *Gītā,* the perfect self has to practice austerities because the bonds created by the action, word and thought prevent the elevation of the self to perfect state. For that, the *Bhagavad Gītā* formulates three kinds of austerities as physical, speech and mental. They are: (i) For physical austerity, the *Bhagavad Gītā* says that one should follow the following activities like service to the as, *Kṣatriyas* and *Vaiśyas;* he has to worship God; he has to show respect to the preceptors and he should abstain from injury to other individuals.[285] (ii) For austerity in speech, the *Gītā* says that the athlete should utter words which are true, gentle, measured, pleasing, beneficial, agreeable and favourable and they should never give pain or sufferings to other's heart. In addition, the *Gītā* advises him less speech to save his energy[286] and he has to practice the habit of sacred recitation of *Vedas.* As far the mental penance, the athlete should keep his *manas* serene, soft and away from the cruelty.

The austerities may also be further classified into three types with respect to the *guṇas.* They are: (i) The austerity with *sattva guṇa* performs the penance with perfect faith and without the desire for the enjoyment of the fruits of his activities. He performs the same without the expectation of honour and even the slightest indication of hypocrisy or ostentation. He does no harm to all and dedicates his actions for the betterment of others.[287] (ii) The austerity with *rājasa guṇa* may not be acceptable because it results in desire towards the fruits of actions.[288] (iii) The austerity with the *tāmasa guṇa* is untenable because it results in foolish ideas, pervasive obstinacy and it degrades the mentality of encourager and the performer to lower level.[289] So, the perfect person always likes to perform the penance by *sattva guṇa* because it helps the individual towards the self-realisation.

To attain the state of Brahman, the perfect self possess faith through his activities as *'manaḥ aveśya'*, *'nityayuktaḥ'* and *'parayā sraddhayā upetaḥ'*.[290] *Manaḥ aveśya* refers to the worship of the Lord with concentrated *manas* to realise the Ultimate Reality. *Nityayuktaḥ* represents the athlete who performs the worldly activities skillfully through *niṣkāmakarma yoga*, i.e., self dedicative rendering of service to humanity to remove other's misery, calamity and the dependence upon the others. *Parayā śradhyā upetaḥ* connotes the self who has strengthened his firm faith upon the Lord through his uninterrupted service to the society. In other words, through perfect dedication of *manas* and a devoted life with solemn faith in God, through rendering service to society and worship of God with faith, the self realises as Lord Himself.[291] The *Bhagavad Gītā* advises the perfect self to get union with the Ultimate Reality by *dhyāna yoga*, 'meditation' and *Sāṅkhya Yoga*, 'intellectual investigation along with the dedication of his actions'. For that the *Bhagavad Gītā* prescribes the systematic paths. They are: (i) *Matparāḥ (Īśvara-paraḥ)* - the perfect self should consider Lord Kṛṣṇa as the Supreme Self. (ii) *Māṁ (Īśvaram) dhyāyantaḥ* - the perfect self has to meditate upon the Lord. (iii) *Mayi (Īśvara) avesita* - the fixation of the *manas* upon the Lord. (iv) *Mayi (Īśvara) manaḥ adhatsva* - the athlete's *manas* should always think about the Lord. (v) *Mayi (Īśvara) buddhiṁ niveśaya* - the fixation of the perfect self's *buddhi* upon the Lord. (vi) *Sarvaṇi karmāṇi mayi (Bramaṇi) saṁyāsya* - the dedication of the athlete's action to the society. (vii) *Ananyena eva yogena upāsate* - the perfect individual should develop feeling of oneness with the Lord.[292]

The text concludes, that, for elevation of one's own self from its lower state to the level of the Ultimate Reality should always think about the Lord,[293] where he gets the right knowledge and unification with the Ultimate Reality. Then he identifies[294] his body, *indriyas, manas, buddhi* and *avyakta* as Lord's lower form and his self as His Higher form.[295] Otherwise, the spiritual self reunites with the Ultimate Reality or the changes withdraw itself to its prime causal centre or the attributes of the self have been arrested because the self itself has been unified with the Ultimate Reality.

The aspirant develops his self as perceiving the Ultimate Reality from every fractions of the universe and forgets his difference from Him. For this the *Bhagavad Gītā*[296] touches the following point: (i) *'ātmanā ātmānaṁ na hinasti'* - it represents the attainment of the supreme knowledge. The athlete eradicates his ignorance and evil by removing the *avidyā* and the *ajñāna*. This helps to perceive the Lord from everywhere. (ii) *'tatoyāti parāṅgatim'* - it helps to realise the self and non-doer and free from doubts and defects the empirical order. In other words, the secured right knowledge results in the active nature of the *prakṛti* as *Kṣetra* and the *ātman* as *Kṣetrajña* who is witnessing the action.[297] One can synthesize the truth of oneness, i.e. the distinction between the *Kṣetra* and *Kṣetrajña* or *puruṣa* and *prakṛti* like the water is being identified with its taste and the sweetness is being identified with the sweetness.[298] If the individual controls his state of *saṁsāra*, his own carnal self becomes a friend to himself and raises its own state towards the liberated state of Divine Self. Otherwise the same self becomes an enemy to himself which degraded self to the level of lower *saṁsāra* state.[299] Here, the lower self through the *jñāna* gained by scriptures, *vijñāna* gathered through his own realisation experiences and maintains the evenness against the pairs of opposite and become the higher self. At this state he does not make difference between the lump of earth, stone and the gold.[300]

This esoteric text explains that the highest *yogin* realises his own self with Brahman.[301] The *Bhagavad Gītā* professes the main characters of the perfect self in series of states where he maintains the equanimity in all circumstances.[302] The *Gītā* explains the series of states as follows: (i) *Samekṛtvā, samobhūtvā* - the realisation of the Brahman in the opposite pairs.[303] (ii) *Sāmye sthitaṁ samaṁ paśyati, ahaṁsamaḥ, samacilltatvam, samadarsanaḥ* - all are representing that the individual perceives Brahman in all beings such as ants and beasts and in all places.[304] (iii) *Sama losṭaśmakañcnaḥ*- the self should perceive the Brahman in all the places, *'Vāsudevaḥ sarvaṃ'*.[305] (iv) The athlete is practices the *yoga* to attain Brahman state where he maintains the balanced mind and follows the Godly life.[306] (v) He controls his *manas* and gets everlasting satisfaction in his own self.[307] (vi) The athlete withdraws his external links with the help of *buddhi*. So, his *manas* abides within the self.[308]

If the self understands its supreme state, it realises its origin from the unmanifested level and ends within the same centre.[309] After getting this balanced mind and perfect knowledge, the merit and the demerit will never incur the aspirant. Then the athlete performs desireless activities with the constant remembrance of Brahman.[310] He performs his action with friendliness and compassion to all living beings. He detaches himself from the worldly happiness and controls his self with firmness and directs his *buddhi* towards Lord,[311] He neither rejoices over nor hates anything. He perceives no difference between *nivṛtti*, 'inaction' and *pravṛtti*, 'action' but considers as one[312] because the realised self thinks itself as 'no agent'. After understanding the self as Brahman, the self does not stoop to lower level by his error in action because of the detachment towards the worldly objects. But the self perceives the Ultimate Reality within the selves of all beings and within his own self. Thus, the self realisation leads to God-realisation and ultimately God Himself.[313]

4.15. SELF WITHIN THE MORAL ORDER

Moral order is an imperative law pertaining to hypothetical character of uniformity which refers to the practical efficacy of human society within their character and conduct in accordance with their nature and rational will. As a theological outlook the moral order works within the Divine Will for the goodness of the society. Theocentrically human beings have to conjoin within the supreme ctasy of Godliness by their obedience to the divine law because the conception of God is considered to be the beginning and the end of the moral order.[314] The text as a theistic scripture suggests the same moral order for the betterment of the society in general and self-realisation in particular through the prescribed duty consciousness, i.e. the *dharma*.

According to the *Bhagavad Gītā, dharma* means the mode of behaviour determined by the individual i.e., regulating the conduct in conformity with one's intrinsic nature towards the right action in right way for social equality and the individual peace. Whereas *adharma* refers to the disharmony of one's nature and his duty towards the wrong action which leads to a society without confirmity and equilibrium. The work as a theocentric philosophy, assumes Lord Kṛṣṇa as the supreme authority for eternal immortal and imperishable moral order.[315] It emphasises that while the individual suffers mental tension within the society the all-progressive Divine Supreme merges with the hearts of the human self for maintaining the equilibrium by divine birth with the tools of wisdom and the righteousness, i.e. the moral equipment to eradicate the evil forces of ignorance and the selfishness. Through the birth of the Divine the new era of *dharma* has been inaugurated where love and mercy has over powered the hatredness and cruelty *dharma* destroys the *adharma;* truth conquers the falsehood and intelligence and Bliss conquer the power of death, disease and sin.[316]

To maintain *dharma* within the society, it says, that, the society splits into several castes on the basis of *guṇas, karma* and conduct but not on the basis of *jāti* or birth, sex and the heredity. *Mahābhārata* also supports the view, that, the whole society of human beings are the blood brothers but they differ only on the basis of specific duties.[317] From the empirical standpoints the *māyā* is acting as a true agent. So, the law of *karma* and the principles of *guṇas* bind the self to a particular duty and paves the way for caste-division. But from the absolute standpoint God is treated as the static and changeless but not as an agent to the worldly order. So, according to the text, the caste division is existed within the society for maintaining the *dharma*. But it will never be applicable to the ultimate standpoint. The Supreme Universal Spirit through which caste-division follows to explicit *svabhāva*, 'inwardness of beings' to outwardness through *svadharma*, 'prescribed duties and they are pre-determined by the Divine Will'. In other words, the individual will be righteous when he acts in accordance with his nature with pure devotion to attain the spiritual perfection. Otherwise, if the aspirant elevates himself through his divine quality, he will reach *sāsvataṁ padaṁ avyayaṃ*, the eternal, and imperishable status. In short, one can say that Lord Kṛṣṇa creates the *svakarma* on the basis of *svabhāva* and law of *karma* but the same is never possible on the basis of birth.[318] The *Cāturvarṇyam* describes the four stages of Hindu ethical life as *brahmacarya*, ' student', *gṛahastha*, 'family man', *vānaprastha*, 'retired age in a forest' and *bhikṣu*, 'mendicant life'. *Varṇāśramadharma* also co-operates with the *sādharaṇa dharma*, 'common duties of all' as *adhairya*, 'steadiness', *kṣama*, 'forgiveness', *śauca*, 'purity', *indriya nigraha*, 'sense control', *dhi*, 'wisdom', *vidyā*, 'learning', *satya*, 'truthfulness', *akrodha*, 'control of anger', *dharma-aradhana*, 'religious duties', *ahiṁsā*, 'goodness to living beings', *satyavacana*, 'truthful talk', *asteya*, 'non-stealing', *brahmacarya*, 'sex-continence', *anupadhā*, 'sincerity of *manas*', *śucidravyasevana*, 'taking pure food', *viśiṣṭadevatā bhakti*, 'devotion of Vedic Gods' and *apramada*, 'watchfulness to avoid transgressions'.[319]

The text formulates the prescribed duties to each caste on the basis of *guṇas*.[320] *Brāhmaṇa* with *sattva guṇa* bears the duties of *sāma*, 'self-control, *dāma*, 'control of the physical organs', *tapaḥ*, 'austerity', *śauca*, 'purity', *kṣānti*, 'forgiving nature', *arjava*, 'sincerity', *jñāna*, 'knowledge', *vijñāna*, 'wisdom' and *astikya*, 'faith'. The *kṣatriya* with the *rājasa* and *sattva guṇas* perform the duties of *saurya*, 'heroism', *tejas*, 'smartness', *dhṛti*, 'power of endurance', *dakṣya*, 'skill', *yuddha chapya phalayanam*, 'not to flee from battle', *dānam*, 'making of gifts' and *īśvarabhāva*, 'power of controlling orders'. The *Vaiśyas* acquire the *rājasa* and *tāmasa guṇas* and followed the duties of *kṛṣhi gorakṣa vanijyam*, 'agriculture, cattle rearing and trade'. Finally the *Śūdras* having the *guṇas* of *tāmasic* and *rājasic* are serving the all.[320] The *Bhagavad Gītā* recommends the caste-division not only to maintain *dharma* of society in the epimenal alone but it also given for perfection of the self. In other words, if one performs the caste-duty he will attain *mokṣa* by cleansing the impurities within the self.[321] The *Gītā* does not support the caste division but it also gives the reason and its importance.[322] The evolution and the all pervasive reality represent that the caste system is based on the *guṇas* of the *prakṛti*, the lower nature of Lord Kṛṣṇa.[323] The *Gītā* does not accept the changing of the caste-duty. So, it emphasizes that doing one's own ordained duty allied with his *guṇas* will never incur sin just as poisonous substance may not disturb the snake with the same substance.[324] If the aspirant changes his caste-duty, he will incur sin because the duty also controlled by the *guṇas* like the fire which is surrounded with smoke.[325]

The *Gītā* stresses that the aspirant has to perform duties with complete detachment from the feelings and motives of self-seeking, pleasure-seeking and elevating the self in higher order by abandoning the fruits of actions. If so goodness or badness does not affect the self. In short, the self maintains the subjective morality from the objective sense of non-moral by cutting the connection between the internal self and the activities of the performer.[326] For this, the *Gītā* does not recommend the *sanyāsa*, to give up actions within the practical order for the purification but grants the mode of *tyāga* to have attachment to worldly activities but to be detached from the fruits of the same activities.[327]

Within the tendency of action without vices and maintenance of good conduct, the text differentiates two kinds of characters as aspirants with *daivi saṁpat*, 'divine equipment' and *asuric sampat*, 'demonic equipment'.[328] Person with *daivi saṁpat* bears the qualities such as *abhaya*, 'fearlessness', *sattva saṁśuddhi*, 'purity of heart', *jñāna yoga vyāvasthitaḥ*, 'steadfastness in knowledge and the proper action with respect to that knowledge', *dānam*, 'givingness', *damaḥ*, 'control of external organs', *yajña*, 'sacrifice' and *śvādhyayaḥ*, 'study as prescribed within the scripture', practicing *tapas*, 'penance', *arjava*, 'sincerity', *ahiṁsā*, 'harmlessness', *satya*, 'truth', *akrodha*, 'control of anger', *tyāga*, 'renunciation', *śānti*, 'peacefulness', *apaisuna*, 'evilness of backbite', *dayā bhūteṣu*, 'kindness to the suffering', *alolupatya*, 'evilness of greedy', *mārdavā*, 'tenderness', *hrī*, 'getting the shame for wrong action', *acapala*, 'absence of fickleness', *tejas*, 'energy', *dhṛṣṭi*, 'fortitude', *śauca*, 'purity' and *adroha*, 'hostility to friends'. The totality of these virtues take the self towards the path of *mokṣa* from *saṁsāra*. The persons with *asuric saṁpat* persist in following bad qualities such as *dambhaḥ*, 'hypocrisy', *darpaḥ*, 'arrogance', *abhimānaḥ*, 'self-conceit', *krodhaḥ*, 'wrath', *paruṣyaṁ*, 'harshness' and *ajñānam*, 'ignorance'. These bad qualities drive the self towards the enslavement within the *saṁsāra* for many births.[329] The divine persons maintain friendly relation with to all animate and the inanimate objects. He follows the path of detachment from the *indriyas* and destroying the influence of *ahaṅkāra* and strengthening the balances *manas* towards the pleasure and pain. The same person persists in good character of endurance, contentment, self control and firm conviction towards the worthily problems. He frees himself from the joy, envy, fear, sorrow and by him the world will never be affected and vice versa. The same aspirant does not want anything, follows purity, clever, unconcerned, not disturbed and he renounces all actions for satisfying his desire. The divine person neither rejoices nor gives or desires and renounces the good and evil.[330] The person with the divine quality always searches the actual nature of the self by perceiving the true knowledge of humility to others, modesty to virtues, innocence or being harmlessness to the living beings, patience for injury, services to the *Ācārya*, purity within the external and the internal conditions and constantly steadfast to attain *mokṣa*.

Unlike the divine lot the person with the *asuric* nature pollute himself with the following worst qualities such as the inefficiency of the performing action to avert evil and the inaction in particular time and place and he will never bother about either purity or conduct or truth. The demonic personalities are concerned with the sense object and they assume that the universe is unreal because there is no basic ground for it as Lord or Reality or invisible cause or *karma*. So, that the universal creatures are the by-product of the seasonal passion. They are performing unholy acts and approach any problem with delusion because their minds are filled with insatiable desires like hope, lust, wrath for the sentient object and full of hypocrisy and arrogance. The same person may bear the materialistic attitude of attaining and storing the material goods with the mentality of ownership and strong egoism. The same person performs the materialist's sacrificial rites with hypocrisy without regarding the ordinance of scriptures with the cruel mentality of selfishness, stubbornness and filled with the pride and intoxication of wealth. They will never pass to heaven but to hell through numerous births within the demoniac wombs because of their *adharma*.[331]

4.16. INDIVIDUAL'S PART WITHIN THE MORAL ORDER

The nature of action can be divided into two ways. They are: (i). The reflex action prompted by the life-function (*jīvana-pūrvaka*) of the individual for the useful ends (*kamapi artha kṛyam*) to the organism. (ii) The conscious and voluntary action directed from the individual's desire or aversion to attain the desirable end and to avoid the undesirable ends.[332] The text reconciles both and declares that the individual's actions are decided by the lower nature of the reality, i.e., *guṇas* in accordance with the five-fold causes viz. the body, the agent, the sense organs, the life-functions and biometry activities and the controlling power of God.[333]

It treats the relation between the *guṇas* with different nature of the actions in accordance with the attitude of the self. The *Bhagavad Gītā* also states that the self is deluded *avidyā* and assumes as agent. From this, one derives that the action done by the individual has been enhanced by the *prakṛti*. The *Bhagavad Gītā* does not refuse to observe the participation of the supreme divine quality or *daiva* in the individual's action as objective causal element or all controlling power of God or luck or destiny or fate or the force which has been accumulated within the past lives.[334] Where the seat or *adhiṣṭhānam* or body refers to the conjoining place of the feelings such as desire, hatred, happiness, misery and the knowledge or the modification of the *prakṛti* or *māyā; kartā* refers to the agent or doer or the enjoyer pertaining to the *upādhi* of the self and *karṇam* refers to the *indriyas* and its activities. *Ceṣṭa* refers to the different distinctive capacities of *karmendriyas, jñānandriyas, manas* and *buddhi* and the *daivam* refers to the self which is derived from the transcendental Supreme Divine sphere.

From this, one can infer that whatever action whether *dharma* as taught by *śāstra* or against the same done by the individual requires the five factors for successful completion.[335] The aspirant who trains his *buddhi* with the help of scriptural knowledge perceives the truth that the spiritual self is only one factor among the five causes of worldly activities. But the person with perverted *buddhi* adheres towards the wrong direction against the scriptural truth identifies the inactive divine self with the five causes and comes to hasty judgment that the pure self is the sole agent of the worldly action.[336]

Ahaṅkāra is the product of the *prakṛti* which assumes the self as agent of the action. If the individual realizes the actual value of the *ahaṅkāra*, the bondage is dissolved. If so, the action should be considered as *dhārmic* because it helps the individual to realise his self and to do goodness to the society. Otherwise, the *ahaṅkāra* may pollute the self and extend the *adhārmic* activities to the society. If the individual realises this, he can perform all actions with duty consciousness without selfishness and desire. Then the spiritual self will never affect the results of his activities.[337]

4.17. GOD'S GRACE UPON THE INDIVIDUAL

The text grants grace as an essential condition for the individuals to achieve perfection. Through the grace the actual meaning of immanent and the transcendental state of the Ultimate Reality is fully understood. In other words, even though, the individual tries to understand the reality by controlling his *manas* and *buddhi* without the grace of the Ultimate Reality, he may not get success because of the implication of *ahaṅkāra* and *avidyā* in the carnal of the embodied self through the past births. The Roman Catholic regards the grace as the *Bhagavad Gītā* does, that, it is nothing but the super natural organism infused with the human self in which the self has been divinized.[338]

The *Bhagavad Gītā* explains liberation as realisation of the self and identifies the same as divine with the Grace of God. Daniel Day Williams in his work called 'God's grace and Man's hope' treats the same as, "The liberal vision sees God working in human history for a progressive achievements of a higher order of life for mankind".[339] Christianity explains the same as an external guidance that comes from the Christ's personal instruction. Where grace has been explained as, "The external help makes easier, the realisation of the natural possibility, together with the natural possibility itself".[340] Here the external help refers to God's grace and the natural possibility connotes the individual's attitude towards its supreme realisation of his self. It resembles the *Bhagavad Gītā's* treatment of the aspirant's desire over his self realisation and the God's grace. Like the text, Christian scripture treats the grace as the omnipotent Divine energy which passes to the finite individual's psychophysical organism as a stream of electricity to help him for his realisation.

The first discourse of the *Bhagavad Gītā* shows the Arjuna's distressed state within the threshold of life between the illumined and confused situation. Arjuna forgets the spiritual state and struggles because of the active participation of the *guṇas*. But he does not forget the situation because he wants to raise his lower state to the higher state. While he raises himself towards perfection the Divine principle acts as *sakhā* and affords His infinite grace over the self. The grace of the Lord helps the individual to avoid the feelings like anxiety, loneliness, doubt and insecurity and helps him to develop the spirituality within himself to push him towards the ultimate state of liberation. So, Arjuna first feels grief of the evils of the war and surrenders himself to the Lord with the utter despondency to get the grace from Him.[341] Here Arjuna represents the individual in the state of self-indulgence, self pity and the hesitation to hurt his own kith and kin because of the excessive attachment with them. This condition has been clearly described by Arjuna's passion to surrender himself to the feet of Lord Kṛṣṇa for His advice and grace where Arjuna says, 'My heart contaminated by the taint of helplessness, my mind confounded about *Dharma*, I ask Thee: Tell me what is absolute good. I am Thy pupil. Instruct me, who have sought Thy grace'.[342] This view indicates the individual's weakness towards the reasoning capacity through doubts, difficulties, attachment, fears, passions and desires. So, to get the right approach from the Ultimate source the finite individual seeks the guidance from the individual's teacher and the Divine principle. S. Radhakrishnan explains the critical situation of the relation between the finite individual and the infinite divine realm through the concept of grace, "When one's world is in ruins, one can only turn within the seek illumination as the gift of God's infinite compassion".[343] In the first verse of the seventh discourse Lord Kṛṣṇa advises Arjuna, 'With the mind intent on Me, O Pārtha, practicing *Yoga*, and finding refuge in Me'.[344]

From this, one can understand the infinite compassion, greatness, strength, power and the grace of the Lord over the individual for his upliftment towards the highest goal of perfection. So, when the individual perceives the finite nature and the critical situation of the circumstance, he has to submit his total consciousness to the feet of Lord. Then without delay the Supreme Lord will bring to bear his power of the grace over the individual for his realisation. The grace of the Lord upon the individual can also be derived from the tenth chapter. Where Lord Kṛṣṇa interested in Arjuna and He describes his different kinds of the disposition of being such as intelligence, wisdom, non-illusion, patience, truth, self-restraint, calmness, pleasure, pain, birth, death, fear, security, innocence, equanimity, contentment, austerity, beneficence and praise and blame.[345]

One can grant the supremacy of the Lord's grace upon the all beings of His descendants. Along with the grace the Lord paves proper ways to perceive the knowledge of the external world and the essential understanding of his own self as identical with Himself.[346] If there is any difficulty for the individual while moving towards the liberating state, God certainly extends his compassion to over-come the same by affording the luminous lamp of wisdom to destroy the darkness born of *avidyā*.[347] In the tenth chapter, Arjuna asks about the divine manifestation of Lord Kṛṣṇa and the Lord does not hesitate to show it but showers His passion upon Arjuna and describes His wonderful glory of the manifestation.[348] From this one can infer that the divinity pervades within the supreme manifested objects for the purpose of liberating the all living beings.[349] The apprehension of the eleventh discourse expresses the deep knowledge of the Lord's grace upon the individual where Arjuna desires to visualize the supreme form of manifestation of Viṣṇu as the infinite wisdom, sovereignty, strength, power and splendour with his own eyes.[350] Here, one can infer the individual's ambition to witness the Eternal Self which dwells in all beings or to understand the view that everything is evolved from the ultimate source.[351] For the transfiguration of Jesus, S. Radhakrishnan refers to Saint Hildegar's report of the "fair human form" who declared the identify that, "I am that supreme and fiery force that sends forth all the sparks of life. Death hath no part in me, yet do I allow it, wherefore I am girt about with wisdom as with wings. I am that living and fiery essence of the divine substance that glows in the beauty of fields . . . . All these live because I am in them and am of their life. I am wisdom. Mine is the blast of the thundered word by which all things were made. I permeate all things that they may not die. I am life".[352]

After revealing His Universal Form, Lord Kṛṣṇa out of excessive compassion and grace converse with Arjuna, 'Thou art not indeed able to see Me with this thy eye alone; I give thee a divine eye; behold my lordly *Yoga*'.[353] Here, the nature of knowledge is categorized as ordinary as well as divine knowledge. The ordinary knowledge is acquired by our own efforts based on the outcome of our *indriyas* and the influence of the intellectual activity which can perceive only the outer forms of the universe. Divine knowledge is acquired by the influence of the supreme grace afforded by the Ultimate Reality which yields the direct knowledge to apprehend the spiritual reality through the medium of intuition. The divine cosmic manifoldness mingles with the individual finite *manas* to form the spontaneous and direct vision of the spiritual realm. Here, one can easily perceive the God's tendency of grace over the individual because Lord Kṛṣṇa Himself gives the divine eye to Arjuna through His lordly *Yoga,* i.e., the great miraculous power of grace.[354] So, one can derive that, beyond the infinite grace of the Lord the finite knowledge will never reach the phenomenal and the noumenal sphere, i.e., manifested as well as the unmanifested form of the Ultimate Reality. The above said apprehension has been perceived by Arjuna which can be seen from the verse, 'There in the body of the God of Gods, the son of Pāṇḍu, then behold the whole world established in one, and separated into many groups'.[355] Where Arjuna's finite knowledge has disappeared and everything merged into one. This reveals the revelation of the Divinity within the earthly life.[356] The greatness of grace can be further studied with the aid of Arjuna's prayer to God to get His forgiveness. Arjuna after witnessing and adoring the glaring splendour of the Universal Form he expects His forgiveness for his past activities springing out of the ignorance.[357] The words of Arjuna reveals the fact that the Reality is related to the individuals as father's affection to son and lover's intimacy to his beloved.

Moreover, Christianity also regards God as father, friend and guardian through its main conception of the Divine love within the teachings of Jesus.[358] After he visualizes blinding blaze of the light from the Universal Form, Arjuna again requests Lord Kṛṣṇa to get back His usual form. At that time Arjuna himself utters about His gracious outlook that, 'Show me that form only, O God; have mercy, O God of Gods, O Abode of the Universe'.[359] The above verse shows that the glorified ever shining light within the metaphysical realm which mingles within the physical field like the teacher and the friend are having the identical hearts towards their sons and beloved.

After withdrawing His Universal Form, Lord Kṛṣṇa addresses to Arjuna, 'By Me, gracious to thee, O Arjuna, this Supreme Form has been shown, by my sovereign powerful of splendour, the All, the Boundless, the Original Form of Mine, never before seen by any other than thyself'.[360] Where one perceives that without the Lord's gracious medium upon the individual through His own supreme power the individual will never attain the knowledge about the all pervasive nature of the Lord within the whole Universe. In other words, the finite individual will never realize the all pervasive feature of the Lord without the aid of the infinite transcendental supreme centre with its grace. Otherwise through grace the infinite realm unites with the finite and the finite gets the power of realising the Supreme Reality as it is. Through the detailed analysis of the grace in the *Bhagavad Gītā*, one can understand the philosophical implication of the same which is considered to be the essence of the Gospel of the *Bhagavad Gītā*. The essence is that if the individual works for the sake of the Lord Himself, if he perceives Lord Kṛṣṇa as the Supreme principle; if he devotes his existence upon the feet of the Supreme; if he detached his psychophysical organs from the worldly affairs and if he eliminates the tendency of hating other beings, he merges with the Godliness.[361]

In the last discourse the *Bhagavad Gītā* unites the Lord's grace with the act of sacrifice, austerity and charity. In other words, if the aspirant performs his own prescribed duty with perfect devotion to Lord Kṛṣṇa as refugee, the grace hailed from Vāsudevaḥ fills the gap between the devoted finite individual's and the infinite Supreme Reality so that the finite individual certainly reaches the abode of Viṣṇu or the state of liberation.[362] Here, one can say that if a wicked person seeks refugee from Lord with the perfect devotion he will reach the highest stage because the grace afforded by the Lord reaches him without partiality where the *Bhagavad Gītā* recommends the state of refugee by the individual to the Lord with steady-mind and firm faith. Then the individual gets grace and peace from the supreme.[363]

In final consideration, if the finite individual practices his actions and takes refugee with the perfect devotion he will definitely earn the Lord's grace. Through the grace he crosses the impossible obstacles which are caused by the perishable *avidyā* within the *saṁsāra* . So, Lord Himself explains the truth to Arjuna as, 'Fixing thy heart in Me, thou shalt, by My Grace, cross overall difficulties; but if from egotism thou will not hear (Me), thou shall perish'.[364] One reviews the merits of devotional actions of the individual with the Lord Kṛṣṇa's effulgent grace because He himself explains the same in His advice to Arjuna. If the aspirant sees the Supreme Reality by thinking as, 'I am myself that' then the result of the sense-object becomes *nirbīja* - 'seedless'. So, the individual gets detachment and attains perfection.[365] The value of grace is strengthened in the last part of the final discourse. In other words, if the aspirant hears the whole Gospel of the *Bhagavad Gītā* with the attentive mind and the state of faith, his faith will be paved the way for liberation. Then the spiritualist destroys his delusion which is caused by ignorance and acquires the highest wisdom.[366] After grasping the total situation of the Divine grace the individual feels himself as an instrument in His hand.[367]

4.18. DESTINY OF THE SELF

Everything whether animate or inanimate objects existing within the universe should have an end. Among animate beings the human beings are considered to be the highest one. Within them, the embodied self is the ultimatum for the particular individual. Pertaining to the above general conception, the *nirvāṇa* of the self is considered to be the final conception. An outlook of the Indian Philosophical system shows that there are two kinds of the ends for the self as the realisation of the self in its own condition within the proper medium and the correct understanding of the not-self, i.e., the material body.

The conversation between Arjuna, the individual self and the Lord Kṛṣṇa, the Brahman, personal God results in self-realisation through detachment and finally the self becomes the Brahman Himself. Here, the Brahman state can be explained as follows with the aid of *Viṣṇu Purāṇa* where it gives explanation for '*Bhagavad*'. According to *Viṣṇu Purāṇa*, '*bhaga*' represents the six attributes as perfect dominion, mighty, glory, splendor, dispassion and salvation.[368] Then the *Purāṇa* adds: 'He is called the Lord (*Bhagavat*), who knows the origin and the end, the coming and the going of beings, what is wisdom and what is ignorance'.[369] Here one can compare the *Bhagavad Gītā's* explanation of *Sthitaprajñā* and *niṣkāmya siddhim* with the Brahman state.[370]

In the Brahman state, perfect self bears the purity of *buddhi* and freedom from illusion, doubt and misconception. Here the self abandons the superfluous luxurious object except the necessary objects for the maintenance of the body.[371] Then the realised person resorting himself in the requested sports as jungle or the sandbank of river or mountain cave because he is always with the Reality. The *Yogin* in Brahmanic state eats little because he has to keep the serenity with the restricted sleep. He maintains the noble austerity in speech, action and thought. In addition, the *ātman* in Brahmanic state always devotionally practices the *dhyāna* through *mantrajapas* upon the visible and the invisible objects of the worldly order.[372] Moreover, the Brahmanic self abandons his egoism, violence, arrogance, desire, anger and greed. Where the athlete should get rid of even the external belongings for the bodily purpose because the property may increase the disturbance towards the passive mind and *indriyas*. So, the aspirant fully eliminates the tendency of 'mine' and leads his existence with peace.[373]

A review of the *Bhagavad Gītā* not only describes the Brahman level[374] but also paves the way to transfer the level to the highest existence of Ultimate Reality as the final destiny of the self. After reaching the Brahman state the self gets absolute serenity where it does not gives or desire towards the failure or success and he always subsists within the Ultimate Reality.[375] The Brahmanic self perceives the Ultimate Reality through the selves of all beings as same.[376]

The Brahmanic self understands the Reality as the casual centre for diverse manifestaiton which is caused by the *upādhis*. Then the Brahmanic self enters into the eternal abode of Godliness through the firm union of love[377] and the tendency as refugee.[378] In other words, the self attains the Ultimate Reality through wisdom and surrendering everything to His feet.[379]

The *Bhagavad Gītā* explains the characters of the embodied self with respect to the *guṇas* within the worldly order. Among the *guṇas*, the *Gītā* recommends the *sattva guṇa* because it helps the self to acquire the knowledge of Brahman and to reach its destiny of Brahman, where the self crosses even *sattva guṇa* and merges with the Ultimate Reality. So, the embodied self attains immortal state and is freed from birth, death, decay and pain.[380]

REFERENCES

1. *Rg. Veda*, 10.72, 81, 90, 121 & 129.
2. *Ch.U.*, 6, 2, 2.
3. *IU*, 8, *ChU*. 3, 19; *SU*. 1, 1; 3, 4.
4. *AU*, 1. 1; *BU*. 1-4; 1-7; *KU*. 4, 6.
5. *BU*, 1, 4, 10.
6. *TU*, 3, 10, 5.
7. *ChU*, 3, 12, 8, 1-6.
8. *MU*, 1, 1, 6-7.
9. *Ibid*., 2, 2. 12.
10. *SU*, 4, 11; *MU*. 6.

11. *SU*, 4, 10.
12. Parrinder, Gloffrey. *Upaniṣads, Gītā and Bible*, pp. 25-28.
13. Hasting, James (Ed.), *Encyclopaedia of Religion and Ethics*, Vol. 2, p. 745.
14. *Ibid.*, p. 746.
15. *BG*, 14. 3.
16. *Ibid.*, 7. 14.
17. *Ibid.*, 7. 15; 16. 20.
18. *Ibid.*, 7. 14-15.
19. *Ibid.*, 8. 17-19.
20. *Ibid.*, 9. 8, 10.
21. *SU*, 6. 16.
22. *mamaivāṁśo jīvaloke jīvabhūtaḥ sanātanaḥ/*
    manaḥ ṣaṣṭhānīndriyāṇi prakṛtisthānī karṣati// — *BG*, 15. 7.
23. *Ibid.*, 13. 8, 23.
24. *Ibid.*, 13. 26; *SU*. 1. 8; 6. 5.
25. *Ibid.*, 15. 1, 3, *KU*, 6. 1; *MU*, 3. 1-2.
26. *Ibid.*, 14. 27.
27. *Ibid.*, 12. 7.
28. *ChU*, 6. 11.
29. *BG*, 2. 18; *SU*. 5. 11-12; *KU*, 5. 4.
30. *Ibid.*, 3. 27.
31. *Ibid.*, 14. 20.
32. *Ibid.*, 8. 1-2.
33. *Ibid.*, 8. 3-4.
34. *Ibid.*, 15. 16-17.
35. *SU*, 1. 10; *MU*, 2. 1. 1-2.
36. *BG*, 4. 24; 9,16, 24; *MaiU*, 6. 16.
37. *Ibid.*, 10. 4-5.
38. *Ibid.*, 18. 59-60.
39. *Ibid.*, 8. 20.
40. *BG*, 6. 7-8; 8. 22; 9.4; 11. 38; 18. 46; *BU*, 3. 8. 8; *KU*, 3. 11.
41. *BG*, 3.5.27; 4.6; 5.15; 9.10.
42. *Ibid.*, 4. 6; *SU*. 4. 60.
43. *Ibid.*, 13. 20; *BU*. 3. 73.
44. *Ibid.*, 8.18-19; 13. 26; *SU*, 1,8, 6. 5.
45. *Ibid.*, 7. 4; 13. 5.

46. *Ibid.*, 9. 8.
47. *Ibid.*, 3. 27.
48. *Ibid.*, 13. 20.
49. *Ibid.*, 9. 8.
50. *Ibid.*, 14. 6.
51. *Ibid.*, 14. 7.
52. *Ibid.*, 14. 8.
53. *Ibid.*, 13. 21, 23.
54. *Ibid.*, 5. 13; *SU*. 3. 18.
55. *Ibid.*, 7. 4.
56. *Ibid.*, 7. 5.
57. *Ibid.*, 5. 14; 7. 4-7; 9. 8-9.
58. *Ibid.*, 15. 8.
59. *Ibid.*, 10. 8.
60. *SU*, 6. 16; *ChU*, 8.31.
61. Satwalkar, Shripad Damodar. *Shrimad Bhagavad Gītā*, Ch.XIII, pp. 83-84.
62. *Ibid.*, 75-76.
63. *BG*, 13. 4.
64. *ChU*, 8.12.3; *MaiU*. 2.5.
65. *BG.*, 13. 2.
66. *upadraṣṭānumantā ca bhartā bhoktā maheśvaraḥ/*
    paramātmeti cāpi ukto dehe asmin puruṣaḥ paraḥ//—*Ibid.*, 13. 22.
67. *KU*, 6. 7.
68. *BG*, 18. 30.
69. *Ibid.*, 18. 31.
70. *Ibid.*, 18. 32.
71. *Ibid.*, 2 . 48-52.
72. *Ibid.*, 18. 51.
73. *Ibid.*, 2. 53.
74. *Ibid.*, 18. 52-53.
75. *Ibid.*, 14. 26.
76. *Ibid.*, 2. 60.
77. *Ibid.*, 2. 62-63.
78. *Ibid.*, 2. 64-65. 68.
79. *Ibid.*, 2. 66-67.
80. *KU*, 6. 10-11.

81. *BG*, 6. 10-19.
82. *Ibid.*, 6. 31-32; *IU*, 4-8.
83. *Ibid.*, 5. 11.
84. *Ibid.*, 3. 5.
85. *Ibid.*, 5. 12.
86. *Ibid.*, 3. 24.
87. *Ibid.*, 3. 32-33.
88. *Ibid.*, 3. 37.
89. *Ibid.*, 14. 7, 12.
90. *Ibid.*, 3. 15; 8. 3; 9. 8.
91. *Ibid.*, 2. 47.
92. *BG*, 2. 47-48; TU, 2-8-1; *MU*, 1-1-8.
93. *BG*, 3. 6.
94. *Ibid.*, 3. 7-8.
95. *Ibid.*, 3. 30; 6.18.
96. *Ibid.*, 3. 17.
97. *Ibid.*, 4. 17-18.
98. *Ibid.*, 4. 19.
99. *Ibid.*, 4. 32.
100. *Ibid.*, 3. 14-15.
101. *Ibid.*, 4. 37.
102. *Ibid.*, 5. 7, 10, 11; 8. 9.
103. *SU*, 2. 14.
104. BG, 12. 11-12.
105. *Ibid.*, 2. 12.
106. *Ibid.*
107. *Ibid.*, 2. 18.
108. *Ibid.*, 2. 22.
109. *avyaktādīni bhūtāni vyaktamadhyāni bhārata/ avyaktānidhānāniyeva tatra kā paridevanā//* —*Ibid.*, 2. 28.
110. *Ibid.*, 8. 18.
111. *Ibid.*, 6. 43; *BU*, 4. 4. 1-6; *SU*, 5. 7-12.
112. *Ibid.*, 2. 20; 5. 10.
113. *Ibid.*, 2. 22.
114. *Ibid.*, 2. 26.
115. *Ibid.*, 3. 27; 13. 20.
116. *Ibid.*, 3. 33.

117. *Ibid.*, 14. 5-18.
118. *Ibid.*, 6. 41-45; *BU*, 4. 4. 2.
119. *Ibid.*, 5.7; 6. 5-6; *KU*, 1, 2.10.
120. *BG*, 2. 48, 50.
121. *Ibid.*, 2. 25; 5. 25; 27-8; 12.4.
122. *Ibid.*, 2. 41.
123. *Ibid.*, 6. 12.
124. *Ibid.*, 6. 13.
125. *Ibid.*, 6. 14.
126. *Ibid.*, 6. 15.
127. *Ibid.*, 6. 37.
128. *Ibid.*, 6. 40.
129. *BG*, 2. 40. 51; 6. 41, 43, 45; 7. 19; *BU*, 4. 4.2.
130. *BG*, 6. 45.
131. *Ibid.*, 15. 7.
132. *BG*, 2. 12-13; *KU*. 2.6; 5. 5; *AU*., 4.4.
133. *Ibid.*, 2. 16.
134. *BG*, 2. 17; *ChU*, 6.2. 1-2; *BU*, 2.1.20, *MU*, 1.1.7.
135. *BG*, 8. 22; 9.4; 11. 38; 18. 46.
136. *Ibid.*, 2. 20-21.
137. *BG*, 2. 22; *BU*. 1. 3; *KU*, 1. 6.
138. *BG*. 2. 22-25.
139. *BG*. 5. 7; 6. 31; 10. 20; 15. 14; *SU*. 2. 14; *ChU*. 8. 1. 5.
140. *BU*, 4-5-15.
141. *BG*, 2. 15.
142. *Ibid.*, 5. 21.
143. *KU*, 4. 1.
144. *BG*, 3. 5, 27; 14. 5.
145. *Ibid.*, 2. 41.
146. *Ibid.*, 2. 62-63.
147. *Ibid.*, 2. 66.
148. *Ibid.*, 2. 25.
149. *Ibid.*, 9. 11-12.
150. *Ibid.*, 16. 4; *KU*. 2-5.
151. *Ibid.*, 17. 5.
152. *Ibid.*, 17. 6.
153. *Ibid.*, 17. 9.

154. *Ibid.*, 17.12.
155. *Ibid.*, 17.18.
156. *Ibid.*, 17.19.
157. *Ibid.*, 18.40.
158. *Ibid.*, 18.8.
159. *Ibid.*, 18.7.
160. *Ibid.*, 18.18-19.
161. *Ibid.*, 18.21.
162. *Ibid.*, 18.22.
163. *Ibid.*, 18.24.
164. *Ibid.*, 18.26.
165. *Ibid.*, 18.28.
166. *Ibid.*, 18.31.
167. *Ibid.*, 18.32.
168. *Ibid.*, 18.38.
169. *MU*, 6.34.
170. *BG*, 3.4; 5.11; 18.5.
171. *BU*, 4.4.22.
172. *BG*, 4.23.
173. *Ibid.*, 3.8.
174. *Ibid.*, 3.9.
175. *TU*, 1-7-4.
176. *BG*, 3.11-13.
177. *Ibid.*, 3.14-15; 14.3-4.
178. *TU*, 2,3.
179. *BG*, 3.19.
180. *Ibid.*, 3.17-18.
181. *Ibid.*, 3.21, 25.
182. *Ibid.*, 3.26-30.
183. *Ibid.*, 3.30; 18.59; 60.66.
184. *Ibid.*, 3.31.
185. *Ibid.*, 3.32.
186. *Ibid.*, 3.38-40.
187. *Ibid.*, 3.41.
188. *Ibid.*, 3.42-43.
189. *Ibid.*, 4.10.
190. *Ibid.*, 4.9.

191. *Ibid.*, 4.16.
192. *Ibid.*, 4.18.
193. *Ibid.*, 4.19-22.
194. *Ibid.*, 4.24.
195. *Ibid.*, 3.28; 5.8; 18.20, 23.
196. *ChU*, 7-1-5.
197. *IU*, 9 -11.
198. *BG*, 4.25; *BU*, 3-2-1.
199. *BG*, 4.26.
200. *Ibid.*, 4. 27.
201. *Ibid.*, 4. 28.
202. *Ibid.*, 4. 29.
203. *Ibid.*, 4. 30-31.
204. *Ibid.*, 4. 32.
205. *Ibid.*, 4. 34-42.
206. *Ibid.*, 13. 24.
207. *Ibid.*, 13. 25.
208. *Ibid.*, 6. 47; 9.23.
209. *Ibid.*, 5. 21-26.
210. *Ibid.*, 12. 6-8.
211. *Ibid.*, 12. 9-11.
212. *Ibid.*, 3. 30; 6. 35; 12. 6.
213. *Ibid.*, 12. 12.
214. *Ibid.*, 12. 20.
215. *BG*, 4. 9-9-10; 12. 11; 18.66; *KU*, 1-2-24.
216. *BG*, 4. 11; 7. 17, 28; 8. 13, 15-16; 10.10; 12. 4, 8, 14 - 20; 18. 54-57& 69.
217. *Ibid.*, 2. 28.
218. *Ibid.*, 2. 63.
219. *Ibid.*, 6. 6.
220. *ChU*, 8. 210.
221. *BG*, 2. 38; 4.22.
222. *Ibid.*, 2. 45.
223. *Ibid.*, 2. 41.
224. *Ibid.*, 2. 58.
225. *Ibid.*, 2. 71.
226. *Ibid.*, 2. 72.

227. *Ibid.*, 3. 8.
228. *BG*, 3. 17; *BU*, 3-5-1.
229. *BG*, 3. 30-31.
230. *Ibid.*, 3. 38-42; 4. 19, 21, 39.
231. *Ibid.*, 4. 36-37, 42; 5. 16.
232. *Ibid.*, 5. 18-19.
233. *Ibid.*, 5. 21, 29.
234. *Ibid.*, 5. 25-26.
235. *Ibid.*, 13. 7-11.
236. *Ibid.*, 13. 27.
237. *Ibid.*, 17. 4.
238. *Ibid.*, 17. 8.
239. *Ibid.*, 17. 11, 18.
240. *Ibid.*, 18. 20.
241. *Ibid.*, 18. 23.
242. *Ibid.*, 18. 26.
243. *Ibid.*, 18. 30.
244. *Ibid.*, 18. 33.
245. *Ibid.*, 18. 37.
246. *Ibid.*, 7. 4-5.
247. *jñānavijñānatṛptātmā kūṭastho vijitendriyaḥ/*
    yukta ityucyate yogī samaloṣṭāśmakāñcanaḥ// —*Ibid.*, 6. 8.
248. *vidyāvinayasaṁpanne brāhmaṇe gavi hastini/*
    śuni caiva śvapāke ca paṇḍitāḥ samadarśinaḥ// —*Ibid.*, 5. 18.
249. *Ibid.*, 6. 9.
250. *Ibid.*, 2. 38.
251. *Ibid.*, 4. 22.
252. *Ibid.*, 5. 19.
253. *Ibid.*, 6. 32.
254. *Ibid.*, 9. 29.
255. *Ibid.*, 12. 18.
256. *Ibid.*, 13. 27-28.
257. *Ibid.*, 18. 54.
258. *Ibid.*, 13. 9.
259. *Ibid.*, 6. 29.
260. *Ibid.*, 5. 25; 12. 4.
261. *Ibid.*, 6. 29.

262. *Ibid.*, 6. 30, 32.
263. *BG*, 2. 29; 7. 3; *KU*, 2.7.
264. *BG*, 2. 42-45, 47, 50, 53.
265. *Ibid.*, 2. 15, 38, 48; 4. 22; 6. 7, 9; 12. 13, 18; 14. 24-25.
266. *BG*, 8. 22; 9. 4; 11. 38; 18. 46; *MU*. 1. 1. 7.
267. *BG*, 2. 51.
268. *Ibid.*, 18. 7-9.
269. *Ibid.*, 2. 52-53; 9. 28; 12. 17.
270. *BG*, 2. 55-57; *MU*, 2. 2. 1; *BU*, 4. 3. 21.
271. *ChU*, 3. 14; 7-6-1.
272. *BG*, 2.62-63.
273. *Ibid.*, 2. 67.
274. *Ibid.*, 2. 64-65.
275. *Ibid.*, 2. 66.
276. *Ibid.*, 2. 71.
277. *BG*, 2. 0; *BU*. 4. 3. 32.
278. *BG*, 2. 72.
279. *Ibid.*, 3. 5.
280. *Ibid.*, 3. 6.
281. *Ibid.*, 3. 7.
282. *Ibid.*, 5. 4-5.
283. *Ibid.*, 5. 3.
284. Satwalkar, Shripad Damodar, *op.cit.*, Chapter V, pp. 268-269.
285. *Ibid.*, 17. 14.
286. *Ibid.*, 17. 15.
287. *Ibid.*, 17. 17.
288. *Ibid.*, 17. 18.
289. *Ibid.*, 17. 19.
290. *Ibid.*, 12. 2.
291. *Ibid.*, 12. 4.
292. *Ibid.*, 12. 6-8.
293. *Ibid.*, 12. 8.
294. *Ibid.*, 13.24.
295. *Ibid.*, 13. 27.
296. *Ibid.*, 13. 28.
297. *Ibid.*, 13. 26 - 29; 3. 27 - 29.
298. *IU*, 7.

299. *BG*, 6. 5-6.
300. *Ibid.*, 6.8.
301. *Ibid.*, 6. 32.
302. *Ibid.*, 15. 5.
303. *Ibid.*, 2. 38, 48; 4. 22; 12.18.
304. *Ibid.*, 5. 19; 6. 29, 32; 13. 9, 27.
305. *Ibid.*, 7. 19.
306. *Ibid.*, 2. 56; 4. 10; 5. 28; 6. 14.
307. *Ibid.*, 6. 20.
308. *Ibid.*, 6. 25.
309. *Ibid.*, 2. 28.
310. *Ibid.*, 2. 50.
311. *Ibid.*, 11. 55; 12. 13-14, 17.
312. *Ibid.*, 3. 27; 4. 18; 13. 29.
313. *BG*, 2. 21; 4. 35; 5. 7, 6. 29-31; 9. 6; 10. 20; 13. 32; 15. 14; *IU*. 6.
314. Hasting, James. (Ed.), *op.cit.*, Vol. 10, p. 833.
315. *BG*, 11. 18; 14. 27.
316. *Ibid.*, 4. 7-8.
317. *Ibid.*, 4. 13; 10. 6; 11. 43 and Radhakrishnan, S., *op.cit.*, p. 161.
318. *BG*. 4. 13; 18. 56.
319. *Ibid.*, 13. 7; 14. 8-9, 13; 17.
320. *Ibid.*, 18. 42- 44.
321. *Ibid.*, 18. 45.
322. *Ibid.*, 18. 46.
323. *Ibid.*, 7. 4; 9. 4.
324. *Ibid.*, 5. 35; 18. 47.
325. *Ibid.*, 18. 48.
326. *Ibid.*, 16. 7; 18. 30.
327. *Ibid.*, 18. 2-3.
328. *BG*, 16.6; *BU*, 1-3-1.
329. *BG*, 16. 1-6; 18. 5-6.
330. *Ibid.*, 12. 13-19; 13.7,11.
331. *Ibid.*, 16. 7-21.
332. Dasgupta, Surendranath, *op.cit.*, Vol. II, p. 515.
333. *BG*, 3. 27; 18, 14.
334. *Ibid.*, 8. 5-6; 18. 56, 58.
335. *Ibid.*, 17. 5; 18. 15.

336. *Ibid.*, 18. 16.
337. *Ibid.*, 3. 27; 18.17, 58-59.
338. *BG*, 4.40, 42; 7.1, 18.76 and Hasting, James, (Ed.), *op. cit.*, Vol. 6, p. 368.
339. Williams, Danial Day, *God's Grace and Man's Hope*, p. 22.
340. Hasting, James (Ed.), *op.cit.*, Vo., l6, p. 365.
341. *BG*, 1. 45; 2. 1, 7; 7.14.
342. *kārpaṇyadośopahatasāvabhāvaḥ pṛcchāmi tvāṁ dharmasaṁmūḍhscetāḥ/ yacchreyaḥ syān niścitaṁ brūhi taṁ me śiṣyas te ahaṁ śādhi māṁ tvāṁ prapannam//* —*Ibid.*, 2. 7.
343. Radhakrishnan, S., *op. cit.*, p. 101.
344. *mayyāsaktamanāḥ pārtha yogaṁ yuñjan madāśrayaḥ/*—*BG*, 7. 1.
345. *Ibid.*, 10.4-5, 12.18-19.
346. *Ibid.*, 10.16; 13.15.
347. *Ibid.*, 10.11.
348. *Ibid.*, 10.41.
349. *Ibid.*, 10.42.
350. *Ibid.*, 11.4.
351. *Ibid.*, 10.8.
352. Radhakrishnan, S., *op. cit.*, pp. 270-271.
353. *na tu māṁ śakyase draṣṭuṃ anenaiva svacakṣuṣā/ divyaṁ dadāmi te cakṣuḥ pasyame yogaṃ aiśvaraṃ//*—*B.G.*, 11.8.
354. *Ibid.*, 10. 7, 18.
355. *tatraikasthaṁ jagat kṛtsnaṁ pravibhaktaṃ anekadhā/ apaśyad devadevasya śarīre pāṇḍavas tadā//* —*Ibid.*, 11.13.
356. *BG*, 11. 52-54; *MU*, 11.2.11.; *ChU*, 7.25.
357. *BG*, 11.41-44.
358. Hasting, James (Ed.), *op.cit.*, Vol. 6, p. 364.
359. *tad eva me darśaya deva rūpaṁ prasīda deveśa jagannivāsa//* —*BG*, 11.45.
360. *mayā prasannena tevārjunedaṁ rūpaṁ paraṁ darśitaṃ ātmayogāt/ tejomayāṁ viśvaṃ anantam ādyaṁ yan me tvadanyena na dṛṣṭapūrvaṃ//* —*Ibid.*, 11.47.
361. *Ibid.* 11.55.
362. *BG*, 3.9; 18. 3, 6-9, 56, 62, 66; *KU*, 1-2-24.
363. *BG*, 18. 62; *KU*, 1-2-24.

364. *maccittaḥ sarvadurgāṇi matprasādāt tariṣyasi/*
atha cet tvaṃ ahaṅkārān na śroṣyasi vinaṅkṣyasi//—*BG*, 18. 58.
365. *Ibid.*, 2. 59.
366. *Ibid.*, 18. 71-72.
367. *BG*, 11.33; 18.73; *ChU*, 7-1-3, 26-2; *MU*, 2-2-8; *IU*, 7.
368. *VP*, 5-74.
369. *Ibid.*, 5-78.
370. *BG*, 2. 54-72.
371. *Ibid.*, 18. 51.
372. *Ibid.*, 18. 52.
373. *Ibid.*, 18. 53.
374. *Ibid.*, 18. 72.
375. *Ibid.*, 6. 15; 18. 54.
376. *Ibid.*, 2. 38; 4. 22; 5. 7, 19; 9, 29; 12. 18; 13. 27.
377. *Ibid.*, 18. 64.
378. *Ibid.*, 18. 55-56.
379. *Ibid.*, 2. 65; 18.66.
380. *Ibid.*, 14. 19-20, 27.

CHAPTER-5

ESSENTIAL NATURE OF SELF AS EXPOUNDED BY ŚRĪ ŚANKARA AND ŚRĪ RĀMĀNUJA

Through this chapter a comparative account of Śrī Śaṅkara and Śrī Rāmānuja about the inner nature of the self with respect to their Commentaries upon the *Bhagavad Gītā* is sharply attempted; and out of it, it is justified that, the understanding of the inner nature of the self helps the individual and the society.

5.1. ŚRĪ ŚAṄKARA'S AND ŚRĪ RĀMĀNUJA'S COMMENTARIES – A REVIEW

As one of the main scriptures of *Prasthānatrayam,* the *Bhagavad Gītā* has been approached by them with their own philosophical notions of 'monism' and 'pluralism'. Śrī Śaṅkara's Commentary is earlier than Śrī Rāmānuja's.[1] He holds his doctrine that, eventhough the Ultimate Reality is unborn, eternal, indestructible, pure, intelligent and free, it appears to the world for the preservation of the spiritual force. He affirms the material principle of the universe as *māyā*, which initiates the wrong perception of the unreal as real. *Māyā* is controlled by Brahman, i.e., indeed it does not exist independently of Brahman. He has equated *ātman* with Brahman. There is a difference because *ātman* is subjected to the influence of *māyā*. He accepts two principles that *puruṣa* alone is real and *prakṛti* is unreal where the matter is the modification of *māyā*. It is neither real nor unreal, but at the final extreme it seems to be null and void, i.e., not at all an existing principle; rather it could be explained as a 'false appearance'. Śrī Śaṅkara supports the *jñāna yoga* as the means to cessation of *saṁsāra*.[2] In his commentary he states, that, all the selves are one and the pluralistic language refers only to the individual bodies. While differentiating the self with body, he comments, that, the selves are qualitatively one as Brahman, and the terms as 'I', 'thou' and 'these rulers' refer only to the material bodies.[3] He advocates, that, by cessation of the *avidyā* through *jñāna*, the individual could experience the pluralistic appearance as false. So, he attempted his commentary to stress the necessity of *jñāna* to reveal the oneness of the self through the proper explanation of the *avidyā*.

Śrī Rāmānuja's Commentary is entirely different from that of Śrī Śaṅkara. He gives importance to the *bhakti yoga* and treats the *karma yoga* and *jñāna yoga* as means to the first. He formulates his Commentary with the philosophical expositions of the *apṛthaksiddhaviśeṣaṇa*, i.e., the existence of the three intertwined realities of *Īśvara*, the *cit* and the *acit*. *Īśvara* is fundamental and supreme; and the *cit* and *acit* are His attributes. He by all means criticizes Śrī Śaṅkara's *māyā* theory and upholds the physical nature as true and real; and they are the bodies to the Brahman as the self to the individual body. Śrī Rāmānuja states that the finite selves are many and they bear intrinsic plurality and individuality for ever. The Ultimate Reality is infinite and transcends the finite selves by its perfection. In the text, the Reality is Lord Kṛṣṇa and He sustains His existence within all the living and non living beings as their *antaryāmi* Brahman.

5.2. ŚRĪ ŚAṄKARA'S VIEWS OF THE SELF

The controversy between Śrī Śaṅkara and Śrī Rāmānuja starts in the twelfth verse of the second chapter and first verse of the thirteenth chapter. The twelfth verse of the second chapter is, 'Never did I not exist, nor thou, nor these rulers of men; and no one of us will ever hereafter cease to exist'.[4] Śrī Śaṅkara commends, that, the self is eternal and exists in past, present and future. He adds, that, the pluralistic language is used to refer to only the death of the material bodies. He comments, that, due to the mental endurance one perceives maniness of the bodies. But this pluralism certainly does not represent the selves, because one self just appears as many with respect to the bodies and due to the specific influence of *avidyā* within the individual. The second verse of the thirteenth chapter is, 'And do thou also know Me *Kṣetrajña* in all *Kṣetras*'.[5] For this he explains that the *Kṣetrajña* within the manifold *kṣetras* is Ultimate Reality. The manifoldness of the individual is due to the various *upādhis*, 'conditions'. These *upādhis* are derivation of the *avidyā*. To understand the reason, it is quite obvious to understand the various metaphysical explanations of the self and the reasons for its false appearance.

Śrī Śaṅkara considers the self as eternal and undifferentiated *sat cit ānanda* 'pure being, pure consciousness and pure bliss'. Pure being represents that the self is the absence of the negation of limitedness and infinite. Pure consciousness refers to the real feature of *svaprakāśa*, 'original nature'. It is neither the substratum of consciousness nor as an object of it, but itself as self-revealing and self-luminous. Pure bliss connotes that, the actual nature of the self which is apart from the falsity of *antaḥkarṇa*, 'mere instrument for pleasure and pain, suffering and sorrow'. This original state transcends the all phenomenal sphere and enjoys the pure freedom and bliss.[6] The embodied self is considered to be the subject-object complex. The subjective element is *sākṣin*, 'pure consciousness' and the objective element is *antaḥkaraṇa*, 'five *indriyas*'. They are as a whole considered to be the active principle of the real agent, the enjoyer and the owner of the merits and demerits of the phenomenal activities. So, the self does not refer to the body but the non-dual universal self. Due to *avidyā* the person indwells in false motion of 'I'-ness and 'My'-ness. The *avidyā* starts at the time of mind clings with the fleeting sensations and ideas. Śrī Śaṅkara says, that, the individuality is nothing but the mere form of the combination of the *vṛtti*, 'mode of *antaḥkaraṇa*' with the object, where the *avidyā* is linked with the internal organ and causes the individuality. The subjective element *sākṣin* connotes the *vṛtti* ignorance in the empirical sphere. In dreaming stage, it works with ignorance. In deep sleep, the *sākṣin* alone works without ignorance, where the *sākṣin* mingles with all existing being as one. Here liberation means destroying the *avidyā* link from the *sākṣin* by the *jñāna*. So, Śrī Śaṅkara argues, that, the self cannot be revealed by others because there is no *vyāpti*, 'invariable concomittance' between the *probans* and the loci of the *probans*.[7]

Māyā is always with the self till *mokṣa*. *Māyā* is not pure illusion. It is *bhāva rūpa*, 'positive wrong knowledge' and *śakti*, 'potency and indescribably real and unreal'. It is neither existence nor non-existence or both. It is considered to be non-existence because Brahman alone is the existence and not the other. It is non-existence because Brahman reveals as the world. So, the shell is mistaken as silver because the silverness is superimposed upon the shellness. But if *brahma*, 'pure descriptive *jñāna*' arises, the *bhrānti*, 'error' is removed from the mind. So, Brahman is the real base of the ground, on which the world appears through *māyā* and it can be realised through *jñāna*.

5.2.1. Śrī Śaṅkara's Doctrine of *Māyā*

The *advaita* can be summarized as *brahma satyaṁ jagat mithyā jīvo brahmaiva naparaḥ*, 'Brahman is the only Reality; the world is ultimately false; and the individual self is non-different from Brahman'. Śrī Śaṅkara distinguishes two kinds of *māyā* as *āvaraṇa* and *vikṣepa*, where the former is the negative aspect of concealment and the latter is the positive aspect of the projection. The positive aspect of *māyā* provides the medium for the reflection and projection of Brahman as *sakti*. The *śakti* is indistinguishable and absolutely dependent upon Brahman. Śrī Śaṅkara differentiates Brahman and *jīva* in accordance with *māyā*. The Brahman unaffected by *māyā* through the positive aspect appears as *Īśvara* and the same Brahman through the negative *avidyā* which exists as embodied *jīva*. With this background, Śrī Śaṅkara formulates nine different characteristic features of the *māyā* or *avidyā*. If one understands the different aspects of *māyā*, it will be very easy to understand his position of monism in the *pāramārthika* state and pluralism in the *vyāvahārika* state. They are: (i) It is *jaḍa*, 'material and unconscious principle' as *prakṛti* in *Sāṅkhya*. It is opposed to pure consciousness or Brahman. Though as *prakṛti*, it is neither real nor independent. (ii) It is *śakti*, 'potency of Brahman'. It is coeval, absolutely dependent, inseparable and non-different from Brahman. The relation between *māyā* and Brahman is *tādātmya*, 'neither identical nor different nor both'. *Māyā* acts as a medium of projection of the world of plurality. (iii) *Avidya* or *māyā* is beginningless. (iv) Eventhough it is not real, it is *bhāvarūpa*, 'positive power'. (v) It is *sat asat anirvacanīya*, 'indescribable and indefinable' because it is neither real nor unreal. It is real because there is no existence apart from Brahman. It is unreal because it projects the unreal world as the real. In other words, *māyā* is not real because it can be removed by true *jñāna* and it is not unreal because it seems to be true as long as it is there with the individual. (vi) It has *vyāvahārikasatta*, 'phenomenal and relative character' and the *vivarta*, 'appearance of the world'. (vii) It is *adhyāsa* and *bhrānti*, 'superimposition of one thing for another like rope as snake and shell as silver'. (viii) It is *vijñānanirasya*, which can be removed by true *jñāna*, i.e., before *vidya*, the *avidya* will not exist. In other words when rope is known the illumination of the rope-snake disappears. (ix) It is *āśraya*, 'locus' and *viṣaya*, 'object'. Both are Brahman only but He is unaffected by them as magician is unaffected by his own magic or the colourless *ākāśa* is unaffected by its colour.

According to Śrī Śaṅkara *māyā* acts as *viparītagrāhikā*, 'absence of knowledge'. It is not only non-apprehension but also misapprehension of the reality. Because of this character the infinite looks as finite, the manifoldness of phenomenal appearance exposing the boundless *ātman* as limited *jīvas* with false notion of plurality and differences among them. The above said appearances are not ultimately real because if one acquires the true discriminative knowledge, all are destroyed. In simple, the Ultimate Supreme Reality through *avidyā* appears as the manifold worlds as pure water appears in the form of dirty foam[8]. He assumes the appearance as the practical reality because he confirms that there is truth even in error and in illusory appearances. He adds, that, so long as one is within ignorance, the world looks real. In other sense, the cause-effect analogy expresses that the main cause of Brahman is independently real and the manifold experiences of effects are only the unreal appearance. Where the manifoldness depend upon the main cause just as the real water appears as in the separated from bubbles, ripples and waves.[9]

He advocates his *advaitic* stand point through various arguments. He explains that the unreal *māyā* cause the real Brahman to appear as the phenomenal pluralism. Śrī Śaṅkara says that if one is entangled within the mud he can get out of it through the same mud and thorn pricked in the body can be removed by the same thorn.[10] Like this, the individual can get self realisation by understanding the *māyā* and its connection with Brahman. Through this he concludes, that, the manifoldness of the unreal selves and the world will appear as real until the realisation of the *jīva* with Brahman through *jñāna* by eradicating the *māyā*. His view reveals that Brahman grants degrees of Realities even in dreams, illusions and errors. According to him the real refers to the absolute real for ever.

Eventhough the Absolute Reality is indeterminate, indescribable, non-dual, beyond speach, mind and description, it brings down within the categories of *buddhi* as an object of our thought, i.e., *Īśvara*. Whenever one thinks within the human limit, he perceives only the conditional *Īśvara*, but beyond the limit the same reality is visualized as monistic Brahman. His description of *Īśvara* is as the *sat cit ānanda* as the perfect Lord on *māyā* and as the soul of souls. *Īśvara* is the immanent ruler as the *antaryāmin*, as the creator, as the sustainer and as the destroyer. The same is the source of everything as supreme universal whole as the object of devotion, as the inspirer of moral order and as the whole bearing identity-in-difference. In comparison, his practical exposition of *Īśvara* is just like that of Śrī Rāmānuja's description of Brahman.

To understand the *māyā* or *avidyā* as the centre for pluralism, there are two theories as *pratibimbavāda*, 'reflection theory' and *avacchedavāda*, 'limitation theory'. *Pratibimbavāda* states that *Īśvara* is the reflection of Brahman in *māyā* and Brahman limited by *avidyā* or its product of *antaḥkaraṇa* is *jīva*. In order to avoid the difficulties of *pratibimbavāda* i.e., how the formless Brahman is reflected within the same centre of *māyā*, Śrī Śaṅkara and his followers answer that both are identical with the original and reflective image, '*bimbapratibimba bhedavāda*'. As for the difficulty in *avacchedavāda*, i.e., how the *māyā* and *avidyā* limit the unconditional Brahman, Śrī Śaṅkara and his followers reconcile the difficulty and support the third theory of *abhdavāda*. The *abhdavāda* says, that, the *Īśvara* and *jīva* are the manifestations of Brahman. Śrī Śaṅkara's monistic system distinguishes the absolute standpoint from the relative standpoint, i.e., *pāramārthika* and *vyāvahārika*, where what is true and one state is not true in another state. The distinction between one *jīva* and the other is true in the *vyāvahārika* level but all are merged and forms the absolute monism in the *pāramārthika* level. He explains, that, even though the absolute is *nirguṇa* when one relates it with the worldly level the same reality seems to be *saguṇa*. So, he affirms his philosophy through the single absolute Brahman in two forms through his doctrine of *māyā*.[11] The non-dual nature of absolute is understood through the discriminative *jñāna* and the process of negation, i.e., negating the known with the unknown which is ultimately true.[12]

Śrī Śaṅkara mixes his total philosophy with the principle of *adhyāsa*, 'wrong *jñāna*'. Due to this *adhyāsa* the pure conscious self relates to the *jñāta*, 'knower' with the *manas* and leads to the pluralistic condition. When the *adhyāsa* disappears by raising the true *jñāna*, the *buddhi* identifies the original standpoint of the self and God as one.[13] The special feature of his philosophy is that he specifies *māyā* as a divine power and a positive entity. *Māyā* bears no beginning and it is subordinated by *jñāna*. Eventhough *māyā* is considered as consort of Parabrahman it is subordinate to the *manas* like illusion to the *jñāna* of *jīva*.[14] In simple, his *avidyā* may be defined as the subjective phenomena of the individual's finitude.[15]

Śrī Śaṅkara gives various reasons for the pluralistic appearance of the *ātman*-Brahman in the *vyāvahārika* state. They are: (i) Due to the association of the modified *upādhis* with Parabrahman in the empirical realm, it appears as many selves. (ii) *Jīvas* being one, the pluralistic appearance represents the *jīvas* with finite ideas. (iii) *Jīvas* are nothing but the Brahman, but its pluralistic appearance is like one *jīva* exists in different bodies. (iv) Empirically *jīvas* are many in accordance with the different *antaḥkaraṇas* and the *upādhis*. It is just like all pervasive air as Brahman, which is assumed as *jīva*, which is within the pot or room.[16] (v) *Advaintins* agree, that, within the empirical order the selves are many because of the numerous mind with its own personalities as the different parts of the *ajñāna*.[17]

Through the theory of *pratibimbavāda* and the example of a jugglar who performs his tricks, Śrī Śaṅkara explains the real nature of self. The theory of *pratibimbavāda* explains that the individual selves are nothing but the reflections of the Universal Self - 'Ultimate Reality' like the reflected image of the sun in the ponds. The manifestation of the sun in the sky differs from the original sun and its actual reflection. Like this, the reflected selves are the partial and imperfect revelations of the Universal Self where the infiniteness of God may not be condensed in the same reflected selves.[18] He describes the same through the illustration of a juggler and his exhibited tricks where the exhibited tricks are not real because it is produced by the juggler. The appearance of the self is not real but mere *māyā* which is always within the self but actually the individual self is nothing but the Brahman Himself.[19] So, when the pure *jñāna* is acquired the *sākṣin* or the seer gets illumined by losing its separate existence. The *Upaniṣad* describes the *jīva* as the combination of the reality and appearance, i.e., self and the not-self with the analogy of two birds on a tree. One bird or *jīva* possesses the ego sense and indulges in worldly activities. Then it missed the opportunity to associate with the substance of the Ultimate Reality. So, it leads to sufferings and sorrows, pleasure and pain with respect to its law of *karma*. At the same time, another bird or the *jīva* knows itself as Reality and the witness of self as *sākṣin* remains as such without any modifications of the worldly activities of the empirical realm.[20] He perceives the different states of the self, by which he proves the identical feature of the *jīva* and the Brahman. For this, he refers to five stages of the consciousness as *jagra*, 'walking', *svapna*, 'dreaming', *suṣupti*, 'sleeping', *turīya*, 'deep sleep' and *turīyātīta*, 'pure self conscious state'. In the first state, the self is having the consciousness of the external objects. In the second state *indriyas, manas* and *buddhi* are working. In this state the self knows the external object through memory and impressions of *saṁsāra*. It results the duality of subject and object. In the third state *ahaṅkāra* and consciousness are working. In the fourth stage the conscious self alone exist and observes the above three states. But in the *turīyātīta* state, eventhough the self exists as Brahman, it realises the all above stated states. Then this state is referred as the state of pure self.[21]

The individual ascribes the qualities of *anātman* to the *ātman* because of the erroneous perception caused by the beginningless illusion or *anādimāyā*. This pluralistic quality can be destroyed by true *jñāna*.[22] By understanding *māyā*, the self is understood as the subject possessed of no attibutes through the distinction of the substance from its attributes by pure *jñāna*. The selves are regarded as eternal, infinite, indivisible, self-luminous and undifferentiated *sat cit ānanda*. In this place the modified feelings of pleasure and pain are realised as the product of different adjuncts, *'antaḥkaraṇa'*.[23]

The explanation of *avidyā* is necessary to evolve *Advaitic* conception of monism. *Advaitic* treatment of the *avidyā* represents the cosmic principle which is responsible for the world of illusion. It is *ajñāna* which is responsible for *bramopādāna*, 'cause of all illusions'. This *avidyā* is *bhāvarūpa*, 'positive entity' and *anādi*, 'beginningless'. It is *anirvacanīya* because it cannot be realised as either *sat* or *asat*. Through the explanation of the *māyā* as *anirvacanīya*, the Brahman can be visualized. Eventhough Brahman alone is real the appearance of Brahman cannot be ignored through proper *jñāna*. So, the plurality is considered to be the *asat*.[24] While explaining the *Īṣṭasiddhi* of *Vimuktātman*, Prof. P.K. Sundaram describes that the plurality of effect is the unreal and the Brahman alone is real through his explanation of the term *'neha nānāstri'*.[25] In the *nānātva*, the suffix *'tva'* explains the meaning of reluctant. So, the plurality does not exist at all in Brahman. The same meaning also can be inferred from the following texts, that, *yatra hi advaitaṃ iva bhavati, taditara itaraṁ pasyati* , 'existence of the plurality and the difference from Brahman are due to the *avidyā* within the individual' and *yatra tvasya sarvaṃ ātmaivabhūt tat kenakaṁ paśyat*, 'experience of the difference will be avoided when true *jñāna* mingle within the individual'.[26]

The locus of the *avidyā* is only within the intelligent self. But due to the *tāmasic guṇa* the individual is unable to distinguish between the self and the *avidyā* except by right *jñāna*. The *tāmasic guṇa* causes pluralistic illusion of the manifestation of the selves because the inherent property of *avidyā* initiates the country of truth or doubt and causes disorder within the perception of the truth like *timira*, 'an eye disease causing dimness of sight'.[27] To understand the monism as such, the place of *vidyā* or *māyā* should be understood within the states of the *vyāvahārika* and the *pāramārthika*. *Advaita* always maintains that anything which is subject to cognition must be real where the *Advaitic* view creates an impression of being real erroneous dream and the normal human experiences, instead of which, they are having different measures of reality. Within the *vyāvahārika* state the pluralistic manifestation of the empirical order is real. This empirical world becomes the real until the individual gets the Brahman intuition. In other words, the unreal empirical order appears as apparently real within the *pratibhāsika* state. So, it should be considered as *mithyā*, 'the false appearance'. The unreality of the *vyāvahārika* state is visualized only in the *pāramārthika* state, where the eternal Brahman is *sat* which bears no-contradiction. In short, in the *vyāvahārika* state there is *pratīti*, 'cognition' and *bādha*, 'substitution of one thing for another' like snake-rope. The same state is not *sat* because there is cognition but it is *asat* because there is sublimation. Since the *vyāvahārika* state is self-contradictory due to its actual form of *māyā* or *avidyā*. *Advaitin* brings out Brahman as *pāramārthika* or absolutely real. It is absolutely real because it transcends the empirical order. In short, the triple experience and the empirical plurality caused by the *māyā* or *avidyā* is verified as the unreal and the Brahman alone is to be considered as real.[28]

Through the *kāryakaraṇa vicāra*, 'technique of cause and effect', Śrī Śaṅkara exposes the monistic standpoint. According to him, the Brahman associated with *māyā* stands as *abhina nimittopādana karaṇa*, 'material and efficient cause'. The *māyā* is indispensable associated with Brahman. Here, the manifold world and the appearance of the pluralism of selves are described through the *vivartavāda*, 'theory of apparent change' of Brahman and not through the theory of *parināmavāda*, 'theory of actual transformation'. In simple, the Brahman can be understood as *vivartaupādānakāraṇa*, 'transfigurative materials cause' and the *māyā* must be *parinnama upādānakārana*, 'transformative material cause'. According to the theory of *vivartavāda*, the pluralistic *vyāvahārika* state, *pratibhāsika* state and *pāramārthika* state beat different levels of ontrological status. In other words, the *pāramārthika* state stands in the highest ontological status and the *vyāvahārika* state stands in the lower. But at the time of proper *jñāna*, the *vyāvahārika* state will become *asat* because the world does not have the same real nature as that of Brahman. In addition to this, *māyā*, the apparent expression is also ultimately *sat* because while *jñāna* illumines *māyā* becomes *mithya*. Considering all these, Brahman appears as pluralistic as well as the efficient cause because of the association with *māyā*. When the individual gets true *jñāna*, the pluralistic unreality of the world and the *māyā* can be negated. Then the Brahman cannot be assumed as the cause of the pluralisitic universe. So, he concludes, that, Brahman alone must be one of the pluralistic appearance and that do is only because of the *māyā*.[29]

Due to *avidyā* in the empirical level, the essential nature of the self as Brahman is conjoined within the five sheaths of *annamaya kośa*, *prāṇamaya kośa*, *manomaya kośa*, *vijñānamaya kośa* and *ānandamaya kośa*. The sheaths of the individual other than the self could be distinguished as three *śarīras* as *sthūla śarīra*, *sūkṣma śarīra* or the *prāṇamaya*, *manomaya* and *vijñānamaya kośas* and the *karaṇa śarīra* or the *ānandamāya kośa*. The essential self seeks to identify with any one of the sheaths and paves the way for pluralistic notion because the sheaths of the different individual express different characteristic features. But according to *Advaita*, the essential self is not that of the sheaths or the three bodies. If one realises the same through proper *jñāna* he can easily understand the identification of the self which is no other than the Brahman.[30]

From the empirical standpoint, the self involves three kinds of *avasthātraya*, 'experiences' as *jāgra*, *svapna*, and *turīya*. These three kinds of experiences are due to the *upādhi* caused by the *avidyā*. Within the walking and dreaming states the *viśva* and *taijasa* are disturbed the self through errors like *agrahaṇa*, 'non-apprehension' and *anyathāgrahaṇa*, 'misapprehensions of the truth'. In the deep sleep stage the self is disturbed by *agrahaṇa* conditioned by *avidyā*. The whole treatment helps to know, that, the above triple stream of experiences is not the essential nature of the self but these are due to *upādhika*, 'adventurous property'. But a person who realizes the actual nature of the self as Brahman by removal of the *avidyā* by *jñāna*, the same individual attains the fourth stage of *turīyātīta* where the individual experiences the state of *ekameva advitīyam*, 'self is one and one only'.[31]

According to *Advaita*, the oneness of *ātman*-Brahman and the pluralistic appearance of the world possess the same grade of reality as the appearance of snakeness in the rope. This kind of non-difference establishes the apparent identity or the illusory nature of the world.[32] *Advaita* also removes the conflict that if *ātman* is Brahman, then Brahman also should be responsible for evilness. For this *Advaita* gives the example of the unchangeable nature of the magician who produces multiple changes without changing them basically. So, Brahman will not change but His power of *māyā* causes the apparent diversity in creation.[33] The apparent multiple effect of the world comes out because Brahman through *vivarta* and *māyā* and *pariṇāma* causes the same. For example, the existence of the pot resembles the Brahman but the inert nature of the pot refers to the active play of *māyā*.[34] While approaching the nature of the self, the *Bhagavad Gītā* explains it as atomic, as agent and as part of God. If it is so, the self must be plural.

But Śrī Śaṅkara observes, that, it is not the nature of the self but the self within the empirical state as *saṁsārin*, where it assumes as such because the self mingles with the *māyā*, i.e., *buddhi, manas* and the *indriyas*.[35]

The pluralistic appearances of the selves and the world are due to the superimposition to the consciousness by memory as something which has previously been observed by the same consciousness as silver within the shell.[36] *Advaita* considers the *anubhūti*, 'consciousness' itself as self which is having the characteristic features of *svayamprakāśa*, 'content knowledge'. It is neither produced nor destroyed and it manifests the other object, but it does not manifest like Brahman. This consciousness is beyond the *vyāvahārika* distinction of knower, known and the knowledge. The *Advaitic* conception of the transcendental and eternal consciousness is undifferentiated and indeterminate. It is *svataḥsiddha*, 'self-evident' or 'self-proved'. Being consciousness as *svyamprakāśa* and unproduced, it does not admit the plural nature. The plurality of consciousness within the empirical state does not imply the actual nature of the consciousness because within the state, the eternal consciousness is governed by the different objects and different finite selves. This is due to the different adjuncts like the single moon which appears as many when reflected by the waves.[37]

5.2.2. Śrī Śaṅkara's Epistemological Background

He maintains the *anubhūti* or consciousness as an independent and eternal existence which is equated with the Ultimate Reality. It refers to the countless knowledge which is neither produced nor destroyed but manifests in everything. But by itself it is not manifested by any other entity because it shines in its own state as *svayamprakāśa*. Śrī Śaṅkara maintains this as the self or the eternal reality or the Supreme Brahman. In the *vyāvahārika* state, the apparent distinction of knower, known and knowledge is not in the self. But the *antaḥkaraṇavṛtti,* 'psychosis of the inner organ' refers to the knowledge which is considered to be the determinant of consciousness.[38] In the *pāramārthika* state, the *antaḥkaraṇa,* 'product of *māyā*' is removed by right *jñāna,* where the pure consciousness exhibits itself as the self. But Śrī Rāmānuja echoes the above conception through the criticism of the knowledge as subjective, to which it belongs and the same as an object to which it refers. He explains, that, knowledge relates with a particular permanent spiritual entity, i.e., the self. In this way, Śrī Rāmānuja rejects Śrī Śaṅkara's view of consciousness as identical with the Ultimate Reality.

Regarding the transcendental consciousness, Śrī Śaṅkara adds, that, the undifferentiated and indeterminate character of consciousness and the knowledge can be understood because consciousness is self-evident and self proved. The materials of the world manifest because of the subjective knowledge which persist within the transcendental consciousness. Eventhough during the waking state, the experience of the consciousness becomes apparent. It can be felt clearly in the state of *samādhi* and *mukti*. In detail, this state can be visualized in the state of pure consciousness as the pure subject and not as an object at any time. Consciousness as *svayamprakāśa,* 'self-luminous' is *nitya,* 'eternal' and it can be neither produced nor destroyed.[39] Since consciousness is unproduced it cannot bear the features of *vikāra,* 'transmutation'.

Because of the characteristic features of *nitya* and *nirvikāra* Śrī Śaṅkara stresses his monistic attitude of *ātman*-Brahman. The plurality refers to the objects which are produced in the conscious realm. They are unreal but depending upon the different objects. Like the One Self which appears as many like the moon appearing as many upon the reflected waves. His conception of the *ātman* can be understood through Prof. S.M. Srinivasachari's explanation of the consciousness as, "The transcendental consciousness which is self-luminous, eternal and immutable is the very self (*ātman*) in so far as it is sentient (*ajaḍa*) unlike an object. True knowledge in other words, is identical with the Reality".[40]

He explains *ātman*-Brahman as *nirviśeṣa* or *nirguṇa* or qualityless. During the deep sleep state, the *tṛpti* status is absent, i.e., cognizer, the cognized and cognition are absent. But the self exist as witness of self. There is no possibility for relative knowledge to justify because he may not be aware of the subject, object and he himself. So, after sleep, the sleep experience is recollected by consciousness in the form of *nirviśeṣa vastu* bereft of distinction. In short, perception while deep sleep proves the self or consciousness as *nirveśaṣa*, 'qualityless'. Śrī Śaṅkara proves the Brahman as *nirviśaṣa*. For this, he says, that, whatever is particularized by name and form should arise from the more general where there is no name and form. For example, a pot and a pan are the *viśeṣas*, 'particulars'. He considers the Brahman as the highest universal, who is beyond distinction where the worlds exist in name and form, i.e., *viśeṣa* as pot and pan. So, the Brahman as *nirviśaṣa* can be seen through the following arguments.

Ātman-Brahman is *nirviśaṣa,* because it is experienced without qualities and distinctions in *suṣupti*. What is experienced without qualities and distinction is *nirviśeṣa*.[41] Śrī Śaṅkara states, that, the *śabda* conveys the non-relational sense. For example, the sentence, 'the flower is red' exposes relational meaning at present context. But the sentence 'this is that *Devadatta*' expresses non-relational knowledge because '*Devadatta*' present in the identical with what is present now and here. In other words, removing the set of determinants, the meaning conveyed here is bare substantive, i.e., *Devadattas* of the identical. In other words, the meaning does not bear *viśeṣanavastu* by the bare substantive of *nirviśeṣanavastu*.[42]

5.2.3. Proximity of Śrī Śaṅkara's Monism to the *Bhagavad Gītā*

The second chapter of the *Bhagavad Gītā* explains the nature of the self as the real, all-pervading, changeless, immutable and indestructible. They are supporting Śrī Śaṅkara's monistic description of the self as Brahman.[43] The seventh chapter[44] and the thirteenth chapter[45] describe the attributelessness of Brahman one ultimate immutable and its manifold appearance within the worldly order. The twelfth chapter explains the *nirguṇa* Brahman as the real nature and the *saguṇa* Brahman as the creation of *māyā*.[46] This also supports the monism of *ātman*-Brahman state. The text has many verses to explain the identity of Brahman and the *ātman*.[47] In order to advance the reason for the illusory appearance of the world, the *Bhagavad Gītā* describes variations of the *guṇas* and the implication of *māyā*.[48]

5.3. CRITISM OF ŚRĪ ŚAṄKARA'S MONISM BY ŚRĪ RĀMĀNUJA'S PLURALISM

Viśiṣṭādvaita criticizes the absolute consciousness through epistemology, i.e., the dual nature of consciousness as subject and object. The consciousness is not a pure subject but an attribute of the self. Śrī Rāmānuja also proclaims the consciousness as *svaprakāśa*, 'self-luminous' and it is knowable. It is not the *Advaitic* conception of the *nitya* because it is immutable but consciousness are many and subject to change through *saṅkoca* and *vikoca*,'contraction and expansion'. Śrī Rāmānuja rejects the *Advaitic* identity of the consciousness with the self but treats as the attribute of the same spiritual entity.[49]

Against the *Advaitic* conception of the self and consciousness as identical, *Viśiṣṭādvaitin* describes it as a medium which manifests the object not for itself but for the self, i.e., it can only show but cannot know.[50] It is like that of the knowledge which functions for the sake of the self as the attribute of the self as substratum. But both are not identical.

In order to substantiate the *Viśiṣṭādvaitin's* doctrine, Śrī Rāmānuja attacks the *Advaitic* principle of *ajaḍa,* i.e., a state of consciousness as being identical with the self from two different angles. As for *Advaitin, ajaḍa* in one sense as *saṁvidāntara nirapekṣa prakāśa,* 'manifestation of the knowledge of an object without depending upon the other knowledge' and the same term represents the other meaning as *jñāna* which is the nature of manifestation or *prakāśarūpa.* For this, *Viśiṣṭādvaitin* criticizes that the consciousness which manifests itself is untenable because it does not manifest itself but for the self. And if it manifests for some other thing, then the statement itself goes against the *Advaitic* conception of the self. So, the above analysis exposes that the *Advaitic* perspectives of consciousness as self, which bears the untenable nature under the conception of *ajaḍa. Viśiṣṭādvaitin* also treats the self as substratum and the consciousness as its attribute through their interpretation of the meaning of self as *jñāta* or knowing subject and *svasmai bhāsamanatvam,* 'manifestation of consciousness for itself'. Regarding *jñāta, Viśiṣṭādvaitin* asks *Advaitin* about the locus for the knowledge or consciousness as *jñānaśraya.* If consciousness is the locus as *advaita,* then it leads to self contradiction, i.e., the same medium becomes a substratum as well as that which understand the same medium is unacceptable. The term *svasmibhāsamanatvam* refers to the manifestation of the consciousness to its substratum and not to itself. Here the term *svasmi* connotes that the self should be the recipient of the manifestation,'*prakāśaphali*' in the empirical order. For this, *Advaita* does not admit but *Viśiṣṭādvaitin* accepts the same.[51]

They state, that, the consciousness is an empirical one which bears the duality of subject and object and not as transcendental consciousness which is considered to be as *ātman*-Brahman. Even Śrī Śaṅkara does not accept the consciousness of the psychosomatic as eternal but only the transcendental consciousness. Regarding this Śrī Rāmānuja draws the main support for the undifferentiated transcendental consciousness of Śrī Śaṅkara from the *pramāṇas*, i.e., no *pramāṇas* support this transcendental consciousness. So, the result is that the consciousness or knowledge is related to subject and object and it exists as qualities to the eternal self.[52] This truth also can be derived from the examination of the *turīya* or deep sleep state by Śrī Rāmānuja. *Advaitin* argues that during the deep sleep state the consciousness perceives the experience as *ajñāna* or ignorance. *Viśiṣṭādvaitin* refuges the above statement that the negation of *jñāna* cannot explicate the experience of that state. So, within the *Advaitin's* statement 'I was not aware of anything all this time', the 'I' the experience of the *sukha svapna* is self, which exists in a quiescent state. Like *Advaitin,* if *ajñāna* is realised by the consciousness within the deep sleep state the *saṁsāra* level may not co-exist with the self. In other words, if pure consciousness is witnessed the experience of the deep sleep where the experience of *saṁsāra* may not be understood because pure consciousness is immutable and indeterminable. But the *saṁsāra* is the outcome of *avidyā* and can be evaded by pure *jñāna*. So, the truth is verified, that, the consciousness is not the pure self and witnesses of the deep sleep experience.[53] This may prove, that, the eternal spiritual self is different from the consciousness.

5.4. ŚRĪ RĀMĀNUJA'S VIEWS OF THE SELF

According to Śrī Rāmānuja selves are different from Brahman each having its own individuality even in *mukti* stage. While commenting on the twelfth verse of the second chapter of the *Bhagavad Gītā* Prof. S.S. Ragavachar quotes Śrī Śaṅkara statement of monism, "Pluralism mentioned is due to the persistent mental habit of looking to the bodies and does not signify a plurality of Spirits".[54] But he criticizes Śrī Śaṅkara's statement and supports Śrī Rāmānuja's views, "While attempting to remove the materialistic delusion of the disciple, the teacher ought not to use language that adopts pluralism that is supposed to be generated by that materialism itself. If he does, we are not entitled to argue that the conception of a plurality of selves is not part of the very doctrine he is inculcating. While liability to death is being negated of the self, that is preciously the text for negating plurality also of it. At bottom both temporarily and plurality are supposed to pertain to the physical aspect of personality. If the latter negation is not effected in the text, it means either that the teaching is imperfect and misleading or that the plurality of selves is a genuine part of the content of teaching".[55] Regarding this, the view is cleared out. For the same, Śrī Rāmānuja explains, that, if absolute monism is correct, then, there is no need of the teachings from the perfect enlightened teacher to other selves. Then there is no possibility for a great seer to be aware of the immediate and complete realization of the Ultimate Reality and conscious of the other selves. In order to reconcile the above gaps, Śrī Rāmānuja strongly recommends *Viśiṣṭādvaitic* views of pluralism.[56]

The second verse of the thirteenth chapter treats the *Kṣetrajña* as *Īśvara*. But Śrī Rāmānuja rejects the above conception of *ātman*-Brahman as identical through the explanation of the term *'api'* which means 'also', where Śrī Rāmānuja explains that Brahman is not identical with the physical world but the language of the identity has been interpreted in the sense of immanence of Him as *antariyāmin*, 'the inner controller'. In this place Śrī Rāmānuja considers the language of identity is not merely valid but it is a necessary factor because the knowledge of the difference between the *Kṣetra* and *Kṣetrajña* and the knowledge of the identity through the conception of *antariyāmin* stands as the body of the supreme Brahman.[57]

In addition Prof. S.S. Ragavachar adds Śrī Rāmānuja's view through which he shakes the *Advaitic* concept. He says, "Does the great God, Vāsudeva, who teaches, know the Ultimate Reality and is He free from ignorance?. If He is, He could have no illusion of other selves and could not, therefore, entertain the ideal of Arjuna's existence and permit Himself to engage in the instruction of Arjuna. If, on the other hand, He has not realised the absolute unity of the *ātman,* He could not, being Himself ignorant, be a teacher of that truth. The *Gītā* tells us that only the seers of truth become teachers property. This dilemma is enough of counterblast to the interpretation advanced".[58] To understand the Śrī Rāmānuja's pluralistic selves; M. Narasimhachari refers to Vedānta Deśika's explanation of the term *Viśiṣṭādvaita*. It includes the *Advaitic* explanation. He says, "The supreme being is only One (*Advaita*). But it has all the sentient and insentient entities (*cit* and *acit*) as its modes or attributes. Though there is thus mutual difference between the modes and the possessor thereof and among the modes themselves, the whole thing is ultimately conceived as a single three-in-one complex unity".[59] Śrī Rāmānuja postulates his pluralistic idea through *satkhyātivāda,* 'realism', *samanādhikāraṇya,* 'co-ordination' and the truth of *jīva* as a *prakāśa* of Brahman. He stresses, that, selves are many and they co-exist with the psychosomatic organism through the transmigration of *saṁsāra* state. At liberation, the realised selves resume the separate and eternal existence as ambiance, where they are not conditioned by space, time and change. Another important fact in connection with the Śrī Rāmānuja's philosophy related to the pluralism is *apṛthaksiddhi* relation, where the *cit* and *acit* are real and ultimate but they are dependent upon Brahman as the attributes depend upon the substance.[60]

Śrī Rāmānuja's *satkhyāti* explains, that, the act of perception as *ātman* and Brahman as one by Śrī Śaṅkara is not that of *anirvacanīyakhyāti,* i.e., inexplicable nature of reality either as real or unreal but non-apprehension where Śrī Rāmānuja considers that the error in perception is only a partial truth and it can be identified as the actual reality by acquiring more perfect and complete knowledge. In this sense, perceiving the plurality of selves within the bodies are not due to the *māyā* but they are real. Śrī Rāmānuja treats the anecdote of shell-silver as the appearance of silver in shell is true because there are some qualities or particles of silver in shell.

Through the philosophy of *satkāryavāda* and the *antaryāmi* Brahman, 'relation of entire world of *cit* and *acit* with Brahman', Śrī Rāmānuja explains the pluralism and the unchangeable state of Brahman. In other words, in the casual state or in the unmanifested state the Brahman, *cit* and *acit* are in subtle form and in the effective or in the manifested state these three are manifested in gross form. Here both are not different in nature. For this, Prof. R. Balasubramanian adds, "That the same substance is the cause and is the effect in another state, and that by the understanding of that substance in its casual state we understood it as existing in another state also owing to the continuity of substance"[61]. In this context, a clarification may be given that eventhough the Brahman is the material cause. He is not a subject who is bearing the changing features and the qualities of imperfection. In order to explain the same Prof. R. Balasubramanian says as, "All change and all imperfection belong only to the beings constituting Brahman's body and Brahman itself is thus proved to be free from all imperfection, a treasure as it were of all imaginable sacred qualities".[62] Eventhough there is plural realities in subtle and gross forms, Brahman is free from changes and imperfections, but there is the presence of the same in *prakṛti* and *jīvas*.

Śrī Rāmānuja explains the self as eternal spiritual entity denoted as the *ahamārtha*, 'the very 'Ego' or 'the notion of 'I'. This view is different from Śrī Śaṅkara's view, i.e., the self is not the 'Ego' because it is only a product of *māyā*, 'illusion'. In this view Śrī Rāmānuja contradicts Śrī Śaṅkara through psychological analysis of the subject, where he criticizes Śrī Śaṅkara's view of the self as not 'I' because it does not persist in the state of *turīyātīta* and *mokṣa*. So, according to Śrī Śaṅkara, if illusory 'I'-ness exists even in *mokṣa* then ignorance would have also co-existed within the state. Since Śrī Śaṅkara's conception of the self is consciousness, he refutes the *ahamārtha* as self but it is the product of *māyā*. Here, Śrī Rāmānuja substantiates his view of 'I'-ness persists in deep sleep and the state of release. After deep sleep the individual puts the statement as 'I slept happily' and 'I was not aware of anything all the time'. The awareness of the self as 'I' represents the prior and subsequent existence of the 'I'-ness. Śrī Śaṅkara stresses his own standpoint that the 'Ego' is not present in deep sleep stage and never recollects the experience of the deep sleep stage because the self as consciousness experiences all as *sākṣin*. Śrī Śaṅkara explains the *sākṣin* as the consciousness qualified per accidents by the internal organ but Śrī Rāmānuja's ego is only the consciousness qualified per proportion by the same internal organ. *Viśiṣṭādvaitin* rejects the experience of sleep because sense organs are not functioning at the time. If consciousness itself is self the presence of the *sākṣin* which experiences the pleasure is untenable because of the presence of *jñāna* immediately after the deep sleep stage. So, criticizing the nature of *jñātṛtva*, 'the act of knowing' and the nature of *sākṣitva*, 'its nature'. *Viśiṣṭādvaitin* rejects the principle of *sākṣin* of *Advaita* through which they substantiate the statement that the self is other than the consciousness through the explanation of the state of deep sleep. Śrī Rāmānuja also stresses that the notion of 'I' has continued even in the state of *mukti*. Where the 'I'-ness does not cause *ajana* to the self but exists in its perfect state because the 'I'-ness in true state does not cause ignorance. If it causes ignorance then the existence of the consciousness itself in deep sleep state causes ignorance. So, in the state of release the perfected 'I'-ness does not cause ignorance to the self. Moreover, if 'I'-ness is absence in the *mukti* state, the attempt to understand the same is inconceivable because if it is absent in that state, then there is no need to study the same even at the time of presence[63]. In other words, the study may not be applicable for anything in concern with the time factor.

According to the epistemological nature of *Viśiṣṭādvaita,* the self is the *jñāna* and not pure consciousness. Consciousness by Śrī Rāmānuja bears two statuses as consciousness of an object and the consciousness of the subject. To assert the features of consciousness, it is not only the consciousness of an object but also somebody's consciousness, i.e., the self in which consciousness is related. So, here the self acts as a *asraya,* 'locus' or 'substance' and the consciousness of the self acts as its attributes. Within this Śrī Rāmānuja distinguishes that realising the self as self may be termed as *dharmibhūtijñāna,* 'substantive consciousness' and conceiving the consciousness of self as its attribute may be the *dharmabhūtajñāna,* 'attribute knowledge'. By elaborating the above conception Śrī Rāmānuja explains that the mere consciousness itself is not the self or one reality as *Advaita.* Connecting *dharma bhūta jñāna* with *apṛthaksiddhaviśeṣaṇa* and the principle of *satkāryavāda,* Śrī Rāmānuja glorifies the relation of *ātmans* with Brahman through the logical and psychological standpoint of *prakāra prakāribhāva,* 'attribute and substance', ontological counterpart of *śarīraśarīribhāva,* 'body and self' and ethical paralalism of *śeṣaśeṣibhāva,* 'means and end'. In the *prakāraprakāribhāva,* the finite selves of *citrūpa,* 'eternal thinking subject' are formed as the essential attributes to the Brahman and *Prakārin.* In the *śarīraśarīribhāva,* Śrī Rāmānuja explains that potential form or in subtle state or in the unmanifested state of *cit* and *acit* are formed as *śarīra,* 'body' of the Brahman in the manifested state. In the *śeṣaśeṣībhāva,* the *cit* is elevated from the boundary of *acit* by getting self-sovereignty where the *cit* is breaking the casualty of *karma* and realising its own nature through the gift of God or His grace and becomes as *śeṣa.* In otherwords, through the *śeṣatva,* 'self realisation of the nature of dependence upon the God', the freed selves move as means to the end, 'supreme Brahman'.[64] Śrī Rāmānuja argues that through epistemology the objects are proved to be *saguṇa,* 'qualified by attributes' and *saviśeṣa,* 'differentiated beings'.

In other words, though his epistemological base, Śrī Rāmānuja formulates his meta-physical standpoint of pluralism. According to Śrī Rāmānuja first *nirvikalpaka*, 'indeterminate perception' follows the second stage of *savikalpaka* or determinate perception. *Nirvikalpaka* perception is perceiving an object for the first time, example, perceiving a cow, where he perceives the same by certain qualities of attributes. In other words, the perceptual knowledge can be expressed in the form of judgment involving subject-predicate relation. When the same individual perceives the second cow, he apprehends the object as qualified. In addition he also perceived the generic character. So, the object perceives in both stages are *saviśeṣa*, 'object qualified by attributes and the definite knowledge of the same'.[65] So, according to Śrī Rāmānuja, through perception, one can argue that each and every object even the selves and Supreme Brahman are bearing definite qualities and they are distinct characters which pave the way for pluralism. Śrī Rāmānuja recommends that the object perceived by inference also should be *śaviśeṣa* because the inference is based on the perception.[66]

Śrī Rāmānuja also supports this view by *śabda*, 'verbal testimony'. For this he advances two kinds of arguments. In general argument, a word conveys meaning which consists of *prakṛti*, 'stem' and, *pratyaya*, 'suffix' and conveys different meaning. That meaning should also have a connection to convey a related meaning, *Viśiṣṭādvaita*. A sentence which consists of above words should convey an object in a relational sense with *saviśeṣa*.[67] In specific arguments, a detailed examination of some of the arguments of the scriptural text proves the object to be *saviśeṣa*. For example, *satyaṁ jñānaṃ anantaṁ brahma* - 'Brahman is real, knowledge and infinite', i.e., Brahman is *saviśeṣa*.[68]

Śrī Śaṅkara elucidates his philosophy of unreality of the pluralism through the proper explanation of the *māyā* or *avidyā*. Eventhough Śrī Rāmānuja accepts the explanation of *māyā* within his principle of law of *karma* given by Śrī Śaṅkara, his explanation of the *māyā, jñāna,* bondage and liberation are different. So, Śrī Rāmānuja formulates his *anupapatti,* the seven-fold objection against Śrī Śaṅkara's theory of *māyā*. They are:

(i) *Āśrayānupapatti*: Brahman may not be the locus of *avidyā* or *māyā*. He may not be the unqualified Brahman as Śrī Śaṅkara because He is pure consciousness or knowledge, then if *avidyā* is ignorance, the unification may not be possible. Individual self also is not the seat because the individuality of the self is due to the effect of *avidyā*. If it is so, there is no possibility of the cause which depends upon the cause. Since it has locus either in Brahman or in the self Śrī Rāmānuja considers the view of *māyā* as pseudo-concept.

(ii) *Tiro-dhānanupapatti*: Since Brahman is self-conscious, self-luminous and self proved the subject of pure knowledge cannot be veiled by the *avidya* like darkness concealing the light.

(iii) *Svarūpānupapatti*: *Advaitin's* conception of the *avidyā* as positive as well as negative may not be fruitful because if it is positive, it is not possible to destroy and there is no necessity to do the same by right *jñāna*. Then *avidyā* is not negative because if it is so, it should not project the world on Brahman. In short, Śrī Śaṅkara's conception of the ignorance is neither positive nor negative and it lacks logical stability.

(iv) *Anirvacanīyatvānupapatti*: *Advaitin* described the *avidyā* as indefinable and indescribable which shows the absurbed self-contraction as either real or as unreal or neither real nor unreal. Śrī Rāmānuja comments that, the reality and unreality are exhaustive and exclusive, i.e., contradictories not contraries. He adds, that, there is no possibility of third alternatives beyond the real or unreal entities. So, Śrī Śaṅkara's conception of the *avidyā* rejects the well established logical corollary, i.e., the law of contradiction and the law of excluded middle.

(v) *Pramāṇānupapatti*: Śrī Rāmānuja attacks the monistic *avidyā* by asking the validity of the same and it is supported by *pramāṇa*. Perception fails because it gives the knowledge of an entity either as the real or unreal. Inference too because it lacks valid mark or middle term and verbal testimony also because they professes the *māyā* as real power creating this universe which belongs to God.

(vi) *Nivartakānupapatti*: *Advaitin* remarks that the unqualified and attributeless knowledge of Brahman wipes out the ignorance. But Śrī Rāmānuja rejects this opinion by arguing that attributeless knowledge is impossible because pure identity is abstraction, discrimination and determination are the basic essential attribute to the knowledge. Hence there is no attributeless knowledge to remove *avidyā*.

(vii) *Nivṛtyānupapatti*: Since *avidyā* is considered to be a *bhāvarūpa*, 'positive entry' and as in *nivartakānupapatti* there is no remover of *avidyā* which explains that the positive entity cannot be removed by the right *jñāna*. Instead of *avidyā* for bondage, Śrī Rāmānuja introduces the concrete reality of *karma* where law of *karma* cannot be removed by right *jñāna* but can be removed by *karma, jñāna, bhakti* and *prasāda*. When *karma* destroys, the *avidyā* evades from the self and this can be possible by the absolute mercy of Lord. At that time the Lord is pleased with the selves who are in constant devotion and extends His absolute grace over the selves.

5.4.1. Proximity of Śrī Rāmānuja's Pluralism to the *Bhagavad Gītā*

For pluralism Śrī Rāmānuja forms extempore francs from the *Bhagavad Gītā*. They are: (i) Supreme reality is Brahman or Puruṣottama or Nārāyaṇa and the selves and matter are His adjectives. To attain His Feet, the spiritual aspiration of *bhakti* and *prapatti mārga* is better means than *karma* and *jñāna mārgas*. (ii) God is beyond that mesh of *māyā* but the selves are brought up into this and they suffer a lot to get *mokṣa*. (iii) To finalize the crisis, God descends to the worldly order through the concept of incarnation out of compassion. The religious belief beyond this is that, God descends to resolve the crisis and make Himself as the object of adoration through which the numerous selves get rid of from the worldly suffering and attain the eternal and spiritual standard. (iv) God descends as Kṛṣṇa, as the teacher of the *Bhagavad Gītā* imparting His message to Arjuna. *Bhakti* is considered as the supreme pathway to *mokṣa*. *Jñāna* and *karma* accelerate the velocity of *bhakti* towards the eternal abode. Śrī Rāmānuja, while approaching pluralism, divides the *Bhagavad Gītā* into three parts. The first six chapter deals about the nature of selves. The middle six chapters stress the supremacy of *bhakti yoga* where God is considered as the object of *bhakti*. The last six chapters describes the nature of *cit* or selves or *puruṣas*, the nature of *prakṛti* or *acit* and the absolute supremacy of the Puruṣottama.[69]

5.5. CRITICISM OF ŚRĪ RĀMĀNUJA'S PLURALISM

Eventhough Śrī Rāmānuja attacks Śrī Śaṅkara's philosophy of monism; the tools used by him are not free from criticisms. They are:

(i) Śrī Rāmānuja remarks that Śrī Śaṅkara's *avidyā* is neither real nor unreal are unnecessary because they do not shake the actual monistic trend. Eventhough Śrī Rāmānuja proves the *avidyā* as unreal, the opinion of Brahman as one does not change because the perception of rope as snake will never change the actuality of the rope, i.e., the wrong cognition of shell as silver does not affect the quality of the shell.

(ii) By rejection the *avidyā* or *māyā* and introducing the law of *karma* to substantiate the reason for the bondage is untenable. As Śrī Śaṅkara's doctrine of *māyā* for cosmic illusion inherent in Brahman as *upādhi* or delimiting adjuncts along with the good as essential attribute for evil, Śrī Rāmānuja proposes the law of *karma* as an essential attribute belonging to the *jīva*. God being the *karmādhyakṣa* or the order of action in the universe proclaims the good and bad, where He introduces *jīva* with appropriate bodies with the power of using the same to their best advantage. In the universe, *jīvas* alone have the moral responsibility for goodness or badness but not the God. Since *karma* causes the endless *saṁsāra*, the *jīva* is not the effect of the *karma*. By using the power of freedom, the individual *jīva* acts in a good way, i.e., through *bhakti* and *prapatti*, the *jīva* has to realise itself and reach the state of *mukti* and the state of *nityamukti*.[70] In other words, if the individuals follows *bhakti* and *prapatti*, the self freed from self-feeling and the relics of the effects of the law of *karma*. The Supreme Lord due to His infinite grace reveals Himself as His own *antaryāmin*. Where the selves realize the union and then resides within the *paramapada*, 'supreme abode'.[71] Śrī Rāmānuja accepts the law of *karma* as beginningless i.e., beginningless *saṁsāra* due to the law of *karma*. It is just like Śrī Śaṅkara's beginningless *avidyā*. In short, by argument one can say that *avidyā* of Śrī Śaṅkara and Śrī Rāmānuja's law if *karma* are beginningless. Then both approach the same problem from different starting point but meet their inefficiency in single point.

(iii) Śrī Rāmānuja's conception of *avidyā* does not conceal the Brahman because Śrī Śaṅkara stresses the point like the clouds which actually do not conceal the sun but valid all the same for sometime. True *jñāna* reveals the Brahman where ignorance fades and darkness disappears when light appears.

(iv) Śrī Śaṅkara approaches *avidyā* as neither positive nor negative entity. His monism is made clear that before *jñāna*, *avidyā* exists as real but after *jñāna* it disappears as unreal.

(v) Even *Advaitins* themselves accept *avidyā* as indiscernible. Since it is an admitted truth this can be realised only when the individual raises his level through his right *jñāna* but not before it.

(vi) Since *avidyā* is neither real nor unreal the law of contradiction and the excluded middle are not over thrown by Śrī Śaṅkara. Śrī Śaṅkara maintains that error or illusion or dream as the real till the time of *jñāna*. Then they become unreal because the reality is realised by the same individual.

(vii) Śrī Śaṅkara's *avidyā* as real or unreal is for the purpose of explaining the nature of superimposition. The super imposition vanishes when the reality is known by right and intuitive *jñāna*, then the self reaches *mokṣa*. Śrī Rāmānuja also accepts this in another form, i.e., *bhakti* and *prapatti* which draw the grace of God for right *jñāna* which ends in *mukti*.

(viii) Within the *apṛthaksiddhaviśeṣaṇa*, Śrī Rāmānuja fails to differentiate the attributive relation of *cit* with Brahman and the same relation of *acit*. Eventhough he adopts the external differences of attributes and substances the same differences lead to the internal also. According to him the selves and matter are attributes of God but in themselves they are considered to be substances. This cannot be stable because it is conjoined only in a relative sense; but it is not a subtle difference. In other words, maintaining *cit* and *acit* as real substance as well as the real attribute bear logical contradiction. When comparing Śrī Śaṅkara's view of the real existence as absolute and the apparent existence as selves and matter, Śrī Rāmānuja's conception may not be tenable, i.e., a substance may not be real if it depends upon God. Since Śrī Rāmānuja reconciles the two extremes of *Upaniṣadic* Absolutism and *Vaiṣṇavistic* Theism, it stands as a main theme for criticism because the relative existence or identity as well as differences of *cit* and *acit* upon Brahman is a mere abstraction. Maintaining absolutism and pluralism or identity and differences are untenable because light and darkness cannot belong to the same status in the same sense.

(ix) Śrī Rāmānuja's qualitative monism and quantitative pluralism are unacceptable because Śrī Rāmānuja himself accepts that, when self realises its own state, the material bodies wil be disappeared. Moreover, his conception of the selves as diverse atomic units of unconsciousness might be the result of his own imagination.

(x) While Śrī Rāmānuja connects the two extremes of empirical as well as transcendental self in a pluralistic way. It bears inconsistency because the individual *jīva* or the 'I' consciousness is subject to finite knowledge and the centre for introspection. But the transcendental consciousness is the self-luminous, self-conscious and changeless through the births and deaths. In other words, there is absolute impossibility to connect the mundane and the transcendental existence.

(xi) While Śrī Rāmānuja combines the *Upaniṣadic* Absolutism and *Pāñcarātras* Theism,[72] he did not substantiate his standpoint. If God is the *antariyāmin* to the *cit* and *acit*, there is no basic philosophical reason for Him to reside in the Vaikuṇṭha with His consort Lakṣmi along with the *nityamukta* and *mukta*. In addition to this, maintaining the selves of *nityamukta* is untenable because philosophically selves are the either in *mukti* or in *baddha* state.

(xii) The relation of selves with *dharmabhūtajñāna* is untenable because if consciousness is the attribute of the selves the quality of consciousness with the character of expansion and contradiction is beyond verification.

(xiii) Śrī Rāmānuja fails to assert the reason for the origin of the law of *karma* upon the pure, changeless and self conscious subject. A close observation reveals that the ignorance due to the law of *karma* of Śrī Rāmānuja is just like Śrī Śaṅkara's *avidyā* or *māyā* because both are formulated on the same concept out of the beginningless *saṁsāra* and *ajñāna*.

5.6. MONISM AND PLURALISM - A CRITICAL ESTIMATE

Śrī Śaṅkara supports the absolute monism and Śrī Rāmānuja modifies the same into pluralism through *apṛthaksiddhaviśeṣaṇa*, i.e., eventhough Brahman, *cit* and *acit* are inseparably unified as a group, the latter two are firmly dependent upon the former.

Advaitin concludes that, *ātman* and Brahman is one in the *pāramārthika* state, which appear as many in the *vyāvahārika* state like a single moon reflected as many in the waves, i.e., through the *bimbapratimbavāda* of *Advaitin*, i.e., one self exhibits as many because of its reflection upon the numerous *antaḥkaraṇas*. In other words, through the *avacchedavāda*, the pure self or consciousness is conditioned by the *antaḥkaraṇa* rather the reflection of the self upon the same like all pervading *ākāśa* conditioned by pot. Where *Viśiṣṭādvaitin* objects, that, in the *vyāvahārika* state the individuals are possessing differences of characteristics as wise and foolish, happy and unhappy which results pluralism. *Viśiṣṭādvaitin* supports pluralism by examining the monism that if one self identifies itself with others, then, it should experience the same from the others.

Prof. P.N. Srinivasachari explains the *Advaitins* idea about the differences of *guṇas* in selves, "What is understood by an opposition is that the qualities do not exist together. That the qualities do not exist together can be known when the difference between the abstrate (in which the qualities inhere) is established; that there is difference between the substrates can be known only when the difference of qualities is established".[73] Regarding the differences of experience, the *Advaitin* contends, that, the experience is like pleasure and pain which are determined by ignorance which automatically leads to the impossibility of experiencing the all recollected experiences of one ordinary individual. When stressing about the highest personality (Prahalāthan and Vamādeva), the *Advaitin* remarks, that, they bear the speciality of recollection of the others, i.e., experiencing the other self as oneself because both the selves are one and the same.[74]

Viśiṣṭādvaitin criticizes the identical nature of selves by arguing the differences of released and bounded selves where if *ajñāna* originates from the Absolute. If so, no one can get the *mukti* and if the *ajñāna* is removed by right *jñāna* the release of the one self would have result of the other selves also. But it is actually not so because the force of *ajñāna* is always existing there. To reject the view, *Advaitin* argues the meaninglessness of the opposite character of the ignorant and wise. So, to criticize the *Advaita*, Prof. P.N. Srinivasachari comments for *Viśiṣṭādvaitin*, "Whether the opposition in question is denied after having accepted opposition in general in some other case or is it denied without admitting the opposition anywhere. If it be denied everywhere it would be absurd even to argue with the opponent in so far as there is no opposition (according to the position held by the *Advaitin*) between one's own view and that of the opponent. If opposition is accepted in some other instances, it is hardly possible to disprove it in the present instance".[75]

Again the *Advaitin* confesses, that, the individuals are determined by differences of *antaḥkaraṇas*. If it is so, *Viśiṣṭādvaitin* remarks that there is a scope to differentiate the self through the external sense organs. Actually it is not so, because the individual recollects what is seen or experienced. So, there must be difference between the selves. As *Advaitin*, if *ajñāna* is located in Brahman, there is no self to attain the *mukti* state. If all the selves are alike, then there is no basic reason as preceptor who teaches the philosophy of *Vedānta* to his disciple. So, the monistic attitude leads to a strong conception of eternal bondage which exists for ever. Then the principle of text which is meant for the purpose of removing the same will be futile. On the other hand, if the bondage rests upon the *jīvas*, then Brahman may not have connection with bondage. Then the distinction between the bondage and liberation will not be a philosophically satisfactory one because everything other than Brahman is illusory. So, *māyā* is as illusory, while free from the bondage is real. In order to overcome the difficulty, there should be many selves each distinct from the other.

While setting aside Śrī Śaṅkara's conception of identity of the self, *Viśiṣṭādvaitin* formulates his view of differences of the same where Brahman is considered to be the *antariyāmin*

Brahman. For this, they substantiate the same through perception, inference and verbal testimony. Eventhough perception fails to perceive the basic differences between the self and *Īśvara*, it helps to recognize the difference in characters. In other words, the individual selves are bearing the law of *karma* and the residue of the unfulfilled desire. This is inferred from the existence of inner urge to get rid of from the above to reach the perfect state of *mukti*.

While criticizing Śrī Śaṅkara's conception of *ātman* and Brahman as the real and the difference as unreal, *Viśiṣṭādvaita* analyses, "For the *Advaitin* himself admits that *Īśvara* and *jīva* are superimposed on Brahman in the form of cause, effect and *upādhi* just as the snake and the crack in the ground are superimposed on the rope; nevertheless of *Īśvara* and *jīva* are identical, then the superimposed snake and the crack in the ground would also become identical which is also absurd as far as our ordinary experience is concerned. The superimposed objects are never identical, much less the substrate and the object superimposed on it".[76] In order to support the view, *Viśiṣṭādvaitin* gives forth the verbal testimony, where the scriptures are supporting the difference between them.[77] The *Bhagavad Gītā* explains the same principle in Kṛṣṇa's word, 'A ray of Myself, the eternal *Jīva* in the world of *Jīvas*, attracts the senses, with *manas* the sixth, abiding the *prakṛati*.[78] *Upaniṣadic* text exposes the *sambandha*, 'relationship' between the self and the Brahman where the differences are also seen within it.[79] *Muṇḍaka Upaniṣad* stresses the distinct characteristic features of the self and the Absolute.[80] *Taitrīya Upaniṣad* brings the differences between the selves even at the state of release.[81]

Even otherwise, if the texts refer to the identity of the two, *Viśiṣṭādvaitin* gives the relationship between Master and servant. About this, *Viśiṣṭādvaitin* continues that, "If such an interpretation are spoken of as one, it would follow that they are identical. It may be argued that matter and *Īśvara* are stated in opposition and as such the former is so far as it is unreal is meant to be sublated by the latter. This will not do since the same interpretation can as well as applied to the statements where *jīva* and *Īśvara* are stated in opposition and as a result of it *jīva* would stand sublated by *Īśvara*".[82]

A close examination of the *mukti* state in *Advaita* is self-contradictory. In this system, *mukti* state is considered to be the *summum bonum* of the particular self, i.e. the attainment of the *puruṣārtha* by the individual through the stages of *dharma, artha, kāma* and *mokṣa*. The *Advitin's* attainment of the same is untenable because they negate the notion of 'I'. In other words, the attainment of *puruṣārtha* without the self bears the meaninglessness of one's own life. Moreover, in the *mukti* state *ātman* identifies itself as Brahman, where *avaccedavāda* falls into conflict because interpreting difference within the example of ether in *ākāśa* as Brahman and the same ether in the jar as *ātman* is creating confusion. So, *Viśiṣṭādvaitin* reconciles the above difficulties by establishing the identity of the Brahman as *antaryāmin* or inner self of the all individuals.

Śrī Rāmānuja's commentary approaches the problem of self, God and the ways of attaining *mokṣa* in an orderly way. There is proper connection with each other through proper justification, so that, the individual understandings of the philosophical output. In his commentary Śrī Rāmānuja does not miss to base the proper description of his epistemology and metaphysical foundation. So, understanding of any crucial problem has come out successful without any criticism. Moreover, his commentary fulfils the practical and theoretical guidelines to follow the spiritual realm to attain the life of *summum bonum* for all personalities who are all being in all the kinds of situations within the sociated order. Eventhough Śrī Śaṅkara theoretically completes his commentary of the *Bhagavad Gītā*, he fails in his practical approach because ordinary human beings may get struggle to understand to follow his doctrines, i.e., the world is *māyā*, a false appearence; and Brahman could be understood through *neti-neti* method through complete *jñāna* approaches the reality through *neti-neti* method. But it could not be denied, that these are beyond to reach the normal personality who is invariably struggled through the odds of the life.

Śrī Śaṅkara and Śrī Rāmānuja approach the nature of self and its characters through the *Gītā* in two different directions with their own specific methodology of epistemology and metaphysics. A close perceptive reveals that, they refer to the same point but from two different standpoints. So, a comparison may be helpful to know the actual facts of the two different approaches in the same verses of the *Bhagavad Gītā*. They are:

(i) Śrī Śaṅkara comments that difference cannot be perceived by perception, inference and verbal testimony and he proves the logical inconsistency. But Śrī Rāmānuja rejects the above issue and says that there is always a difference within the dependent entity of *cit* and *acit* and the independent entity of Brahman. Eventhough both differ, they justify their standpoint through their elaborated arguments.[83]

(ii) Regarding the relation of the self and the consciousness, Śrī Śaṅkara affirms that both are identical. But Śrī Rāmānuja points out, that, since consciousness is related to the subject and object, it should not be identified as the self, He said that there is no eternal, self-luminous and undifferentiated transcendental consciousness. So, consciousness is the attribute to the basic eternal substratum-the self.[84]

(iii) Śrī Śaṅkara formulates the doctrine of *māyā* to illustrate the pluralism as illusory appearance. But Śrī Rāmānuja rejects the same through his seven-fold criticism upon the doctrine of *māyā* and elogically proved that the subject and the object of the universe as many.

(iv) Śrī Śaṅkara says,. that, the self is not a knowing subject because it is eternal and changeless. But Śrī Rāmānuja professes, that, eventhough the self is considered to be the subject it does not change its originality. Regarding this problem, Śrī Śaṅkara approaches from the transcendental point of view and confirms the consciousness as *svataḥsidha*, 'self-dependent, eternal and undifferentiated pure *jñāna*' which is Brahman. But Śrī Rāmānuja approaches the same from empirical standpoint of consciousness related to subject in one point and object in another point. So, Śrī Rāmānuja strongly condemns the universal consciousness and professes the pluralistic state.

(v) As a final consideration, Śrī Śaṅkara appraises the non-dualism as the ultimate truth and maintains the individual self as unreal. But Śrī Rāmānuja through the proper epistemology and metaphysics establishes the individual selves as real, eternal and spiritual entities which are distinguished from the other selves.

(vi) Śrī Rāmānuja through the principle of *apṛthaksiddhaviśeṣaṇa* accepts the dependent plurality, i.e. the pluralistic *cit* and *acit* are forming the nodes and attributes to the body of Brahman. In other words, Brahman Himself willed to be many so that He manifested Himself as the pluralistic modes and attributes of the sentient objects of the manifold Universe. By negating plurality Śrī Śaṅkara affirms monism that the absolute supremacy of *ātman*-Brahman is the real and all other matters are the unreal because they are the products of *māyā*.[85]

So, by considering the comprehensive analysis and a proper review of the commentaries of *Advaita* and *Viśiṣṭādvaita* with their relevances to the individual as well as the social necessities, the author of this work may be humbly and personally expressed his opinion. That is, Śrī Rāmānuja, by taking into the social need and the feasiblity of intellectual set up covering the ordinary to the highest esteem of the mentioned humanistically justified the metaphysical as well as the epistemological approach towards the esoteric understanding of the *Bhagavad Gītā*.

REFERENCES

1. Radhakrishnan, S., (1948). *The Bhagavad Gītā,* pp. 16-17.
2. Mahadeva Sastri, A., *The Bhagavad Gītā,* pp. 2-6.
3. *BG,* 2.12.
4. *na tvevāhaṁ jātunāsaṁ na tvaṁ neme janādhipāḥ/ na caiva na bhaviṣyāmaḥ sarve vayaṃ ataḥ paraṃ//* —*Ibid.,* 2.12
5. *kṣetrajñaṁ cāpi māṁ viddhi sarvakṣetreṣu bhārata/* —*Ibid.,* 13.2
6. Chaudhuri, Anil Kumar Roy, *Self and Falsity in Advaita Vedanta,* pp. 65-101.
7. *Ibid.,* p.99.
8. *Brah. Bhāṣyā,* IV, 3,20; 1, 4, 7.
9. *Katha. Bhāṣā,* I, 3, 13; II, 2, 11, III, 3.1.
10. Joshi Shanti, *The Message of Śrī Śaṅkara,* p. 92.
11. Narasimhachari, M., Deevasenapathi, V.A. & Balasubramanian, R. *Perspectives of Theism and Absolutism in Indian Philosophy,* pp. 45-46.
12. Shanti Joshi, *op. cit.,* p. 132.
13. Krishna Warrier, A.G., *The Concept of Mukti in Advaita Vedanta,* pp. 308 & 312.
14. Narasimhachari, M., Deevasenapathi, V.A.& Balasubramanian, R. *op. cit.,* pp. 47-48.
15. *Ibid.,* p. 311.
16. Joshi, Shanti, *op. cit.,* p. 131.
17. *Ibid.,* pp. 353-354.
18. Sastri, Kodileswar, *An Introduction to Advaita Philosophy,* p. 119.
19. *Ibid.,* p. 121.
20. *MU,* III-1.
21. Chaudhuri, Anil Kumar Ray, *Self and Falsity in Advaita Vedanta,* p. 79.
22. Shanti Joshi, *op. cit.,* p. 75.
23. Chaudhuri, Anil Kumar Ray, *op. cit.,* pp. 110-101.
24. Narasimhachari, M., Deevasenapathi, V.A. & Balasubramanian, R. *op. cit.,* p. 57.
25. Sundaram, P.K., *Advaita Metaphysics,* pp. 38-39.
26. *Ibid.,* p. 40.

27. Sastri, Mahadeva, *op. cit.*, p. 323.
28. Narasimhachari, M., Deevasenapathi, V.A., & Balasubramanian, R., *op. cit.*, pp. 55-56.
29. *Ibid.*, pp. 59-60.
30. *Ibid.*, p. 61.
31. *Ibid.*, p. 62.
32. Vireswarananda, Swami, *Brahma-Sūtra*, pp. xx-xxi.
33. *Ibid.*, p. 167.
34. *Ibid.*, p. xxiv.
35. *Ibid.*, p. xxix.
36. *Ibid.*, pp. 7-8.
37. Srinivasachari, S.M., *Advaita and Viśiṣṭādvaita*, pp. 42-43.
38. Srinivasachari, S.M., *op. cit.*, p. 41.
39. *Ibid.*, pp. 42-43.
40. *Ibid.*, pp. 34-44.
41. Balasubramanian, R., *Some Problems in the Epistemology of Ramanuja*, p. 15.
42. *Ibid.*, pp. 17-18.
43. *BG*, 2. 11-15.
44. *Ibid.*, 7. 6-7.
45. *Ibid.*, 12. 12-16.
46. *Ibid.*, 12. 1-5.
47. *Ibid.*, 6.31; 13. 29-34.
48. *Ibid.*, 3.27; 5.15; 7.13-16; 25; 14-23; 15.7; 18.61.
49. Narasimhachari, M., Deevasenapathi, V.A. & Balasubramanian, R. *op. cit.*, p.10.
50. Srinivasachari, S.M. *op. cit.*, p. 58.
51. *Ibid.*, p. 59.
52. *Ibid.*, p. 60.
53. *Ibid.*, p. 46.
54. Raghavachar, S.S. *Śrī Rāmānuja on the Gītā*, p. 11.
55. *Ibid.*, pp. 11-12.
56. *Ibid.* p. 12.
57. *Ibid.*, pp. 143-144.
58. *Ibid.*, p. 144.
59. Narasimhachari, M., Deevasenapathi, V.A. & Balasubramanian, R., *op. cit.*, pp. 1-2.

60. Balasubramanian, R., *op. cit.*, pp. 5-6.
61. *Ibid.*, p. 67.
62. *Ibid.*
63. Srinivasachari, S.M., *op. cit.*, pp. 62-65.
64. *Ibid.*, pp. ix, 16, 40 & 50.
65. Balasubramanian, R., *op. cit.*, pp. 7-8.
66. *Ibid.*, p. 13.
67. *Ibid.*, p. 16.
68. *Tait*, II. i. 1.
69. Ragavachar, S.S., *op. cit.*, p. xiv.
70. Narasimhachari, M., Deevasenapathi, V.A. & Balasubramanian, R., *op. cit.*, pp.12-13.
71. Srinivasachari, P.N., *Ramanuja's idea of the Finite Self*, pp. 90-91.
72. Dasgupta, Surendranath, *History of Indian Philosophy*, Vol. III, p. 12, Vol., p. 537.
73. Srinivasachari, S.M., *op. cit.*, p. 70.
74. *Ibid.*, p. 77.
75. *Ibid.*, p. 72.
76. Srinivasachari, S.M., *op. cit.*, p. 75.
77. *M.U*, 3-1-2, *Śvet. Up*, 1.6 & *Tait. Up*, 2-5-2.
78. *BG.*, 15.7.
79. *Br. Up.* 5-7; *Śvet. Up.* 11-3.
80. *Mund. Up.* 1-1-9, *Śvet. Up.* 6-8 to 10.
81. *Tait. Up.* 1-7, *Mund. Up.* 3-1-3.
82. Srinivasachari, S.M., *op. cit.*, p. 76.
83. *Ibid.*, pp. 175 & 180.
84. *Ibid.*, p. 175.
85. Ragavachar, S.S., *op. cit.*, p. 151.

CHAPTER-6

RELEVANCE OF THE SELF TO THE MODERN WORLD

6.1. IMPORTANCE OF THE BHAGAVAD GĪTĀ'S TEACHING

The world civilizations and institutions have gone through a radical change because of the social conditions like monarchism, racism, fascism, communism, etc. Specifically Hindu society is subverted because of its internal agitations within the religious believes of various sects with their respective perspectives. The scientific laws weaken the human confidence and question the basic doctrines of religion in the economical as well as the sociological ground. The days of plenty and prosperity have caused the defects and poverty, confrontations and conflicts in every walks of life and in all domestic spheres of the society. The implications of *varṇāśramadharma* have resulted in chaos and confusion to the society because of its wrong identification, i.e., the society perceives it not by based on the *guṇas* and the nature of work but by *varṇā*, i.e., the status by birth. In the modern days, the people are getting interests towards the material pleasures rather than the spiritual. Every country is very much interested to increase their standard of living with the sophisticated equipments. The scientific inventions are bringing into lots of pleasures of different kinds and the multiple varieties to the people. In simple, pleasure is equated with material comfort but not with the spiritual maturity.

Scientific advent and industrial revolution have brought a thorough change in the productive function and the relation between the different classes of the society. While they are attempting to increase their own standard of living, automatically the conflicts arise between the classes and nations. It results helplessness to the humanity for the peaceful co-existence. At present, every place is Kurukṣetra and every day is a day of unwanted and irresistible battle. Our modern world has witnessed the unbearable horrors of the two world wars and it is also threatened by the impending third world war due to the dominance and the wrong notions towards the name and fame. As the consequence, along with the usual weapons like the atom bomb, hydrogen bomb etc., the dominant nations even piled the dangerous weapons made out of chemicals which may inhumanely kill the masses in total. They are even ready to destroy the whole humanity by initiating to change the DNA (deoxyribonucleic acid) of the chromosomes of the living organisms, irrespective of human and animals. It proves, that, they are the weapons in the hands of *asuras* for the purpose of destruction and not in the hands of *devas* for the purpose of protection; and also for the welfare of humanity.

Mounting material goods do not create peace and pleasure but only pain and sorrow, because some groups only materially progressed; so to say, the social equilibrium has been radically upset. In other words, at the one end, the society has a class of idle rich who think, that, work is not for them but for the toiling masses. Then, there are the rich who think, that, the working class must work in order to get more wealth. Then there are persons who want to work but they are unable to get work in this machine age. Then, there are persons who do not wish to work but live a life of ease and idleness on the misplaced charity of religious minded people. Thus the two extremes, the idle rich and the idle poor are both the products of two different kinds of our social life as the capitalist/

industrialist; and the persons with the sense of religious pietism. This upsetting equilibrium and the consequent change of values have relegated religion to a secondary place.[1]

The cause for the sordid and painful situation lies in the misunderstanding, that, the religion is based on superstitious believes; and the science is based on the empirically verified truths through the empirical tests of the physical phenomena. It is equally believed, that, science advocates materialism and dispensing with spiritualism. But a careful study of the history of scientific thought exposes the plausible truth, that, science is not advocating materialism, even though it is not fully accepting spiritualism in the religious terminology. The scientists like Darwin, Huxley and Spencer have advocated, that, life is determined by the organic changes. Thus the material law which prevailed in nature and human development are determined by biological change as man evolved from monkey. But the views of law of nature are changed when the scientists went deeper into the mystery of life. In detail, matter cannot by itself evolve but with the life energy behind the matter. So, the verified truth is, that, the matter is only a matter through the embodiment of life. So, the life is determined by the organic changes which are nothing but the nature brought out in the bodies of living organism. By understanding the phenomenal truth, the scientist go deeper and deeper into the mystery of life and invent the fact, that, through the natural change, the matter cannot by itself evolve life; rather, it has gradually unfolded itself through matter, which is considered to be the embodiment of life.

Through the 'Theory of Relativity', Albert Einstein frames a new ideology in the radical change of the concept of matter and life. He says, that, the object that one perceives is not really as it is seen, but the atoms mingling in a perpetual motion. So, if it splits up, the enormous energy will be let loose tremendously, i.e., the matter is nothing but the crystallized energy of spirit.[2] From this, one can say, that, the matter in external appearances is false. The form may change or not, but the contained energy may not be mutable or distortable. Also, in the views of Einstein, space and time do not exist independently. Every object is relative to other object and the knowledge of the objects is therefore relative and not absolute. So, the present day science upholds the non-materialistic view of life force; and the scientific indepth study of the universe reveals, that, the metaphysics is an essential part of physical theories. Based on the proper study of the science and its discovery towards the benefit of the society and individual, the understanding of the scientific outlook upon the inner nature of the atoms and the feature of the every individual subjects of the universe expressively reveal the fact, that, the metaphysical approach towards the reality would be an essential part of the physical theories. In it, it is no doubt, that, the philosophical speculations support our enquiry into the practical field. So, the advancement in the scientific techniques totally change the notion of metaphysical speculations upon the principle of natural philosophy, which in turn, automatically directs the humanity towards the spiritual advancement.

The philosophical speculations support our enquiry in the practical fields, i.e., the science helps to discover the truths and the religion protects the origin and the actuality of the natural process. With this, one can unveil the dogmatic religious faith to unique revealed truths. So, scientists are realizing the importance of religion and they are believing the existence of a Super Force. But on the other extreme, the religious leaders and their perceptions are being drawn in the wave of materialism and they have failed to fulfill the expected service, because they are doing only lip service to the religion. So, this practical perspections all these paraphernalia of external religion is evanescent. Behind these external formalities religion looses its soul and it is becoming a screen to cover a selfish and materialistic mentality, which consequently left out a great void in the religious field.[3]

The teachings of *Gītā* are not barren dogmas, but a lively art of reality and thereby help to understand the true meaning of life. Indeed, we should not forget and avoid thinking even, that, the causes of the individual diseases as well as the pollution of the society of the current century lie upon the fanatic attachment towards the materialism. For this, the *Gītā* relevantly says, 'How can a man, O Arjuna! Who knows it as the imperishable, the eternal, the unborn, the not decaying, cause anyone to be slain? whom can he slay? Just as a man puts on fresh cloths after discarding worn-out ones, so does the embodied self, discarding worn-out bodies, proceed to take up new ones. Weapons do not cut it, fire does not burn it. Neither does water wet it; nor wind dry it'.[4] So, by understanding the eternal nature of the self, the individual should focus himself towards the spiritual side, rather than the materialistic attachment. From the above never lasting words, it is understood, that, since the self is spiritual, the materialistic attitude would not fulfill the life mission. So, the present generation has to turn away from it to understand the spiritualism. Regarding this the *Gītā* relevantly states, "Enjoyment born of objective contacts, indeed, cause pain only. Son of Kuntī! They have a beginning and end; the Sages do not delight in them.".[5] So, the text foresees, that, if the individual enjoys the bliss through the spiritual exercises, it becomes the divine by itself.

Attachment to the materialism putforths the selfish development. It results the baseless continuum, through which if the survival of the fittest is the rule, one wants to live at the cost of others. For this *Gītā* advises, 'Giving up wholly all desires born of mental constructions and controlling, on all sides, the senses with the help of the resolute intellect; anchoring the mind in the self, think of nothing whatsoever'.[6] So, by understanding the sacred truth, it is earnestly asserted, that, the selfless service to the humanity is urgently in need of to march towards the spiritualism.

Materialistic waves and the irresponsible men make the importance of the teachings of the *Bhagavad Gītā* more required than ever before. Its teachings concern with the inner nature of the self are not the barren religious dogmas but a lively art of life. It emphasizes one to realize the eternal reality and thereby to understand the unity of life. For the convenience of the proper approach, the importance of teachings of the *Bhagavad Gītā* is classified into two major divisions, as teachings to the individuals and to the society. Indeed the discussions may neatly unveil the dark side of the society and lead it to march towards the brighter perspectives.

6.2. THE TEACHINGS TO THE INDIVIDUALS

6.2.1. *Niṣkāmyakarma Yoga*

The *Gītā* prefers renunciation in action, *'karma yoga'* than renunciation of action, *'karma saṁnyāsa'*. Through *karma yoga,* he will never commit sin because it helps the individual to realize his own self. For action to inaction, the *Bhagavad Gītā* says, "And even the maintenance of the body would not be possible for him by inaction".[7] The *Bhagavad Gītā* advises the individual to get the knowledge through the desireless action.[8] If the individual performs the *niṣkāmyakarma yoga,* he separates his spiritual self from the worldly entanglements. Then the result of the action does not influence the self towards the worldly order. So, in due course the individual could realize his own self and attain *mokṣa.*[9] The work also advises the individual to dedicate all the fruits of his actions to the feet of the Ultimate Reality. While dedication, he understands his finite nature and expects the grace from the Supreme. So, during dedications, the finite self unites with the Infinite Reality. For the unity, the *Gītā* through the words of Kṛṣṇa advices Arjuna, 'With this do ye nourish the Gods, and the

Gods shall nourish you, thus nourishing one another, ye shall attain the supreme good'.[10]

For the realization of the supreme truth through *niṣkāmyakarma yoga,* Swami Prabhavananda and Christopher Isherwood jointly write, "Freed from fear and desire, he offers everything he does as a sacrament of devotion to his duty. All work becomes equally and vitally important. It is only towards the result of work success or failure, praise or blame that he remains indifferent when action is done in this spirit. Kṛṣṇa teaches that it will lead us to the knowledge of what is behind action, behind all life; the ultimate reality. And, with the growth of this knowledge, the need for further action will gradually fall way from us, We shall realize our true nature, which is God".[11] By understanding the theme, each and every person of this world has to do action without fail. If he performs the action without desire of the result, he will move one step upward to realize his own self in the divine realm,[12] where he understands *daiva*[13] as the Supreme Controller to decide the individual's action. The individual also understands, that, the action of his own has been already decided by the Lord. But doing the same action, through the *niṣkāmyakarma,* he can nullify the result of the action not to incur the self through the strong belief, that, the Ultimate Reality directs him to perform the activity. For that, through *niṣkāmyakarma yoga,* the *Gītā* does not sanction war or non-violence but recommends duty based on *svadharma* and *svabhāva.* In other words, the *Gītā* states, that, if a person performs the same *yoga* based on his *svadharma* and to destroy the *adharma* of the society, he will realize the self as it is, which in turn will lead to the state of *mukti.* So, the *Gītā* says, that, if an individual performs the action disinterestedly, he himself and the society will be gained the highest spiritual status within the religious and moral order.[14]

Along with the understanding of the social good, if the same individual sacrifices the result of his action to the divinity through *niṣkāmyakarma yoga,* the Almighty gives hope for perfection. For this, the *Gītā* proclaims, 'Renouncing all actions in me, with thy thought resting on the Self, being free from hope, free from selfishness, devoid of fever, do thou fight. Men who constantly practice this teaching of Mine with faith and without caviling, they too are liberated from actions'.[15]

Herewith, the views are also to be added about the intrinsic values of individual's detachment towards the fruits of the action and the total emancipation towards *mukti.* Absolute control over the senses as sensual detachment and abstinence with the result of the actions are the reflection of the acquisitions and enrichment of spiritual qualities. It is the *niṣkāmyakarma yoga,* the highest contribution of the *Gītā* to the world community. For this, the esoteric Celestial Song conveys the message, 'Giving up the fruits of works, the *Yogin* attain disciplined peace; the non *Yogin,* attached the fruits by force of craving is bound'.[16] Indeed, the preaching of *Gītā* which centers around the detachment and duty implicitly calls for a certain quality of status and opportunity. It provides the right scenario for the observance of the duty without bias and any kind of avarice. In this context, detachment towards life is not a negative state of mind but a positive stand of control over it and discrimination of the good and bad in concern with the society. Devotees in the path of work perform action only with body, mind and senses and intellect but foresaking the attachment to its result for the purification of the heart. This is possible when a man becomes *sthitaprajñā,* who has the steady wisdom which is the way to the serene happiness, i.e., *mokṣa.*

6.2.2. Suggestions to raise the Lower Self to Higher Self

The *Gītā* advises the individual to raise his carnal self to spiritual self. To lift the self, it recommends to do work which is ordained by nature. Out of it, the individual can get happiness and peace. During the time, the *karma yogin* should welcome the difficulties and distractions and through them, he should test his strength and conviction. If the individual overcomes the drawbacks through patience and perseverance, his self progresses towards the spiritual realm. For this, the individual should be away from the desire and inclinations towards the fruits of action; and he should realize the supreme good in his life.[17]

The *Gītā* sanctions not the perishable worldly goods for natural pleasure, but the imperishable bliss for *mukti*. The *Gītā* does not offer the earthly prosperity to the bound self, but it helps to lead towards the Ultimate Reality by removing ignorance and delusion. The text explains, that, the ignorance and delusion arise from the individual's attachment towards the fruits of his actions. So, if the individual controls his senses through desireless actions, he attains the highest peace.[18] The *Gītā* not only professes the philosophical theme but also emphasizes the practice than the expounding new philosophical doctrines. For this, it describes the characters for *sthitaprajñā* in the last portion of the second chapter, the way of practicing *yoga* in the sixth chapter, *guṇas* of the aspirants in the twelfth chapter and the spiritual *jñāna* and the explanation of the divinity in the thirteenth chapter.

It suggests ethical teachings for character building to purify the mind by discarding the lust and greed. It also adds the devotional love towards the Brahman.[19] In the sixth chapter, it explains the way of getting perfect *jñāna* through *dhyāna* where it reconciles the spiritual illumination and philosophical doctrines through practice. Along with this, the immortal work imposes the need of equanimity of *manas* with purity and calmness. Then only *buddhi* can help self realization and God realisation. For this the *Gītā* says, "Evenness is called *Yoga*".[20] To stress the equanimity, the *Gītā* reconciles the two extremes of pleasure and pain, profit and loss, victory and defeat, success and failure, good and evil, heat and cold and friends and foe. So, even though the individual is caught in conditions of the two extremes, it realizes its own immortality because of the balanced mind, where the self tides over the wills and trials, limitations of obstacles in nature and realise the supreme bliss.[21]

In the eleventh chapter, God Himself stresses the highest nature of all pervasiveness within the whole universe and the immanent nature within the sentient and non-sentient. From this, one can easily understand, that, God is not partial but generous to all. It is worthwhile to say, that, He is above the level of human love. So, there will be no meaning to differentiate the two extremes except to admit the balanced attitude towards the same. To explain the truth, the *Gītā* avers, "In a *brāhmana* endued with wisdom and humanity, in a cow, in an elephant, as also in a dog, and in a dog-eater, the wise see the same".[22] Through this simple truth, it could be added, that, he should love other selves with balanced mind as your self. In other words, through the love and balanced attitude, the *Gītā* transcends the universal brotherhood to universal love because it reaches the highest status where the individual self identifies itself with all Universal Self. The *Gītā* formulates different *sādhanas* as *jñāna yoga, karma yoga, bhakti yoga* and *prapatti yoga* to attain the perfect state. It recommends the practical ways, rather to express the doctrines to attain the final goal. While emphasizing the practical side, the text is not missed to frame the laws for spiritual practices. It advises the people to face and overcome the drawbacks, difficulties and perplexities in the spiritual progress towards the higher status of life.

While raising the self to higher level, many individuals get fear by doubting his own status as house-holder. He looses his own will-power to resist the temptations and obstacles and feels, that, spiritual life is not for him but for the *saints* and *mahātmās*. But the *Gītā* never treats the people as ordinary person and higher but generally advises the individual not to indulge in the self-ruinous thought of despair and hopelessness.[23] It adds, 'By action only, indeed, did Janaka and others try to attain perfection. Even with a view to the protection of the masses thou should perform (action)'.[24] This teaching should be considered not for Arjuna alone but to the whole humanity. The *Bhagavad Gītā* does not admit, that, *saṁnyāsins* alone can attain *mukti* but the *karma yogin* also reaches the same state. To stress the fearlessness to Arjuna, Lord Kṛṣṇa says, 'Killed, thou wilt reach heaven; victories, though wilt enjoy the earth. Wherefore, O son of Kuntī, arise, resolved to fight'.[25] While emphasizing the same point, Vidyaprakasha-nanda proclaims, "So, the first command of the *Gītā* is to free the mind from all defeatist thought and feelings, never to yield to suggestions of helplessness and despair, in short to be fearless in the face of the most overwhelming obstacles and difficulties, and make steady progress with unswerving faith in God, Guru and One's own self."[26] So, while practicing the above *sādhana*, the aspirant should bear a stout heart, mental gut and firmness and the law of moderation by avoiding the two opposed extremes in all matters.[27]

The *Gītā* advises, that, every object of the universe must be utilized carefully and efficiently, especially the human body, '*indriyas, manas* and *buddhi*' to cross the *saṁsāra*. It even includes, that, over practice of *yoga* results in the damage to the physical body. For control of mind in moderation, the text says, 'By whatever cause the wavering and unsteady mind wanders away, from that let him restrain it and bring it back direct under the control of the self'.[28] For the upward progress of the self, the individual should not have any doubt about the divine existence. For that, he has to accept the scriptural truth and the reality of the universe. If not, he may bear his own opinion which gives rise to the illusions and delusions. To explain this truth, the text says, 'He obtains wisdom who is full of faith.'[29] In the series of births, the individual's mind is polluted because of the attraction towards the material world through the sensual pleasures; so that, the mind departs from the immortal self, where the mind reacts, rebels, struggles and refuses to proceed further to aid the lower nature of self to become the higher state. For this, the *Gītā* gives an answer in its sixth chapter. In it, the teachings are helpful to individual to cultivate the self through discipline, self-efforts and control of the mind by study, meditation and with the company of holy man. For this, the *Gītā* advises the aspirant to practice mental control for ever to destroy the *māyā* because lust, greed, over indulgence and sensual pleasures and hatredness will overcome and destroy the *sādhaka's* mind. In other words, the individual has to think about Brahman until his death because the *māyā* can enter at any moment and throw him away from the Divine Centre. The Celestial Song always emphasizes, that, the lower self should understand the pain, suffering and the perishable nature of the sense-object. It should permanently fix itself with the higher self by aversion towards the vulgar and the result of sense-object contact by the discriminative *jñāna*. So, if the individual develops the dispassion towards the pleasure drawn from the sense-object contact, the mind realizes the self through steadfastness of his meditation within the spiritual advancement.[30]

For the practice of dispassion, the *Gītā* prescribes every day practices for destroying the doubts, difficulties of physical, mental and the upliftment of the lower self to higher self by morally and spiritually. It lays special emphasis to avoid anger. For this the text says, 'From wrath arises delusion, from delusion failure of memory; from failure of memory, loss of conscience; from loss of conscience he is utterly ruined'.[31] So, anger and passion arise out of *rājasa guṇa* and out of them man degrades himself from his status to demon and he may not distinguish the difference between right and wrong. At the end, the total society will collapse because the passion which is the outcome of anger is the deadly poison, which could slowly pollute the society through the individuals' minds, words and deeds.

The *Gītā* advises, that, whenever the individual's mind is tempted towards the material pleasure, he should follow the *Gītā's* teachings to overcome the same to lift the lower self to higher self. Then the individual gets satisfaction, joy and peace. In describing the evil effects of worldly pleasure, the *Gītā* says, 'For, the mind which yields to the roving senses carries away his knowledge, as the wind (carries away) a ship on water'.[32] All human beings irrespective of their learning or ignorance, rich or poor and high or low born are subject to fear of death. But this esoteric text through its teachings exposes the immortal nature of the *ātma* and the mortal nature of the body. While *ātma* is eternal and *sat, cit, ānanda,* the body alone is like a torned cloth and it can be removed and thrown out through the series of births. By explaining the perishable features of body, the text explains the sameness of *ātman*-Brahman, the self is qualityless and *Kṣetrejña* or Brahman. The *ātman* should perceive the eternal nature of the self as he was and he is as same. Through the constant adherence of the same, he has to dehypnotize himself from delusive fear of death. So, if he senses the actual truth, the lower self steps up towards the divinity.

The *kāma,* 'sensual desire' is considered to be the foremost opposite force of hatred, greed and *'jñāniyo nityavairina',* 'eternal enemy of the *jñānī*'. The *Gītā* through its teachings boosts the *ātman* to strengthen his heart by permanent sentient of guarding the immortal nature. To it the *Gītā* says, "Triple is this, the gate to hell destructive of the self: lust, wrath and greed. Therefore, these three, one should abandon".[33] Moreover, the *ātma* gathers the power resources and determined effort through his series of past births to eradicate the *kāṃa* from the individual nature. Even though the world has separate individuals from the reality, one likes waves, bubbles and foam, which are the different forms of the water. Like this, consciousness is same for all created sentient object. If the lower self wants to attain higher nature, it should not hate and harms the other selves. Understanding this, he has to believe the Lord's declaration as the surest way to eradicate the uncharitable downward progress to the lower nature of self.

The *Bhagavad Gītā* emphasizes, that, the universal factors of possession and position, prosperity and practical life of the finite self are nothing. The individual should contemplate the mysterious power which pervades within the universe. If one understands this, he may not mind the egoism and pride; and he shall follow the humble means to meet out his necessities. If the individual is enlightened this vision, he will perceive the facts, that, everything in nature is perishable; and *ātman*-Brahman alone will be real. He may also understand the bitterness through his proper enquiry through *jñāna* and unite his self with the Supreme Reality. So, if the individual perceives the truth, he will overcome the pride of power and property; then, the lower self will reach the higher state without any restriction.

6.2.3. *Svadharma*

The *Bhagavad Gītā* explains *svadharma*, as, "Devoted each to his own duty, man attains perfection; how one, devoted to one's own duty, attains success, that do thou hear.[34] The *Gītā* explains, that, every individual has to perform action without aiming at the result with respect to his *svabhāva*, the spiritual temperament and the essential characters. Along with this, *Gītā* does not recommend to perform other's duty. It says, 'Better is one's own duty (though) destitute of merits, then the duty of another well performed. Doing the duty ordained according to nature one incurs no sin'.[35] So, understanding of the society as castes by *svadharma* and *guṇas* the *Gītā* says, 'The fourfold caste has been created by Me according to the distribution of energies and actions though I am the author thereof, know Me as non-agent and immutable'.[36] The above said caste system helps the society in all its perspectives. They are: (i) It recognizes four functions of the economical side of the social man in the society, i.e., the religious and intellectual the political, the economical and the servile functions. (ii) The cultural aspects stresses that each class should have its own religious custom, ethical rule, suitable education, training, family ideals and disciplines. (iii) The system brings the society totally towards the religious sanctions. (iv) The individual will understand the indestructible nature of self and he can get rid of the feeling of 'mine' and 'thine'. If one sincerely follows solemnly the principle of *svadharma* as directed by Lord's Will certainly finds the kingdom of God. So, through *svadharma*, even with the human body, the individual can get the blissful nature.

One has to perform *svadharma* without expecting reward, which is easy to say and to understand, but very hard to practice. Every individual could be distinguished as outer body and self. With this understanding, one has to perform one's own prescribed duty. If it is so, he could understand, that, the external body is not an end but a means to realize his essence. Metaphysically, the *svadharma* and the *svabhāva* inclined with *paradharma*, i.e., doing necessary spiritual service to the others, are the internal and external self expressions. They could be considered as the execution and attainment of the *dharma*, which in turn leads towards the holy feet of the Puruṣottama. To the *Gītā*, Supreme Spirit, who brings out the individual essence of its existence. The three *guṇas* are not the innermost crux of the Highest but an outward scheme of exercise and practices of the individual existence. In this direction, each and every individual self has the power of divinity, in it, the divinity guides the being towards perfection. So, the inner significance of the *svadharma* and *svabhāva* are, 'the integral ideal of Divine Nature and Divine law'.

Saint Vinoba stresses the important features of this concept as, (i) After perfection, the seeker needs to leave the crooked ways of *adharma* and *paradharma* and take the natural path of *svadharma*. (ii) The body perishes every moment. Understanding this let the individual use it for the sake of *svadharma*. When there is need, let him not hesitate even to give the body for the sake of *svadharma*. One should be constantly aware that the self is imperishable. So, he should remove the distinction of 'mine' and 'thine'. With this, he has to do his duty without expecting any reward. One who follows solemnly the way directed by Lord's will surely find himself in the kingdom of God, where he realizes his self.[37] According to the *Gītā*, one has to perform *svadharma* with the attitude of *niṣkāma*. This practice is called *karma yoga* which is easy to say and understand but hard to practice. Every object can be distinguished as outer body and inner self. In this way, he has to perform his own prescribed duty, then, he comes to know, that, our external body is not an end but a means to realize the eternal truth *niṣkāma*.

The total system with the *svadharma* and the *svabhāva* and *varṇāśramadharma* with the attitude of brin the society towards the spiritual realm through the realization of self by performing the prescribed duty. In other words, to bring out a unified and harmonious result, the society systematizes its work to get a total upliftment through the spiritualistic and a peaceful atmosphere. On the way of systematizing their society and the work, the Gītā gives much importance to the *guṇas* of the particular individual. So, the work done by him may have an inherent value to attain the realized state of the self.

6.2.4. Right Perspectives of the Law of *Karma*

'*Karma*' means the causation of things or an order or '*ṛta*', 'cosmic law' in the moral and social world. It results in the good or bad conduct to the individual. It decides the destiny of the individual, i.e. *karma* fixes the transmigration of the self from one birth to the next with respect to its nature of *karma*. This law of *karma* is responsible for the inequalities in humanity and tragedy of the individual. It shows an apt path to perceive the good conduct for *mukti* through compassion, perfect way of work, detachment and devotion.[38] With this background, the *Gītā* shows the apt path to decide Arjuna's destiny, whether to fight with his kith and kin or not. In other words, Arjuna as a warrior by temperament should fight because there is no greater good for a warrior; and through his duty to fight, he has to realize himself but not because of its nature which is disagreeable. In addition, the individual has to do the allotted duty rather than abstention from that because action is better than inaction.[39] Apart from the above, it prescribes good conduct through the technique of non-attachment towards the reward and renunciation of the good or bad. Compromising the above situation Parrinder Gloffrey quotes Dasgupta's statement, i.e., "The great solution of the *Gītā* is the compromise it advances between the worldly life of allotted duties and the hermit life of absolute renouncement and between a life of lawful and proper enjoyment and the absolute extinction of desires. The program that it proposes is, on the one hand, that we purify our minds, purging them of all attachments and passions by dedicating all the fruits of our actions to God; and yet, on the other hand, that we continue to perform all the duties belonging to our particular caste or stage of life".[40] This statement is self expressive.

The way of faith and devotion to God leads to *mukti* through Lord's grace, where the individual must do action with respect to the state of his own. If it is so, the grace hails from the Lord's abode and helps the individual to overcome his difficulties and to reach perfection. Even though the individual will be restricted to perform his action, the nature or the *guṇas* and the situation will make him to perform the same action. But if he gets the *prapatti mārga* to God, he will attain peace because of His healing grace. In short, through proper action with respect to his *guṇas*, the duty consciousness and the belief in His grace help the athlete to attain the perfect state of *mukti*.

Arjuna's status in the war-field refers to the common man's critical position in the toiling society. Arjuna as a human being bears compassion and ridicules the nature of war and cruelty of killing others.[41] For this, S. Radhakrishnan comments, "He is stressing the physical pain and the material discomfort which were face involves. The main end of life is not the pursuit of material happiness. We are bound to miss it as we approach the end of life, with its incidents of old age, infirmity, death. For the sake of an ideal, for justice and love, we must stand up to tyranny and face pain and death. On the very edge of the battle, Arjuna losses heart and all worldly considerations persuade him to abstain from the battle. He has yet to realize that wives and children, teachers and kinsmen, are dear not for their own sake but for the sake of the self".[42] Moreover, Arjuna experienced the desperate situation because of his unknown condition about the nature of duty and the reality beyond delusion. For duty, the *Gītā* stresses, that, the duty should be done with respect to his state and his situation, i.e., Arjuna should fight because it is his caste duty.[43] In order to understand the reality beyond delusion, the text explains the perishable nature of the body, the imperishable nature of the self, the metaphysical implication of the *niṣkāmyakarma yoga,* balanced state of the mind towards the opposite extreme and the *prapatti mārga.*[44]

Gītā does not support the tendency, that, all our actions are ordained by the law of *karma* and the helpless situation of our free will, i.e., entire actions are not pre-determined but self determined. The *Gītā* accepts the dual capacity of pre-determinism in the sense of effects of our own past *karma* result present action and the self-determinism. The individual can control and regulate his action through his discrimination and determination. While the *Bhagavad Gītā* explains the responsibility of *daiva,*[45] it gives importance to human efforts.[46] This concept is verified with the *Bhagavad Gītā.*[47] That is, Lord Kṛṣṇa, after giving all the kinds of advices, he lets Arjuna to take the final decision of his own. If one understands the importance of self-determinism, he can understand the ideology of *summum bonum* of life, which is not through the greatest good for the greatest number, but purification of the self by knowing its actual essence and its place in action. Along with this, he can realize his self as the Universal Self.[48] In other words, happiness of the humanity is possible by establishing peace between the conflicting forces. So, the *Gītā* explains the individual self as the Ultimate Reality. To explain the truth, the *Gītā* says, 'Whose has his joy within and his pastime within, and whose has his light within only, that *Yogin* attains Brahman's bliss, himself becoming Brahman'.[49]

6.3. TEACHINGS TO THE SOCIETY

The *Gītā* conveys the following message to the society for its total upliftment in moral, spiritual, social, religious and economical orders.

6.3.1. Detachment towards Materialism

The cause for the diseases of the present century lies in the fanatic attachment towards the material pleasure. Because of the destructive nature of the matter, one's life mission may not be fulfilled. The present day generation is turned towards the teachings of the *Gītā* because they can realize themselves as the spiritual beings of God. This feelings of the self realization as *satcidānanda* will be slowly released them from the bondage of the materialistic *māyā*.

During the current era, one wants to live at the cost of others. So, the survival of the fittest rules a nation. In other words, *avidyā* causes the curtain to fall before the self and keeps the society away from the realization of its own. In order to avoid the implication of the *avidyā* no more, the society needs the selfless service and detachment towards materialism and *niṣkāmakarma* for the welfare of the humanity.

6.3.2. Universal Self through Love

Through the philosophy of all selves as the same and the concept of *ātman*-Brahman as one as expounded by *Upaniṣads* and not only the human beings but also the animate and the inanimate objects of the universe are same, the *Gītā* directs the humanity towards the concept of Universal Self. From this source, the philosophy of Universal Brotherhood springs up. This could be possible through the realization of life through ripening of the heart with love. If the individual indulges in ignorance and selfish desires, he becomes hard and cruel where prayer, worship and meditation may not aid the athletes to the perfect state of liberation. On the other hand, if the individual's heart is filled with love, devotion, knowledge and meditation, he will be matured towards the ultimate goal through identifying the other selves as his own. If he fails to realize the nature of other selves by love, the devotion upon God may not have value. Then, it means not a service to God but sheer offence against Lord because the universal form of the Almighty is nothing but to constitute of all living and non-living creatures of the universe. So, the *Gītā* throughout its teachings instructs the aspirants to do no injury to others but to express pure love. The *Gītā* emphasizes the practice of meditation, worship, discrimination by *jñāna;* and they are are not possible without love in universal application to all living beings. To explain the concept, the *Bhagavad Gītā* appropriately conveys, "But those who worship Me, renouncing all actions in Me, regarding Me Supreme, meditating on Me with exclusive devotion (*Yoga*) for them whose thought is fixed on Me, I become ere long, O son of Pritha, the deliverer out of the ocean of the mortal *saṁsāra*."[50]

The princely quality of love is *adveṣṭā sarvabhūtānām*, 'no hatred of any creature in the universe'. In other words, the universal love is the real result of the all *yogas*, meditation, knowledge and action . The *Gītā* says, that, the aspirant should understand the universe as the manifestation of the love and the highest realization of the same is through his *jñāna*. Moreover, he has to practice the realization through effulgent love in his every day life, so that, he can eliminate all ill-will and hatred towards all creatures. If the individual practices the *yogas* with love, he can easily attain the supreme state, where the universal love eradicates the mental conflicts among the individuals. Then self-realization leads to God-realization. Here, the overflowing love for all creatures is considered to be the greatest virtue than worship of His lotus feet and the company of holy devotees because the perfect devotion and *jñāna* emerge from the love. In short, the *Gītā* recommends, that, if the humanity seeks self-realization, the individual should bear disinterested love towards all creatures and radiant love and mercy for the suffering individuals.[51]

6.3.3. Middle Path

Renunciation of action is not possible for liberation because without action man cannot survive for a second. *Saṁnyāsin* who renounces all action and absolute absorption in a solitary place is very difficult. But all people who live in this world are *saṁsārins* who need realization of their own selves through the philosophy of action. So, the *Gītā* does not advise elimination of worldly activities but through which the individual can reach the ultimatum. Arjuna stands as an ideal example, because initially, he refuses to fight because of the delusion of *māyā*. But at last he fights because the advice gained from the Lord about the middle path. Lord Kṛṣṇa understands the impact of *māyā* upon Arjuna's mind and He eliminates it by His divine *jñāna*. So, Arjuna considers the fight as a holy sacrifice with the remembrance of the Lord Kṛṣṇa and the understanding himself as an agent of the almighty. To it, the Gītā explains, 'Abandoning all righteous deeds, seek Me as thy sole Refuge; I will liberate thee from all sins; do thou not grieve'[52]; 'Out of mere compassion for them, I abiding in their self, destroy the darkness born of ignorance, by the luminous lamp of wisdom'.[53] The remembrance of the Lord reveals the truth, that, surrendering the fruits of action and performing the prescribed duty with the constant remembrance of the Lord are necessary. In other words, the work is transformed into worship by the way of dedicating the result of the actions to the feet of the Lord.

6.3.4. Harmonization of the different *Yogas*

The *Bhagavad Gītā* prescribes *karma yoga, bhakti yoga, dhyāna yoga* and *jñāna yoga* for culturing the lower self to that of higher nature. Among this, the particular path is determined by the individual through his *guṇas,* taste and temperament. Even though, the individuals are supporting their own way as superior to others, the *Gītā* never supports any path, but gives equal importance because the ultimate end is the same for all ways. Within the society many are inclined to practice the *karma yoga,* because they find pleasure and delight from action and render service to the society. For this, the *Gītā* describes the nature of *karma* and *niṣkāyakarma yoga.* So, the aspirant may not blindly incur sin because of the wrong action. In other words, the *Gītā* unveils the secret, that, the selfless and desirelessness towards the fruits are much important for *karma yoga* to lead a perfect life.[54] Others who are emotional with the feelings of love and affection may follow the *bhakti yoga,* through which they can worship, pray and utter the name of the Lord for thousand times in hundred ways and find effulgent joy from their personal selected deity. The *Gītā* supports the *bhakti yoga* for the aspirant to raise himself to the higher level through devotion and faith in the object to inward and find the ultimate source in them. In other words, through the *dhyāna yoga* or control of *indriyas* and *manas,* the individual has supreme satisfaction and finally reaches the state of *mukti.* Then, there are aspirants who are all rational and they through *jñāna yoga* analyze, discriminate and accept the truth. Through discrimination and the will power towards the rational enquiry of real from unreal, matter from spirit, the individual self transforms the lower standard of self to the higher state of divinity. So, a real conception of the *yogas* certainly reveals the balanced status but the controversies among them are only due to *avidyā*. Swami Vivekananda stated for the above situation, 'The reconciliation of different paths of *dharma*, and work without desire are the two special characteristics of the *Gītā*'.[55]

6.3.5. Value of Self Determinism

Gītā advises everybody to get self determinism to achieve their goal as they feel, think and decide. By supporting the concept, Gītā proclaims, 'Elevate the self by self; do not weaken the self. Self alone is the self's foe. The self is the friend of that self by which the self has been subdued. The self alone operates as the foe to the self'.[56] Every activity of the individual is encircled only with his self through the varied percepts of the mind. It activates the human personality, i.e., the internal unfolded thinking externally exposed through the activities. If this verdict is understood, the society as a whole would uplift spiritually.

6.3.6. Need of the Universal Brotherhood

The notion of plurality of selves disintegrates the individual as well as the society, because the unified thinking adds boost to morality to perform any kind of work with vigor and strength. As such, the conception of the Universal Self as *puruṣas* and *prakṛti* are the equal spiritual force of the Puruṣottama, unites not only the individual but also the animate and inanimate objects. From this, the philosophy of the Universal Brotherhood springs up, which indirectly unveils the spiritual nature of the humanity. For this Lord Kṛṣṇa utters, 'I am not lost to him who beholds me everywhere and beholds everything in me; neither is he lost to me. Confirming to unity, the *Yogin* who adores me present in all beings, lives in me, no matter how he appears to live. Arjuna! He, who sees alike pleasure pain in all beings, on the analogy of his own self, is deemed the supreme *Yogin*'.[57]

6.3.7. *Sāttvika Jñāna*

Naturally *jñāna* can be identified as two lines as the vision of the whole and the vision of the part. In the *Vedāntic* days metaphysics, physics, psychology, sociology, economics, natural science, physiology and religion were all one; different partial aspects of the one reality. The *Vedāntic jñāna* can be understood as intuitive and inductive than rational and deductive. On the other hand, the *jñāna* of the modern age is rational and deductive because it is based on observations and experiments. The analytical system is the basis for the modern knowledge. Modern scientist fails to take the synthetic views of findings of all sciences. The knowledge of man emphasized by the *Gītā* is called integrated knowledge which remains correct and even scientific. It is more useful at present than it was. So, through the *sāttvika jñāna,* the modern society has to find out the common source of energy as Ultimate Reality; and it should act in accordance to attain and to understand the same in all its walks.

6.3.8. Evolution of the World Religion

Generally, the philosophical doctrines of each and every sect are for the betterment of the society, but they differ only in their means. Instead, if they eradicate the different religious faiths and have a common verdict among them, definitely there will be a firm union and healthy development in social status in all walks of life. For the world religion, all the secretarians may join within the sense of *niṣkāmyakarma yoga* and with common means, through which they can rectify the errors of the past and utilize common lofty principles for the highest good of the humanity. For this, the *Bhagavad Gītā* affords much philosophical scope and helps the humanity, by which the finite individual reunites within the infinite through selfless dedicated services. If one follows each and every verses of the *Bhagavad Gītā,* he can understand, that, it is formulated by Veda Vyāsa to the humanity out of sheer compassion through the spiritual conversation between Lord Kṛṣṇa and the chosen devotee Arjuna. In other words, if the individual crosses the *saṁsāra* state through proper direction, the whole humanity will by-pass the same state to the perfect state. Then, definitely there will not be any sufferings but ever blooming bliss of the spirit.

Right perception of truth, beauty and bliss are the ultimate aims of the *Bhagavad Gītā*. It helps the individual to perceive and enjoy the same through his life, so that, it is an eternal miracle of the universal significance without minding the nations, races, religions and creeds and the people of all temperaments and the conditions. So, the *Gītā*, as the universal non-sectarian scripture, generously sets asides all the manifested differences and identifies the cause of all the causes, the force of all the forces with the ultimate reality. The world community should march towards the reality to get the rightful status bereft of differences based on colour, caste and creed. The human self as spiritual force tossed in the whirlwind of modern socio-economical and religious problems and cultural identity crisis could get the hope to attain the solace from this classical text.

The above teachings of the *Gītā* state, that, all sciences, all religions and all philosophies are directed towards the services to the humanity. In this sense, the *Bhagavad Gītā* is a non- sectarian universal scripture which sets aside all the humanly manifested differences and intuitively identifies the eternal cause for all causes, the supreme force for all forces that cause and force is the ultimate reality. Yes! certainly, the present world has to march towards this eternal journey for its ever blooming existence for all ages.

REFERENCES

1. Divatia, H.V., *The Art of Life in the Bhagavad Gītā*, p. 169.
2. *Ibid.*, p. 144.
3. *Ibid.*, pp. 146-147.
4. *BG*, 2: 21 - 23.

5. *Ibid.*, 5: 22.
6. *Ibid.*, 6: 24, 25.
7. *śarīrayātrāpi ca te na prassiddhyed akarmaṇaḥ//* — BG, 3. 8.
8. BG, 18. 66.
9. BG, 12. 8.
10. *devān bhāvayatānena te devā bhāvayantu vaḥ/*
    parasparṁ bhāventaḥ śreyaḥ paraṃ avāpsyatha// — BG, 3. 11.
11. Prabhavananda, Swami, Isherwood Christopher, *Bhagavad Gītā*, p. 139.
12. *Ibid.*
13. BG, 18. 14.
14. BG, 3. 25.
15. *mayi sarvāṇi karmāṇi saṁnyāsyādhyātmacetasā/*
    nirāśīr nirmamo bhūrtvā yudhyasva vigatajvaraḥ //
    ye me mataṃ idaṁ nityaṃ anutiṣṭhanti mānavāḥ/
    śraddhāvanto anasūyanto mucyante te api karmabhiḥ//
    — BG, 3. 30 - 31.
16. *Ibid.*, 5.12.
17. Balbir Singh, *Essence of Bhagavad Gītā*, pp. 143-144.
18. BH, 2. 62 - 64.
19. Vidyaprakashananda, Swami, *Gītā Makaranda*, p. 46.
20. *samadvaṁ yoga ucyate//* — BG, 2. 48.
21. *Ibid.*, 2. 15, 38, 45, 48, 50, 53, 56 - 7, 64, 71; 3. 18, 30, 4. 22; 5. 3, 19-20, 6. 7-9, 29, 32; 9. 29; 12. 3-4, 13, 18-19; 13. 28; 14. 24-5 & 18. 53-54.
22. *vidyāvinayasaṁpanne brāhmaṇe gavi hastini/*
    śuni caiva śvapāke ca paṇḍitāḥ samadarśinaḥ// — *Ibid.*, 5. 18.
23. Vidyaprakashananda, Swami, *op. cit.*, p. 79.
24. *karmaṇaiva hi saṁsiddhiṃ āsthitāḥ janakādayaḥ/*
    lakasaṅgrahamevāpi saṁpaśyan kartum arhasi// —BG., 3. 20.
25. *hato vā prāpsyasi svargaṁ jitvā vā bhokṣyase mahīṃ/*
    tasmād uttiṣṭha kaunteya yudhāya kṛtaniścayaḥ// —*Ibid.*, 2. 37.
26. Vidyaprakashananda, Swami, *op. cit.*, p. 80.
27. BG, 6. 17.
28. *yato yato niścarati manaścañcalaṃ asthiraṃ/*
    tatastato niyamyaitad ātmany eva vaśaṁ nayet// —*Ibid.*, 6. 26.
29. *śraddhāvaṁl labhate jñānaṃ* — *Ibid.*, 4. 39.

30. Vidyaprakashananda, Swami, *op. cit.*, pp. 83-84.
31. *krodhād bhavati saṁmohaḥ saṁmohāt smṛtivibhramaḥ/ smṛtibhraṁśād buddhināśo buddhināśāt praṇaśyati// —BG.*, 2. 63.
32. *indriyāṇāṁ hi caratāṁ yan mano anuvidhīyate/ tadasya harati prajñāṁ vāyur nāvaṃ ivāmbhasi// —Ibid.*, 2. 67.
33. *trividhaṁ narakasyedaṁ dvāraṁ nāśanāṃ atmanaḥ/ kāmaḥ krodhas tathā lobhas tasmād etat trayaṁ tyajet// —Ibid.*, 16. 21.
34. *sve sve karmaṇy abhirataḥ saṁsiddhiṁ labhate naraḥ/ svakarmaniratāḥ siddhiṁ yathā vindati tac chṛṇu// —Ibid.*, 18. 45.
35. *śreyān svadharmo viguṇaḥ paradharmāt svanuṣṭhitāt / svabhāvaniyataṁ karma kurvan nāpnoti kilbiṣam// —Ibid.*, 18. 47.
36. *cāturvarṇyaṁ mayā sṛṣṭaṁ guṇakarmavibhāgaśaḥ/ tasya kartāram api māṁ viddhyakartāram avyayaṃ// —Ibid.*, 4. 13.
37. Vinoba Bhave, Acharya, *Talks on the Gītā*, pp. 191-206.
38. Parrinder, Gloffrey, *Upaniṣads, Gītā and Bible*, p. 110.
39. *BG.*, 2. 31; 3. 5; 3. 24.
40. Parrinder Gloffrey, *op. cit.*, p. 112.
41. *BG.*, 1. 35.
42. Radhakrishnan, S., *Bhagavad Gītā*, pp. 94-95.
43. *BG*, 2. 31.
44. Parrinder, Gloffrey., *op. cit.*, pp. 122-123.
45. *BG*, 18. 24.
46. Divatia, H.V., *op. cit.*, p. 120.
47. *BG*, 18. 63.
48. Divatia, H.V., *op.cit.*, p. 124.
49. *yo antaḥsukho antarārāmas tathāntarjyotir eva yaḥ/ sa yogī brahmanirvāṇaṁ brāhmabhūto adhigacchati// —BG*, 5. 24.
50. *ye tu sarvāṇi karmāṇi mayi saṁnyāsya matparāḥ/*
ananyenaiva yogena māṁ dhyāyanta upāsate//
teṣāṃ ahaṁ samuddhartā mṛtyusaṁsārasāgarāt /
bhavāmi nacirāt pārtha mayyāveśitacetasāṃ// —Ibid., 12. 6-7.
51. Vidyaprakashananda, Swami, *op. cit.*, pp. 51-52.
52. *sarvadharmān parityajya māṃ ekaṁ śaraṇaṁ vraja/ ahaṁ tvā sarvapāpebhyo mokṣayiśyāmi mā śucaḥ// —BG*, 18. 66.
53. *tesāṃ evāmukampārtham ahaṃ ajñānajaṁ tamaḥ/ nāśayāmy ātmabhāvastho jñānadīpena bhāsvati// —BG*, 10. 11.

54. Radhakrishnan, S., *The Theism of Bhagavad Gītā*, p. 90.
55. Vidyaprakashananda, Swami, *op. cit.*, p. 51.
56. *bandhur ātmā atmanas tasya yenātmaivātmanā jitaḥ/*
    anātmanas tu śatrutve vartetātmaiva śatruvat//—BG, 6. 6.
57. *yo māṁ paśyati sarvatra sarvaṁ ca mayi paśyati/*
    tasyāhaṁ na praṇaśyāmi sa ca me na praṇaśyāti//
    sarvabhūtasthitaṁ yo māṁ bhajaty ekatvam āsthitaḥ/
    sarvathā vartamāno api sa yogi mayi vartate//
    ātmāupamyena sarvatra samaṁ paśyati yo arjuna/
    sukhaṁ vā yadi vā duḥkhaṁ sa yogī paramo mataḥ//
    —*Ibid.*, 6. 30-32.

CONCLUSION

Though the metaphysical treatments of the self by *Bhagavad Gītā* reasonably resembles the Indian philosophy; in its elucidate explanations, it deviates from their inconsistent ideas. It includes four parts. In the first part, a comparative account of the explanation of self by this esoteric text along with the other systems of Indian Philosophy is included. In the second part, the various explanations about the characteristic features of the self as expounded by all the systems of Indian Philosophy are sharply dealt with, within which the *Gītā's* stand is comprehensively incorporated. In the third division, the views of Śrī Śaṅkara and Śrī Rāmānuja about the self through their Commentaries upon this text are necessarily condensed. As such, in the fourth part, the relevance of the self to the modern world with special reference to the individual and the society are appropriately placed.

I

In relation to the heterodox systems, the text has no relation with *Cārvāka* because it explains the self with respect to the human values of *dharma* and *mokṣa*; and considers the consciousness as the innermost essence of the self. But *Cārvāka* describes the consciousness as the epiphenomenon and the by-product of matter. The *magnum opus* is conceptually allied with the philosophical treatment of Jainism. But the Jaina's '*madhyamaparimāṇa*' and the self as light particles which pervade the space are reconciled by this monumental text. It explains the self as the eternal and spiritual entity which is bound within the psychophysical material body with respect to its law of *karma*. The esoteric text explains the concept of *nirvāṇa* as Buddhism does, but with a minute variation. The *nirvāṇa* of the *Gītā* is spiritual integration of self with the Supreme Principle. But Buddhism describes it as blowing out of the self into nothing and absolute stoppage of births and deaths and sufferings and sorrows. It differs from Buddhism, i.e., the latter explicates the insubstantiality of self in different degrees; but the former views the self as eternally spiritual substance and co-equal with Ultimate Reality.

The *Gītā* is utmost similar to the orthodox systems. It could be authentically placed under spiritualistic absolutism because the explanation of the self is similar to *Upaniṣadic* monism and *Advaitic* non-dualism of *ātman*-Brahman. It accepts the theistic absolutism because of its doctrines of *'vasudevaḥ sarvam'*, *'apṛathaksiddhiviśeṣaṇam'*, *'dharmabhūtajñāna'* and *'antariyāmin brahman'*. The *Bhagavad Gītā* resembles the realism for its metaphysical treatment of the *puruṣa* and the *prakṛti* as real for self realisation and liberation. But it deviates from the same, i.e., it does not resemble the pluralistic realism of *Nyāya Vaiśeṣika* because it treats the self as *jaḍa* with the accidental property of consciousness. The text rejects the pluralistic realism of *Mīmāṁsā* because it does not believe the existence of God as creator and destroyer. The metaphysical treatment of the *Gītā* links with the dualistic realism of *Sāṅkhya* with an exception. The text considers the *puruṣa* as the higher nature and the *prakṛti* as the lower nature, i.e., the two sides of Ultimate Source, Puruṣottama, whereas the former accepts only the *puruṣa* and the *prakṛti*.

A corroborative study expresses the relation between the *Gītā* and the Indian Philosophical systems of *Sāṅkhya, Yoga*, Jainism and Buddhism. Though the text resembles *Sāṅkhya* in the philosophical standpoint and terminological affinities, it also deviates from the system. The *Bhagavad Gītā* refers to the term *'sāṅkhya'* into two ways, i.e., as to distinguish the path of knowledge and the performance of prescribed duties;

and to explain the way of union with God through *jñāna*. More specifically, it uses this term as 'wisdom' or 'knowledge' and *yoga* as the performance of duty without expecting any reward. By reconciling the both, the text professes, that, through contemplative knowledge and desire less action, the individual could attain self realization. *Sāṅkhya* philosophy treats the *puruṣa* and *prakṛti* as two independent realities. But the *Gītā* synthesizes the duality through the doctrine of Parabrahman and the philosophy of *Kṣetra* and *Kṣetrajña*. *Sāṅkhya's* explanation of the *triguṇatīta*, the person who transcends the *guṇas* resembles *sthitapajña* of the *Bhagavad Gītā*. As a link with *Sāṅkhya*, the *Bhagavad Gītā* adds Lord Kṛṣṇa, the Puruṣottama as the twenty-sixth category along with the *Sāṅkhya's* twenty-five categories. In addition to the explanation of *mukti*, the *Bhagavad Gītā* refers to the destruction of the *māyā* through *jñāna* and the realization of *Paramātman* through His grace. But the *Sāṅkhya* system describes the same as the isolation of the *puruṣa* from *prakṛti*. In the *Gītā*, the higher form of the *puruṣa* and the lower form of *prakṛti* emerge from the unmanifested *pradhāna* under the control of Puruṣottama, Lord Kṛṣṇa, where the varied manifestation is initiated by His Divine Will. But in *Sāṅkhya*, the *puruṣa* and *prakṛti* are independent realities, where the diversified manifestation starts by the disturbance of the equilibrium of the *prakṛti* in the presence of the *puruṣa*. In this text, the *guṇas* are considered to be the qualities of the *prakṛti*. But in the *Sāṅkhya*, the *guṇas* by themselves constitute the *prakṛti* in their equilibrium state.

The *Bhagavad Gītā* resembles the *Yoga* system in the state of attaining *mukti*. The work recommends the middle path for *Yogins* to get union with the *Paramātman* but the latter recommends the complete stoppage of our mental and physical activities through the prescribed *sādhanas* in a lonely place. Through the *yogas* of the text, one can get the equanimity and steadfastness in the worldly order but Patañjali Yoga's *samādhi* helps him to isolate his self from the world. The text resembles

Jainism in the metaphysical explanation of the self, the law of *karma,* the presence of rebirth with respect to the preponderance of *guṇas* in the last birth and the division of *jīvas* and *pudgala* as *prakṛti* and *puruṣa.* But *Jainism* differs from it, i.e., it categorizes the selves as *mukta, baddha, trasa* and *sthāvara;* it divides the *karmas* as *mohanīya karma, antarīya karma, jñānavaraṇīya karma* and *darśanavaraṇīya karma;* and it treats the *kārmic* forces as infra-atomic particles.

The *yoga* of Buddhism reveals the pessimistic approach to the world. For that, one has to disregard the desire and train his mind to look upon his fellow beings as nothing. He should pass through the purificatory processes like sense-control, to offer gifts, the fearlessness of death and the feeling of extinction of the phenomenal order. But the *Gītā's yogas* are optimistic and they can be practiced even by an ordinary man. There is no universal compassion as friendliness and happiness with others in Buddhism to reach equanimity but the *Bhagavad Gītā* also includes the same.

II

The Lord Kṛṣṇa's emphathetic word explains the manifestation of the self with reason. It argues, that, in the unmanifested state, the spiritual *puruṣa* and the material *prakṛti* are kept in constant and it is controlled by the Supreme Reality, Puruṣottama. Then the manifestation of the contingent beings are evolved from the unmanifested *pradhāna* by the copulative activity of Lord Kṛṣṇa, the efficient cause as father and Brahmā, the material cause as mother. During manifestation, the animate and the inanimate beings emerge from Lord Kṛṣṇa's divine creative power of *māyā,* which is nothing but the conglomeration of *sāttvaika, rājasa* and *tāmasa guṇas.* The *Gītā's* view of manifestation reveals, that, Lord Kṛṣṇa Himself pervades within the individual self as *aham* and the mental qualities as His divine essence. It is being understood, that, every activity of the universe and the individual is derived from the *prakṛti,* i.e., the *guṇas.* The *puruṣa* does not act but experiences the whole activities of the individual and the universe. So, *puruṣa*, the individual self and Puruṣottama, the universal are acting as mere witnesses, i.e., the *guṇas* alone act as agent.

Through the study of *Kṣetra* and *Kṣetrajña*, the relationship between spiritual self and material body is understood. It reconciles the *prakṛti* and *Kṣetra*, where the former refers to the instrument to form the individual body and the universe; and the latter refers to the entire body of the individual and universe. The *Kṣetrajña* refers to the *puruṣa* which is the active conscious principle; and it acts as a witness or knower of the *Kṣetra*. After reconciling the both, the *Gītā* explains, that, if one understands this, the individual may realise his original duty in his circumstance with respect to the predominated *guṇas* to reach the supreme state of *mukti*. If one understands the *buddhi* with the preponderance of *guṇas* through *indriyas* and *manas*, he can control the same to realize his self. So, through *niṣkāmakarma yoga* and the suppression of the *guṇas*, he could concentrate his mind which helps him to realize its reality through *buddhi*.

The self transmigrates from one birth to the next. Before manifestation all the selves of animate and the inanimate beings are indistinct and constant. During manifestation, selves pass through many births and deaths until they return to their unmanifested state. During transmigration, the self throws out the bodies repeatedly until its union with God through self-realization. The *rājasa* and *tāmasa guṇas* are binding the self within lower level through the crudity of knowledge, wrong faith, utter firmness in his activities, unusual habits and the practices of unrefined speech, mind and body. If so, the lower selves forget the wisdom of the reality due to the ignorance which binds the *indriyas* to the worldly level. After expressing the above truth, the text recommends the presence of *sattva guṇa* to raise the lower self to that of higher. The lower self becomes the higher one through self-control, selflessness, understanding the value of action to inaction- *niṣkāmakarma yoga;* the perfect devotion to God; and the dedication of his fruits of the actions to the welfare of the humanity. Along with this, the self-discipline; stead-fastness and non-attachment; and the control of desire, anger and greed are helpful to become the higher nature. So, in the higher state, the self identifies its *indriyas, manas* and *buddhi* as Lord's lower form, the *prakṛti;* and his actual self as His higher form, the *puruṣa.* If so, the *vāsanā* of the past births is weakened and finally it will be fully nullified. In that state, the higher self realizes the many branched wisdom as one and enjoys the supreme peace and happiness. Then, the higher self resembles the Supreme Reality, i.e., *ātma* as *Paramātma* and *nara* as Nārāyaṇa.

To shift the lower self to higher, the *Bhagavad Gītā* recommends *jñāna yoga, karma yoga* and *bhakti yoga,* etc., and through which the different kinds of lower selves attain the higher status. Through the *yogas,* the *puruṣa* within the *prakṛti* separates itself and conjoins with the Puruṣottama through reflective, emotive and active mind to reach the spiritual realm. Through *karma yoga,* the lower self disciplines the human will for the divine purpose to realize the eternal reality through *niṣkāmyakarma yoga* and dedication of the fruits of actions to the holy feet of Lord. Through the *bhakti yoga,* the distinction of the creature and creator is reduced by perfect devotion, by adoring His qualities, by singing His praises and doing services to Him with the aid of His grace. Through *jñāna yoga,* the self through knowledge realizes the nature of self, God, the drawbacks to follow the paths, the means to rectify the drawbacks; and through the process it also matures and attains the holy feet of the Lord Kṛṣṇa. So, through the all kinds of *yogas, rājasa* and *tāmasa guṇas* are transformed into *sattva guṇa,* where the individual mystically experiences the bliss of the Reality.

The self with reference to morality represents the right character and conduct in accordance with its nature and rational will. The *Bhagavad Gītā* as a theo-centric scripture assumes Lord Kṛṣṇa as the supreme authority for the moral order. This moral order helps the society for its upliftment through the individual's duty-consciousness, i.e., *dharma*. To maintain *dharma*, the text, splits the society into four castes with their prescribed duties on the basis of *guṇas, karma,* nature of duty and conduct. The Song Celestial does not accept the change of caste-duty because doing one's ordained duty with respect to the *guṇas*, the individual will never incur sin. Based on the *dharma*, the *Bhagavad Gītā* differentiates two kinds of personalities as aspirants with the *daiva sampat* and the individuals with the *asura sampat*. The former always leads his life to realize his own self for *mokṣa* but the latter pollutes himself with worst qualities like lust, wrath and greed; and he is always kept away from the divinity. The *Bhagavad Gītā* emphasizes, that, eventhough the individual tries to understand the Ultimate Reality through controlling his *manas* and *buddhi*, he may not get success without His grace, because, as such, the impact of the *ahaṅkāra* and *avidyā* which predominantly overcome the essential nature of the carnal self. While understanding the reality, it recommends two kinds of knowledge as the ordinary and the divine. The former is acquired by one's own effort based on his *indriyas* and the intellectual activities; but the latter is acquired by the influence of Supreme Grace of the Lord, which helps him to apprehend the Reality through intuition.

A critical study of the *Gītā* explicates the truth with proper analysis. It advocates, that, if the individual performs his worldly activities, he will never understand the divinity. Instead, if he perceives Lord Kṛṣṇa as the Supreme; if he devotes his existence to the feet of Him; if he detaches his psychophysical complex from the worldly order; if he eliminates the tendency of hatredness towards all beings; and if he considers himself as an instrument in the Lord's hand, then, the individual automatically merges with the Godliness.

The ultimate destiny of the self is considered to be the *nirvāṇa*. It is not as that of Buddhism, but self realization and its union with the Reality. For this, the *Gītā* recommends the suppression of the *buddhi, manas* and *indriyas* to isolate the self and to realize its immortal nature. In that state, the self gets absolute serenity, where it maintains the equanimity and always subsists in the Ultimate Reality. To attain the proper destiny, the Glorified Song recommends *sattva guṇa* because it helps the self to acquire knowledge about the Brahman. Then the self crosses even the *sattva guṇa* and merges with Him as *triguṇātīta*.

III

The views of Śrī Śaṅkara and Śrī Rāmānuja about the self with respect to their Commentaries upon the *Bhagavad Gītā* are necessary to apprehend the inner nature; and out of the study, the relevance could be properly justified.

Through his commentary Śrī Śaṅkara professes, that, all the selves are one and the pluralistic languages such as 'I', 'thou' and 'these rulers' refers to only the material bodies. He affirms, that, the material principle of the universe is *māyā*, and is controlled by the Brahman. He equates *ātman* with Brahman, but there is a difference because *ātman* is subjected to the influence of *māyā*. Giving prime importance to *jñāna yoga*, he advocates, that, by cessation of the *avidyā* through *jñāna*, the individual can perceives the pluralistic appearance as false, because they are the by-products of the *māyā* in the temporal order; and which is organized by Brahman who is associated with it.

Śrī Śaṅkara explains, that, the *Kṣetrajña* or *puruṣa* within the *Kṣetras* is only Reality and the manifoldness of the individuals is only because of the various *upādhis* and *vṛtti*, the mode of *antaḥkaraṇas*. He professes, that, in the *vyāvahārika* state, the spiritual *sākṣin* connotes the *vṛtti* and *avidyā* but in the *pāramārthika* state, the *sākṣin* alone exists. By explaining *māyā*, he verifies, that, the pluralism will appear as the real until the realization of the *jīva* and Brahman through *jñāna* by nullifying the effects of *māyā*. He also exposes his monistic conception through the principle of the *adhyāsa*, the erronious *jñāna*, i.e., due to the *adhyāsa*, the self relates to the *jñāta*, the knower with mind; and it leads to the pluralism. But when *adhyāsa* disappears by *jñāna*, the *buddhi* identifies the original standpoint of the self and Brahman as one. By analyzing the different states like *jāgra*, *svapna*, *suṣupti*, *turīya* and *turīyātīta*, Śrī Śaṅkara explains the monism, i.e, the self in the *turīyātīta* state is Brahman. Through *kāryakāraṇa vicāra*, the technique of cause and effect and *vivartavāda*, the theory of apparent change, he explains the pluralism as false.

Unlike Śrī Śaṅkara, through his Commentary, Śrī Rāmānuja gives importance to *bhakti yoga* with the philosophical exposition of *apṛthaksiddhaviśeṣaṇa*. By criticizing former's *māyā* theory, Śrī Rāmānuja states, that, the finite selves are many; physical nature is true as well as real; and they bear intrinsic pluralities and individualities for ever. Śrī Rāmānuja criticizes Śrī Śaṅkara's explanation of absolute consciousness by analyzing the dual nature of consciousness as subject and object. He unlike Śrī Śaṅkara argues, that, consciousness is not *nitya* but it is many and subject to change through *saṅkoca* and *vikāsa*, the contraction and expansion. So, he rejects the *Advaitic* identity of the consciousness with the self but treats as its attribute. So, rejecting the principle of *sākṣin*, Śrī Rāmānuja substantiates, that, the self is other than the consciousness. So, 'I'-ness, the self even continues its existence in the *turīyātīta* and *mukti* states. He postulates his pluralism through *satkāryavāda*, the realism; and *samanādhikāraṇya*, the co-ordination. He also substantiates his stand with the philosophical views of *jīva* as a *prakāra* of Brahman; the divinity exists everywhere as *antaryāmin*; and the relation of *cit* and *acit* with Brahman as *apṛthaksiddhi*. In the casual state or in the unmanifested state, the intertwined organic whole is in subtle form and in the effective state or in the manifested state, these three, i.e., *cit*, *acit* and *Īśvara* are in the gross form. There are plural realities in the subtle and gross forms, but Brahman is free from the changes and imperfections.

Śrī Rāmānuja's criticism of Śrī Śaṅkara's doctrine of *māyā* also bears remarks, i.e., the *avidyā* of Śrī Śaṅkara and the law of *karma* of Śrī Rāmānuja are beginningless to the self. In this context, both are approaching the same problem from different starting points but meet their inefficiency while placing the proper reasons. Maintaining *cit* and *acit* as the real substances and as the real attributes bear a logical inconsistency because the real may not be dependent upon anything. So, Śrī Rāmānuja's reconciliation of the two extremes of *Upaniṣadic* Absolutism and *Vaiṣṇavitic* Theism stands for criticism because maintaining absolutism and pluralism or identity-in-differences in the same level is untenable. His qualitative monism and quantitative pluralism are unacceptable because he himself accepts, that, the material bodies are going to disappear when the self realizes its own state. To unite the mundane and transcendental existence through pluralism is an inconsistent one because the individual *jīva* is subject to finite knowledge but transcendental self is not as such because it is eternal and exists beyond time and space. Even if one accepts the *Viśiṣṭādvaitic* stand, the view is substantiated, i.e., if God is the *antariyāmin* Brahman, there is no reason for Him to reside at Vaikuṇṭha with His consort Gòddess Laksmi with *nityamukta* and *mukta*. Here, maintaining the *niytamukta* is untenable because philosophically the selves are either in *mukti* or in *baddha* state. Anyhow, in religious sense some of the dogmatic views may be beyond the philosophical discussion; rather it may be acceptable within the realm of faith. But to him, it needs much of analysis to settle down the some of religious issues. Śrī Rāmānuja's *dharmabhūtajñāna* is untenable because if the consciousness is the attribute of the selves, then the consciousness with the feature of expansion and contraction is beyond verification.

In a nutshell, Śrī Śaṅkara and Śrī Rāmānuja approach the self with respect to Brahman and the world into two different direction with their distinct epistemology and metaphysics. A comprehensive perspective of the both shows, that, eventhough Śrī Rāmānuja's pluralism bears criticism, he fulfils the practical and theoretical guidelines to the spiritual realm through fulfiment of the phenomenal activities. But Śrī Śaṅkara theoretically completes his work but fails in the practical field because ordinary human beings may get struggle to follow his doctrines of *māyā* and the realization of the Ultimate Reality through *neti-neti* method.

IV

The study is relevant to this modern world because the world community changed towards the materialistic and scientific advancement rather than that of the spiritual. Attachment with material goods, inventions of modern weapons and the wrong identification of *varṇāśramadharma* have changed the society upside down. This drastic situation is due to the misunderstanding of religion as a superstitious belief. Our upsetting social equilibrium of idle rich and idle poors change the values and put the religion in a secondary place. But our modern scientific inventions are bridging the science and philosophy. Scientists through their research give importance to religion and accept the existence of super spiritual force which helps to invent new things. Though one generation believes the importance of religion as essential, the other loses its soul and make the religion as an external appearance to cover their selfish and materialistic attitude. But understanding the metaphysics of the self in the *Bhagavad Gītā* generously rectifies these defects and helps humanity to lead a life of peace with bliss of the divinity. For the individual, the *Gītā* recommends renunciation of the fruits in action and not the renunciation of action. Through this, the individual gets self-realization and out of it, he attains the self content and fullness of the action, spiritual enjoyment and the understanding of the Reality. In this respect, it advises the individual to dedicate all the fruits of his actions to the feet of Lord Kṛṣṇa. For the dedication, the Lord showers His grace upon the individual.

The *Bhagavad Gītā* supports the individual to raise himself to higher level through the purification of mind by penance, charity, conduct etc. For that, he has to remove his ignorance and delusion; he has to build up his character by discarding the lust and greed; he has to maintain the equanimity to the opposite pairs; and he has to feel other selves as his own. For the same, he should be away from the thought of despair, helplessness to others, the fear of death; and lust, wrath, and greed. Along with them, he should bear tough heart, firm mind and the law of moderation. In addition, the individual should always think about Brahman until his death because *māyā* can enter at any time to drawback the self from the higher status of spiritual advancement into the lower level of materialistic attachment. It grants, that, every individual should perform his *svadharma* in accordance with his *svabhāva*. If it is so, he will never incur sin. So, the text unanimously supports, that, the total system of the society becomes spiritual through self-realization through the performance of the prescribed duties.

It professes, that, the law of *karma* is responsible for the inequalities and the tragedies in the society. If the individual performs his duty sincerely as the direction of the *Gītā*, he can get *summum bonum* of life; and through which, he realizes his self and the Universal Self. The Song Celestial says, that, all our activities are not determined by the law of *karma* without the aid of our free will. The entire activities are not pre-determined by other external force apart from his self, but self determined. Reconciling the both, the *Gītā* explains, that, the individual controls and regulates his activity through his discrimination and determination along with the *daivic* force. Like the individual, if the entire society performs the *niṣkāmyakarma yoga*, it becomes superb because, the results of the works will reach the others. Then, out of it, they, by eradicating their *avidyā* through proper *jñāna* can realize their selves as *sat cit ānanda.*

Through love, the individual can perceive the Ultimate Reality within the animate and the inanimate beings. Along with this, the sense of universal brotherhood evolves from the love, so that, the mental conflicts, ill-will and hatredness among the individuals will be vanished. Then, the self realizes its own status as the spiritual force of the cosmos and leads to perfection.

The *Bhagavad Gītā* does not recommend either *saṁnyāsa* or *saṁsāra* but the middle path. Through the middle path, the individual can realize his own life and helps the society for its goodness, so that, he reaches the blissful feet of Lord Kṛṣṇa.

Eventhough it professes *jñāna yoga, karma yoga, bhakti yoga* etc., as the paths towards the realization, the different kinds are only because of the variations of the *guṇas,* taste, temperament and efficiency of the particular individual in the society. They lead to one goal, i.e., *mukti.* If a person bears *avidyā,* he perceives only contradiction among them, but a person with knowledge treats all as one. So, the text stands as a world scripture, within which, all human beings can attain perfection through their desired paths.

The knowledge of the *Gītā* is considered to be integrated and scientific for all the times because it is intuitive and inductive rather than rational and deductive. So, through the *sāttvika jñāna,* the modern society finds out the ultimate source of energy as spiritual. Instead of various religious sects with distinct philosophical doctrines, if there is a single religion with a common belief, there will be a firm union and total development of the world society. If one closely observes the tenets of the *Bhagavad Gītā,* he can certainly assert, that, it helps for the world religion with a casteless, colourless and creedless society through its versatile outlook with cosmopolitan vista.

BIBLIOGRAPHY

Abhedanda Swami. (1969). *Bhagavad Gita the Divine Message*, Calcutta.

Agrawala, V.S., (n.d.). *The Song Celestial*, Varanasi.

Alexander Neil (1903). *Gita and Gospel*, Calcutta.

Alladi Mahadeva Sastry, *The Bhagavad Gita*, Madras.

Anil Baran Roy. (1963). *The Gita*, Pondicherry.

Arnold, Edwin (Trans). (2002). *Bhagavad Gita: The Song Celestial*, New Albian Press.

Arnold, Sir Edwin. (1930). *The Song Celestial or the Bhagavad Gita*, London.

Aurobindo. (1922). *Essays on the Gita* (2 Vols). Madras.

Ayyangar, Satyamurti S. (1980). *Srimad Bhagavad Gita*, Madras.

Baba, Bhagavan Sri Sathya Sai. (1980). *Geetha Vahini*. Prasanthinilayam, Andhra Pradesh.

Baba, Bengali. (1944). *Shrimad Bhagavad Gita*. Lahore.

Bahm, Archi, J. (1970). *The Bhagavad Gita*, Bombay.

Balasubramanian, R. (1978). *Some Problems in the Epistemology and Metaphysics of Ramanuja*, Madras.

Balbir Singh. *Essence of Bhagavad Gita*, New Delhi.

Balbir Singh. (1981). *Atman and Moksha*, New Delhi.

Balbir Singh. (1979). *The Conceptual Framework of Indian Philosophy*, Meerut.

Balvalkar, S.K. (1943). *The Bhagavad Gita*, Poona.

Banerjee, Nikunja Vihari. (1974). *The Spirit of Indian Philosophy*, New Delhi.

Banerjee, V.V., *History of Western Philosophy*, Lucknow.

Barbara Stoler Miller. (2004). *The Bhagavad Gita*. London.

Bajaj Prem Nath. (1975). *The Role of Bhagavad Gita in Indian History*, New Delhi.

Belwalker, S.V. (1948). *Bhagavad Gita Trichotomy vs Triune Unity*, Poona.

Besant, Annie, (1906). *Hints on the Study of the Bhagavad Gita*, Chennai.

Besant, Annie. (1961). *The Bhagavad Gītā: The Lord's Song*, Madras.

Besant, Annie & Bhagwan Das, (1979). *The Bhagavad Gita*, Madras.

Betai, Ramesh, S. (1970). *Gita and Gandhiji*, Ahmedabad.

Bhagwan Sri Ramana Rishi. (1960). *The Song Celestial*, Tiruvannamalai, Tamil Nadu.

Bhagwat, Ramchandra Keshav. (1979). Jnaneshwari *(Sri Jnanadeva's Bhavartha Dipika)*, Madras.

Bhaktivedanta Swami Prabhupada, A.C. (1972). *Bhagavadgita as It Is*. New York.

——. (1984). *Light of the Bhagavad Gita*, Singapur.

Bhave, Acharya Vinoba. *Talks on the Gita*, Madras.

Bolle, Kees, W. (1979). *The Bhagavad Gita*, London.

Bose, Dilip. (1981). *Bhagavad Gita and Our National Movement*, New Delhi.

Bramachari Gitananda. (1930). *The Gita Idea of God*, Madras.

Brooks, F.T. (1909). *The Bhagavad Gita*. Srirangam, Tamil Nadu.

Burway, M.W. (1981). *Bhagavad Gita*, New Delhi.

Burway, Mukund Woman Rao. (1916). *Glimpses of the Bhagavad Gita and the Vedanta Philosophy*, Bombay.

Buitenen, J.A.B.Van. (1974). *Ramanuja on the Bhagavadgita*, Varanasi.

Caleb, C.C. (1911). *The Song Divine or the Bhagavad Gita*, London.

Castell, Alburey. (1965). *The Self in Philosophy*, London.

Chakravarti, Pulinbihari. (1975). *Origin and Development of Samkhya System of Thought*, New Delhi.

Chatterjee, R.K. (1987). *The Gita and Its Culture*, New Delhi.

Chaudhuri, Anil Kumar Ray. *Self and Palsity in Advaita Vedanta*, Calcutta.

Sharma, Chandradhar, *Critical Survey of Indian Philosophy*, Delhi.

Chatterjee, Mohini, M. (1960). *The Bhagavad Gita*, New York.

Chidbhavananda, Swami. (1969). *The Bhagavad Gita*, Tirupparaithurai, Tiruchirappalli.

Chinmayananda, Swami. *The Holy Geeta*, Bombay.

——. (1985). *The Bhagavad Geeta*, Vol. I-XII, Bombay.

Chintamon Hary Chund, (1874). *A Commentary on the Text of the Bhagavad Gita*, London.

Chilate, Mahadeo Parashuram. (1953). *Bhagavat Gita and Hindu Dharma*, Poona.

Tiwari, Chitra, *Sutras in Manu*, Delhi.

Coomaraswamy, Ananda. (1956). *Buddha and the Gospel of Buddhism*. Bombay.

Dasgupta, Surendranath. (1975). *A History of Indian Philosophy* Vol. I-IV, Delhi.

Date, V.H. (1971). *Brahma-Yoga of the Gita*, New Delhi.

Davies, John. (1979). *The Bhagavad Gita*, Delhi.

De Riencourt, Amaury. (1960). *The Soul of India*, New York.

Desai, Mahadev. (1951). *The Gita according to Gandhi*, Ahmedabad.

Deshmukh, C.D. (1976). *Bhagavadgita*, Secundrabad.

Deussen, P. (1912). *The System of Vedanta*, Chicago.

Deutch, Eliot. (1969). *The Bhagavad Gita*, New York.

Dharma Theerthaji. (1944). *Yoga for all or the Religion of the Gita*, Lahore.

Dhar, Mohini Mohan. (1919). *Krishna and Charioteer*, London.

Roy, Dilip Kumar, (1974). *The Bhagavad Gita: A Revelation*, New Delhi.

Divatia, H.V. (1970). *The Art of Life in the Bhagavad Gita*, Bombay.

Dreamer. (1902). *Studies in the Bhagavad Gita*, London.

Durrani, F.K. Khan. (1929). *The Bhagavadgita: A Criticism*, Lahore.

Edgerton, Franklin. (1964). *The Bhagavad Gita*, New York.

Edward, Paul, (Ed.). (1967). *The Encyclopaedia of Philosophy*, London.

Easwaran, Eknath, (1986). *Like a Thousand Suns*, 2 Vols, Petaluma.

Entwistle, A.W. (1982). *Vaisnava Tilakas*, London.

Wood, Ernest, *The Bhagavadgita Explained*, Texas.

Farguhar, J.N. (1904). *The Age and Origin of the Gita*, Calcutta.

Farguhar, J.N. (1917). *Gita and Gospel.*

Feuertein, G.A. (1974). *Introduction to Bhagavad Gita*, London.

Gandhi, Mahatma. *The Bhagavadgita*, New Delhi.

Gandhi, M.K. (1945). *Gita the Mother*, Lahore.

Gauchwall, Balbir Singh. (1967). *The Concept of Perfection in the Teachings of Kant and the Gita*, Delhi.

Geoffrey, Parrinder. (1974). *The Bhagavad Gita*, London.

Goswami, C.L. and others. (1947). *Srimad Bhagavad Gita*, Gorakhpur.

Goyanka, Jayadayal. (1973). *Srimad Bhagavadgita*, Gorakhpur.

Greenless, Duncan. (1962). *The Gospel of Sri Krishna*. Madras.

Gunaji, N.V. (1957). *Geeta*, Bombay.

Gune, N.P. *The Shrimat Bhagavad Gita*, Poona.

Hanmant Rao, K. (1916). *Fragrant Essence of Geeta*, Ahmedabad.

Hastings, James Ed. (1956). *Encyclopaedia of Religion and Ethics*, New York.

Ray Chaudhuri, Hemchandra, (1975). *Materials for the Study of the Early History of the Vaisnava Sect*, New Delhi.

Hill, W.D.P. (1928). *The Bhagavad Gita*, Madras.

Hill, W. Douglas, P. (1973). *The Bhagavad Gita*, Madras.

Hiriyanna, M. (1970). *Outlines of Indian Philosophy*, London.

Hume, R.E. (1951). *The Thirteen Principal Upanishads*, Oxford.

Singh, Indu Prakash, (1977). *The Gita*, Bombay.

Jagadeesan, N. (1977). *History of Sri Vaisnavism in the Tamil Country (Post-Ramanuja)*, Madurai.

Shastri, Jagadish and McLeod.(1938). *Bhagavad Gita*, Lahore.

Jitender. (1993). *Dialogue Divine*, Saharanpur.

Joshipura, J.M. (1980). *Realities of Bhagavad Gita*, Bombay.

Joshi, Shanti. (1968). *The Message of Sankara*, Allahabad.
Joshi, V.M. (1916). *A Gist of Mr. Tilak's Gita Rahasya*, Banaras.
Juan Mascaro. (2003). *The Bhagavad Gita*, London.
Judge, William and Grosbire Robert. (1942). *Notes on the Bhagavad Gita*, Los Angeles.
Kalelkar, Kakasahab. (1967). *The Geeta as Jeevan-Yoga*, Bombay.
Kalidas Shastri, Rajavaidya Jivaram. (1937). *Sri Bhagavad Gita*, Kathiwad.
Kaji, Chargantal, G. (1909). *The Philosophy of Bhagavad Gita*, Rajkot.
Kamala Roy. *The Concept of Self*, Calcutta.
Kanto Keshob. *The Message of the Gita*, Gauhati.
Kasinath Trimbak Telang. (1983). *The Bhagavad Gita*, Delhi.
Kaveeshwar, G.W. (1971). *The Ethics of the Gita*, Delhi.
Khair, Gajanan Shripat. (1969). *Quest for the Original Gita*, Bombay.
Kher, B.G. (1960). *The Art of Life in the Bhagavad Gita*, Bombay.
Krishna Warrier, A.G. (1983). *Srimad Bhagavad Gita Bhasya of Sri Sankaracharya*, Madras.
Kumudranjanray. (1931). *Evolution of the thoughts in Bhagavad Gita* or Evolution of Gita, Calcutta.
Kuppuswami, A. (1974). *Shri Bhagavad Gita*, Kumbakonam, Tamil Nadu.
Laird, John. (1924). *The Idea of the Soul*, London.
Lal, R.B. (1970). *The Gita in the Light of Modern Science*, Bombay.
Lingesh Mahabhagavat of Kurtkoti, Pandit. (1918). *The Heart of the Bhagavad Gita*, Baroda.
Mahadevan, T.M.P. (1976). *Philosophia Perennis in the Bhagavad Gita*, Madras.
Mahadeva Sastri. (1961). *The Bhagavad Gita*, Madras.
Mahadev Desai. *The Gita according to Gandhi*, Ahmedabad.
——. (1946). *The Gospel of Selfless Action or the Gita According to Gandhi*, Ahmedabad.
Mahesh Yogi, Maharishi. *Bhagavad Gita*, England.
Maheshwar. (ed). (1978). *Bhagavad Gita in the Light of Sri Aurobindo*, Pondicherry.

Mainkar, G. (1938). *Sankara and the Moksha Passages in Bhagavad Gita*, Poona.

Majumdar, Sachindra. (1991). *The Bhagavad Gita*, Fremont, C.A.

Mascaro Juan. (1970). *The Bhagavad Gita*, London.

Mathai, P.S. (1956). *A Christian Approach to the Bhagavadgita*, Calcutta.

Mehta, Rohit. (1953). *The Bhagavad Gita* and our Age, Guntur.

Mikhailov, F.T. (1980). *The Riddle of the Self*, Moscow.

Minor, Robert N. (1982). *Bhagavad Gita*, New Delhi.

Misra, H.N. (1963). *Ethics Aristotle and Bhagavadgita*. Kanpur.

Misra, Tulsi Ram. (1924). *Srimad Bhagavad Gita*, Lucknow.

Misra, Sharda. (1979). *Krishna Speaks to you again*, New Delhi.

Mishra Umesha. (1954). *The Bhagavadgita: A Critical Study*, Allahabad.

Mitra, Pramada Dasa. (1897). *The Bhagavad Gita*, Banaras.

Modi, P.M. (1955). *The Bhagavadgita: A Fresh Approach*, Baroda.

Mookerjee, S. (1935). *The Buddhist Philosophy of Universal Flux*, Calcutta.

Morarji Desai. (1978). *A View of the Gita*, New Delhi.

Mukherjee, Radhakamal. (1999). *Bhagavad Gita*, Delhi.

Mullick, Bulloram. (1894). *A Land-marks of the Ethics according to the Gita*, Calcutta.

Munshi, K.M. (1960). *Bhagavad Gita and Modern Life*, Bombay.

Murdoch, John. (1902). *The Religious and Moral Teachings of the Bhagavad Gita Examined*, Madras.

Murti, T.R.V. (1955). *The Central Philosophy of Buddhism*, London.

Nagaraja Rao, P. The *Bhagavad Gita and the Changing World*, Ahmedabad.

Narasimhan, P. (1939). *Gita*, Madras.

Nataraja Guru (tr. from the Sanskrit). (1981). *Nitya Chaitanya Yati* (with Explanatory Dialogue), New Delhi.

Nataraja Guru (trans.). (1981). *The Bhagavad Gita*, Ghaziabad, U.P.

Narasimhachari, M. Deevasenapathi, V.A., Balasubramanian, R. (1978). *Perspectives of Theism and Absolutism in Indian Philosophy*, Madras.

Narayabagiah, Prakash Chaundra. *An Introduction to the Study of the Bhagavad Gita*, Calcutta.

Nikhilananda, Swami. (1952). *The Bhagavad Gita*, New York.

Noel, Sheth. S.J. (1984). *The Divinity of Krishna*, New Delhi.

Otto Rudolf. (1939). *The Origin of the Gita*. (Tr. by Turner), London.

Padmanabhan, C.M. (1916). *A Critical Study of the Bhagavad Gita*, Madras.

Pandey, R.K. (1979). *The Concept of Avatars*, Delhi.

Pandya, J.J. (1944). *The Holy Gita*, Rajkot.

Panoli, Vidyavachaspati. (1979). *Gita in Śankara's Own Words*, Madras.

Paradkar, M.D. (1970). *Studies in the Gita*, Bombay.

Parrinder Geoffrey. (1975). *Upanishads Gita and Bible*, London.

Geoffrey, Parrinder, (1974). *The Bhagavad Gita a verse translation*, London.

Patel, Baburao. (1962). *Bhagavad Geeta*, Bombay.

Paul, Deussen. (1976). *Outlines of Indian Philosophy*, Delhi.

Phillipson Coleman. (1928). *The Trail of Socrates*, London.

Prabhavananda Swami, Isherwood, Christopher. (1951). *Bhagavad Gita*, New York.

Prabhupada, A.C. Bhaktivedanta Swami. (1972). *Bhagavad Gita as It is*, Bombay.

Pradip Tirtha, Maharaj, Srila Bhakti. (1948). *Bhagavad Gita*, Calcutta.

Pringle Pattison, A.S. (1917). *Idea of God*, Oxford.

Radhakrishnan, S. (1927). *Indian Philosophy*, Vol. I & II, London.

Purohit, Swami Shri. (1938). *The Geeta*, London.

Radhakrishnan, S. (1946). *The Theism of the Bhagavad Gita*, Banaras.

Radhakrishnan, S. (1948). *The Bhagavad Gita*, London.

Radhakrishnan, S. & Charles A. Moore. (1973). A *Source Book in Indian Philosophy*, New Jersey.

Rajagopalachari, C. (1964). *Bhagavad Gita*, Bombay.

Ragavachar, S.S. (1969). *Sri Ramanuja on the Gita*, Mangalore.

Rale, Vasant, G. (1959). *Bhagavad Gita: An Exposition*, Bombay.

Ramdas, Swami. (1976). *Gita Sandesh*, Bombay.

Ramakrishnan, S. (1948). *The Bhagavad Gita*, London.

Ramanujacharya, V.K. (1922). *Introduction to the Bhagavad Gita*, Madras.

Vyas, Ramnarayan, (1977). *The Bhagavata Bhakti Cult and Three Advaita Acaryas*, Delhi.

Ramanathan, V. (1982). *Bhagavad Gita for Executives*, Bombay.

Ranade, R.D. (1959). *The Bhagavad Gita as a philosophy of God Realisation*, Nagpur.

Roy, Dilip Kumar, *The Bhagavad Gita a Revelation*, Delhi.

Roy, R.N. (1981). *The Bhagavad Gita*, Allahabad.

Roy, S.C. (1941). *Interpretations of the Bhagavad Gita-Book I Bhagavad Gita and Modern Scholarship*, London.

Runes, Dagobert D. (Ed.). (1945). *The Dictionary of Philosophy*, London.

Ryder, Arthur, W. (1929). *The Bhagavad Gita*, Chicago.

Sampathkumaran, M.R. (1969). *The Gitabhasya of Ramanuja*, Madras.

Sargeant, Winthrop. (1979). *The Bhagavad Gita*, New York.

Sarma, D.S. (1928). *The Gita and Spiritual Life*, Madras.

Sarma, D.S. (1945). *Lectures and Essays on the Bhagavad Gita*, Madras.

Sastri, Kodleswar. (1926). *An Introduction to Advaita Philosophy*, Calcutta.

Satcherbatsky (Tr.). (1927). *Conception of Buddhist Nirvana*, Leningrad.

Satwalekar, Shripad Damodar. (1944). *Shrimad Bhagavad Gita* (4 Vols). Aundh.

Shankar, Pandit Bhavani. (1928). *The Doctrine of the Bhagavad Gita*, Bombay.

Sharvananda Swami. (1933). *Religion and Philosophy of the Gita*, New Delhi.
Sharan, Mahesh Kumar. (1977). *The Bhagavad Gita and Hindu Sociology*, New Delhi.
Sharma, Arvind, (1986). *The Hindu Gita*, London.
Sircar, Mahandranatha. (1929). *Mysticism in Bhagavad Gita*, London.
Sivananda, Swami. (1957). *Shripad Bhagavad Gita*, Rishikesh.
Sivananda, Swami. (1982). *The Bhagavad Gita*, Garhwal, India.
Srinivasachari, P.N. (1928). *Ramanuja's idea of the Finite Self*, London.
Srinivasachari, P.N. (1943). *The Ethical Philosophy of the Gita*, Madras.
Srinivasachari, S.M. (1961). *Advaita and Visistadvaita*, Madras.
Srivastava, A.K. (1980). *Bhagavad Gita Economic Development and Management*, New Delhi.
Stafford Betty, L. (1978). *Vadiraju'a Refutation of Sankara's Non-Dualism*, Delhi.
Stanford Ann. (1970). *The Bhagavad Gita*, New York.
Steven J. Rosen (ed). (1992). *Vaisnavism*, New York.
Subbayya, Swami. (1917). *Bhagavad Gita*, Madras.
Subba Rau, S. (1906). *The Bhagavad Gita according to Shri Madwacharya's Bhasya*, Madras.
Subba Rao, T. (1931). *Philosophy of Bhagavad Gita*, Madras.
Sundaram, P.K. (1980). *Advaita Metaphysics*, Madras.
Suzuki, T. (1900). *The Awakening of Faith in the Mahayana*.
Swarupanand, Swami. (1926). *Shrimad Bhagavad Gita*, Almora.
Swarupanand, Swami. (1967). *Shrimad Bhagavad Gita*, Calcutta.
The Oxford Dictionary of Quotations (II Ed.), London.
The Encyclopaedia Americana, Vol.25. (1959) Washington D.C.
The Pail Tipitaka (ed.). London.
Thadani, N.V. (1933). *Bhagavad Gita*, Karachi.
Thirugnansambandam, P. (1978). *Bhagavad Gita*, Madras.
Thomson, Cockburn, J. (1954). *Bhagavad Gita*, Chicago.
Thomas, J. (1959). *Bhagavad Gita*, London.

Tilak, G. (1936). *Srimad Bhagavadgita-Rahasya or Karma Yoga Sastra*, Poona.

Tilak, Bal Gangadhar. (1971). *Srimad Bhagavadgita-Rahasya*, 2 Vols., Poona.

Toleni, P.S. *Gita-My Guide*, Bombay.

Toynbee, A. (1970). *The Hindu Testament*, Bombay.

Upadhyaya, Kashi Nath. *Early Buddhism and the Bhagavad Gita*, Delhi.

Utgihar, N.B. (1918). *Garbe's Introduction to Bhagavad Gita*, Bombay.

Vadekar, D.D. (1928). *Bhagavad Gita a Fresh Study*, Poona.

Van Buitenen, J.A.B. *Ramanuja on the Bhagavadgita*, Delhi.

Van Buitenen, J.A.B. (1981). *The Bhagavad Gita in the Mahabharata*, Chicago.

Varadachari, V. (1982). *Agamas and South Indian Vaisnavism*, Madras.

Vasant G. Rele. *Bhagavad Gita — An Exposition*, Bombay.

Vasudevarai, R. (1938). *The Heart-Doctrine of the Bhagavad Gita and its Message*, Madras.

Vasudeva Row, R. (1946). *Introduction to the Study of Srimad Bhagavad Gita*, Madras.

Vaswani, T.L. *Gita: A Bible of Humanity*, Poona.

Vaswani, T.L. *The Bhagavad Gita: The Song of Life*, Poona.

Vaswani, T.L. (1960). *The Gita and the Modern World.*

Vaswani, T.L. *The Bhagavad Gita: An Interpretation*, Poona.

Venkatanarayana Nayudu, J. (1948). *Essential Teachings and Sadhanas of the Bhagavad Gita*, Madras.

Venkateswarananda. (1982). *Song of God*, New York.

Venkateswaran, R.J. (1982). *Bhagavad Gita for Peace of Mind*, Bombay.

Verma, K.M.P. (1980). *Kant and the Gita*, New Delhi.

Vidyalankara, Ishwara Dutt. (1930). *Ramanuja's Com.on the Bhagavad Gita*, Hyderabad.

Vidyaprakashananda, Swami. (1980). *Gita Maharanda*, Chittoor.

Vinoba. (1932). *The Essence of Quran*, Varanasi.
Virajeshver, (1977). *Science of Bhagavadgita*, Delhi.
Vireswarananda, Swami. (1972). *Srimad Bhagavad Gita*, Madras.
Vireswarananda, Swami. *Brahma Sutra*, Calcutta.
Vivekananda, Swami. *Thoughts on the Gita*, Mayavati.
Vyas, R.N. (1985). *The Bhagavad Gita and Jivana Yoga*, New Delhi.
Wadiya, Sri Jaya Chamraja. (1963). *The Gita and Indian Culture*, Bombay.
Warren, H.C. (1915). *Buddhism in Translation*, Cambridge.
Warrier, A.G. Krishna. (1981). *The Concept of Mukti in Advaita Vedanta*, Madras.
Williams Daniel Day. (1946). *God's Grace and Man's Hope*, New York.
Yati, Nitya Chaitanya. (1981). *The Bhagavad Gita*, New Delhi.
Yogananda, Paramhamsa. (2006). *The Essence of the Bhagavad Gita*, Gurgaon, India.
Zachner, R.C. (1969). *The Bhagavad Gita*, Oxford.

JOURNALS

Philosophy and West

David White. *Proto Samkhya and Advaita Vedanta in the Bhagavadgita*, Vol. 29, No. 9. October 1979.
Keith E. Yandell. *On Interpreting the Bhagavadgita*. Vol. 32, No. 1, January 1982.
MUS, Paul. *The Problematic of the Self*, Vol. 29, No. 4, 1959.

Prabudha Bharata

Venkatrama Iyer, M.K. *The Finite Self: Its Nature and Destiny*, March 1966.

Philosophical Quarterly

Vol. X, No. 4, December 1970.
Vol. VI, No. 1, March 1966.
Vol. XVI, No. 1, April 1940.
Vol. VII, No. 2, July 1931.

Review of Philosophy and Religion
Vol. VI, No. 1, March 1935.
Vol. II, No. 1, 1942.

Vedanta Kesari
Vol. XXVII, May 1940, April 1941.
March 1964
February 1967.
November-December 1982.
September, October, November & December 1982 and January 1983 issues.
January 1983.
May 1983.
March 1983.

Bhavan's Journal
Vol. 29, No. 1, August 1-15, 1982.
Vol. 29, No. 9, December 1, 1982.
Vol. 29, No. 13, February 1.
Vol. 29, No. 14, Feburary 16.

The Adyar Library Bulletin
Vol. XLIV-XLV, 1980-81.

Articles

Bajaj, Prem Nath. *The Bhagavad Gita: Philosophy of a frustrated Society* (*Caravan*, January) (Second) 1981, No. 688 and February (First) 1981 No. 689 Fortnightly of National Resurgence. Editor and Publishers Viswa Nath.

Rangaswami, J. *Attuvitattiṉ māyāvātattai maṟuttu viśiṣṭāttuvitam moḻium ēḻuvitamāṉa poruntāmaikaḷ-mutal pākam (Septavidha Anūpapatti of Viśiṣṭādvaita to Refute Māyāvāda -First part), Āyvukkōvai*, 1997, pp. 35-39.

------------------. *Attuvitattiṉ māyāvātattai maṟuttu viśiṣṭāttuvitam moḻium ēḻuvitamāṉa poruntāmaikaḷ-mutal pākam (Septavidha Anūpapatti of Viśiṣṭādvaita to Refute Māyāvāda -Second part) Āyvukkōvai*, 1998, pp. 41-45.

------------------. *Attuvitattiṉ māyāvātattai maṟuttu viśiṣṭāttuvaitam moḻium ēḻuvitamāṉa poruntāmaikaḷ-mūṉṟāṃ pākam (Septavidha Anūpapatti of Viśiṣṭādvaita to Refute Māyāvāda -Part III) Āyvukkōvai*, 1999, Part I, pp. 49-52.

------------------. *Attuvitattiṉ māyāvātattai maṟuttu viśiṣṭāttuvaitam moḻium ēḻuvitamāṉa poruntāmaikaḷ-Nāṉkām pākam (Septavidha Anūpapatti of Viśiṣṭādvaita to Refute Māyāvāda-Part IV) Āyvukkōvai*, 2000, Part I, pp. 57-60.

------------------. *Relevanance of Bhagavad Gītā's Teachings in Modern Ages.Tamil Civilization*, Tamil University, Vols.14 -18, March. 1996-Dec. 2000, pp. 51-55 (Released on Aug. 2002).

------------------. *Māyāvātam-oru kaṇṇōṭṭam (Māyāvāda—An Outlook), Āyvukkōvai*, 1994, pp. 56-60.

------------------. *Refutation of Śaṅkara's Māyāvāda by Śrī Rāmānujā and Śrī Jñānadeva – A Critical Study*. International Institute of Tamil Studies, Chennai.Vol.62, December, 2002. pp. 91-118.

------------------. *Śrīvallabharum cuttāttuvitamum, (Śrī Vallaba and His Philosophy of Śudhādvaita), Tamiḻiyal Āyvu*, International Society for Tamil Cultural Studies, Madurai, 1994, pp. 169-172.

Sundaram, P.K. *Voice of Samanvaya (A Journal of the C.P. Ramaswami Aiyar Foundation*, Vol.V, combined issue of April and October, 1980, No.1 and 2, pp. 19-27, 47-50, 51-57 and 58-64.

Van Buitenen J.A.B. *A Contribution to the Critical Edition of the Bhagavadgita (Journal of the American Oriental Society*, 85 (1965), pp. 99-109.

INDEX

B

C

D

E

G

T